How The

ECONO

WOR

AN INVESTOR'S

TRACKING THE

SECOND E

How The
Economy
Works

AN INVESTOR'S GUIDE TO TRACKING THE ECONOMY

SECOND EDITION

Edmund A. Mennis

NEW YORK INSTITUTE OF FINANCE

NEW YORK • TORONTO • SYDNEY • TOKYO • SINGAPORE

Library of Congress Cataloging-in-Publication Data

Mennis, Edmund A.
    How the economy works : an investor's guide to tracking the economy /
Edmund A. Mennis. — Rev. and expanded ed.
        p. cm.
    Includes bibliographical references and index.
    ISBN 0-7352-0076-9 (pbk.)
        1. Economics.   2. United States—Economic conditions—1981–   3. Investments.
I. Title.
HB171.M523   1999
332.67'8—dc21   98-25274
                                                                CIP

Printed in the United States of America

10 9 8 7 6 5 4 3 2 1

This publication is designed to provide accurate and authoritative information in regard to the subject matter covered. It is sold with the understanding that the publisher is not engaged in rendering legal, accounting, or other professional service. If legal advice or other expert assistance is required, the services of a competent professional person should be sought.

—From the Declaration of Principles jointly adopted by a Committee of the American Bar Association and a Committee of Publishers and Associations.

ISBN 0-7352-0076-9

ATTENTION: CORPORATIONS AND SCHOOLS

Prentice Hall books are available at quantity discounts with bulk purchase for educational, business, or sales promotional use. For information, please write to: Prentice Hall Special Sales, 240 Frisch Court, Paramus, New Jersey 07652. Please supply: title of book, ISBN, quantity, how the book will be used, date needed.

 NEW YORK INSTITUTE OF FINANCE
An Imprint of Prentice Hall Press
Paramus, NJ 07652
A Simon & Schuster Company

On the World Wide Web at http://www.phdirect.com

Prentice Hall International (UK) Limited, *London*
Prentice Hall of Australia Pty. Limited, *Sydney*
Prentice Hall Canada, Inc., *Toronto*
Prentice Hall Hispanoamericana, S.A., *Mexico*
Prentice Hall of India Private Limited, *New Delhi*
Prentice Hall of Japan, Inc., *Tokyo*
Simon & Schuster Asia Pte. Ltd., *Singapore*
Editora Prentice Hall do Brasil, Ltda., *Rio de Janeiro*

TO TRES

For her patience, encouragement and understanding

Preface to the Second Edition

Although we are deluged with statistical data about the status of the economy, sorting the data, understanding it, and interpreting it are difficult tasks even for a professional economist, let alone the average individual. This book originated in a series of reports I prepared for my clients to explain and interpret for them the recurring batch of statistics available in the financial press. When three years of these reports had accumulated, I was urged to put them together in a book; *How the Economy Works* is the result.

The first edition of the book was received favorably, but a good deal of the information in it is now out of date or has been completely revised. Moreover, when the first edition was published, the economy was on the brink of the 1990–91 recession. Now the United States has experienced a prolonged period of economic growth with little sign of the inflationary pressures that ordinarily accompany the latter stages of an expansion—a situation so unusual that some observers are calling it a "new era." It remains to be seen whether we are in such a new era or it is just the same old phrase that crops up whenever the economy's performance differs from expected patterns. In any event, the data that continue to stream in still require understanding and interpreting to determine where we were and where we may be going.

The charts and other economic data in this edition are current as of June 1998, so that most of the charts with monthly data reflect information through May. At that time, the effects of the Asian crisis were just beginning to impact the U.S. economy. In addition, the effects of a major strike at General Motors were not yet evident in the data. These events stress the need for continuous evaluation of what is going on in the economy in historical perspective, which this book tries to provide.

A new development in checking on the economy is the ready availability of data on the Internet. Anyone with a computer and a modem now can get the full texts of almost all statistical reports shortly after they are issued rather than waiting for the abbreviated reports that come later on TV, in the newspapers, and via other media. While this provides prompt access to much more information than before, information overload can often cause more confusion than enlightenment. Hopefully, this book will help sort out the important from the unimportant and provide perspective on what should be watched and why. Also, you can now easily access original sources and make up your own mind instead of having to rely on others.

A new chapter has been added to this book describing how and where to get economic and financial information on the Internet. I was fortunate to be able to call on my son, Liam, to provide the expertise in writing Chapter 12 on how to track the economy using this new resource. He also has been an invaluable aid in teaching me how to use the Internet and has cheerfully answered my many questions to make this great tool less intimidating. My debt to him is substantial.

I want to express my appreciation to Robert P. Parker, Chief Statistician, and Brent Moulton, Associate Director for National Income, Expenditure and Wealth, of the Bureau of Economic Analysis of the U.S. Department of Commerce for helpful criticisms of Chapters 2 and 3. I also want to thank Sheshunoff Information Services for permission to use in Chapter 13 some of the material in the chapter "Managing Trust Investments" that I wrote for their *Trust Department Management Manual*. I also acknowledge permission from The Conference Board, New York,

NY, to use the information on the consumer confidence index in Chapter 4 and on business cycles in Chapter 9. The information on investment returns in Chapter 13 is copyrighted in 1998 by and has been used with the permission of Ibbotson Associates, Chicago, IL, which reserves all rights to the material. [Certain portions of this work were derived from the copyright works of Roger G. Ibbotson and Rex Sinquefield.]

My greatest obligation remains to my wife, Tres, who has patiently given me the time and encouragement to complete this revision. She also has brought a non-economist's perspective to the material in the book by insisting that I explain my ideas without economic jargon and use simple English instead. I am truly grateful.

Edmund A. Mennis
Palos Verdes Estates, California

A Note from the Author

Throughout the book, a number of abbreviations are used frequently. As a handy reference, the following explanation of them may be useful:

BEA   Bureau of Economic Analysis,
          U.S. Department of Commerce
CBO   Congressional Budget Office
CPI   Consumer price index
ERP   *Economic Report of the President*
FOMC   Federal Open Market Committee
FRB   Federal Reserve Board
GDI   Gross domestic income
GDP   Gross domestic product
GNP   Gross national product
IMF   International Monetary Fund
NIPA   National income and product accounts
OASI   Old age and survivors insurance
OMB   Office of Management and Budget
OPEC   Organization of Petroleum Exporting Countries
PPI   Producers Price Index
SCB   *Survey of Current Business*

About the Author
and
About the Contributor

Edmund A. Mennis is Editor of *Business Economics*, the quarterly professional journal of the National Association for Business Economics. He is the Editor and an author of three manuals designed for community banks, and he also edits and writes economic analyses for the monthly *Bank Funds Management Report*. He has edited and written monographs on investment portfolio management for state and local governmental bodies and is a coauthor of a manual on the use of derivative securities in fiduciary accounts. He also has written or edited more than 60 books, monographs, and articles in the fields of financial analysis and economics.

He has been an independent economic and financial consultant since 1982. Prior to that, he held a number of positions in investment management organizations and had sixteen years' diversified experience as economist, financial analyst, and member of the investment committee of the Wellington Fund, a billion-dollar mutual fund in Philadelphia.

Dr. Mennis is a Chartered Financial Analyst and served as president and a trustee of the Institute of Chartered Financial Analysts. He has received a number of professional awards from the Financial Analysts Federation and the Institute of Chartered Financial Analysts for his contributions to the profession of financial analysis and the education of professional investors. He has been elected a Fellow of The National Association for Business Economics, and in 1996 he received the David L. Williams Lifetime Achievement Award for exceptional service to that organization. He is a member as well as past chairman of the Conference of Business Economists. He holds a Ph.D. degree in economics and finance from New York University Graduate School of Business Administration.

Liam Mennis (Chapter 12) is Director of Consulting Services for General Management Resources in Pasadena, California. He has more than twenty years of diversified business and information systems experience in management, consulting, and technical support.

Prior to joining GMR, he held a variety of positions, specializing in information technology strategic planning, operations and automated systems assessment, financial services—financial planning and securities brokerage—and general business litigation. His background also includes twelve years in hardware and software development and support with Hewlett-Packard, CACI, Sperry Univac, and Electronic Data Systems (EDS). He holds an MBA in Finance and Production and Operations Management from The Graduate School of Management, University of California Los Angeles (UCLA).

Contents

Chapter 1
Why Bother About the Economy? 1

Chapter 2
What Is GDP Anyway? 13

Chapter 3
Measuring Price Changes 25

Chapter 4
Tracking the Consumer 39

Chapter 5
Following the Business Sector 67

Chapter 6
The World Overseas 89

Chapter 7
Government and the Economy 111

Chapter 8
Interest Rates and Monetary Policy 135

Chapter 9
Economic Trends and Cycles 159

Chapter 10
Understanding Corporate Profits 181

Why Bother About the Economy?

Each day, we are subjected to a lot of economic information, whether from newspapers, radio, television, or the Internet. This information is just a small piece of a very complicated mosaic that makes up the economy, and it may be expressed in technical jargon that is difficult for a non-economist to understand. Economic information often appears obscure and confusing, and it is little wonder that the average individual questions whether it's worth trying to understand how the economy works.

Understanding the health of the U.S. economy is very important if we are to be better informed citizens and voters. Moreover, knowledge of the economy may influence a choice of careers or a change in jobs. Fluctuations in the economy affect the stability of a job. Understanding how the economy works also helps to make sound investment decisions.

Most people are constantly making decisions about what to consume and how to invest. "Investment" is a word often used to mean just buying and selling stocks, an exercise that many individuals have little or nothing to do with. Nevertheless, the surge in mutual fund sales in the past several years has significantly increased the number of people who own stocks indirectly, which has intensified their interest in the economy, corporate profits, and the financial markets.

Many more investment decisions other than buying or selling stocks are made every day. For example, investment decisions are made when buying or refinancing a home and deciding whether to use a fixed or variable-rate mortgage. Buying high-ticket items and paying either with cash or credit is an investment decision. Taking out a personal loan is an investment decision; so is deciding whether to put money aside in a savings account, a money-market fund, a bank certificate of deposit, or a U.S. Treasury bond. All of these decisions are influenced by movements in interest rates, which in turn are affected by movements in the economy.

Future income may be affected by changes in the economy. The value of a pension plan is affected by changes in interest rates and stock prices. While this may not be too important if pension benefits are set by salary levels and years of service, it is critical if retirement benefits are related to the market value of a pension, profit sharing, or thrift plan. Some employee benefit plans offer a selection, allowing a combination of investments—and that combination may be changed from time to time. What are the best choices at any given time? It may not be last year's best investment performer.

The list could go on, but the point is clear. Everyone makes decisions that affect his or her future economic well-being. These decisions will improve with a better understanding of where the economy is, where it is going, and how to track its changes. The goal of this book is to make that task easier.

ECONOMICS AND THE ECONOMY

Economics is the social science that deals with the allocation of scarce resources. It is concerned chiefly with the description and analysis of the production, distribution, and consumption of goods and services. However, this book is not designed to be an economics text; it has other objectives.

This book is intended to enable the reader to understand and interpret the flood of economic information provided by the news media, government, and private sources. A good deal more economic information is available; just coping with economic information covered in the financial press is a sufficiently ambitious task.

A major challenge in understanding current data is to put it in some sort of perspective. The latest information may be expressed as a percentage change from last month or a year ago. Looking back over a period longer than a month, is the trend of the data up, down, or indeterminate? How does this information relate to other information at hand or to information still to come? How does this information provide a perspective of what is going on in the whole economy? Is business getting better or worse?

One method of providing needed perspective is to plot the data on a chart to show the movements for a period of several years or longer. Consequently, this book has many figures. Remember, the figures are as important as the text; it is worthwhile to spend a few minutes looking at each, trying to understand the story it has to tell.

If it is important to know how the economy affects us, where does one start? A basic assumption is the logical relationship that flows from the economy to corporate profits, and from those profits to stock prices. The path of the economy also influences interest rates. This chapter will develop these relationships.

The following terms are introduced in this chapter:

Gross domestic product (GDP). The measure of the output of goods and services in the economy;

Corporate profits. The estimate of the current income received by corporations as a part of the income generated by GDP;

Standard & Poor's 500 (S&P 500) Stock Price Index and *S&P earnings per share.* The combined prices and earnings of a group of 500 large, successful corporations;

Price-earnings (P/E) ratio. The price of a stock divided by its past or expected earnings providing a measure of comparative valuation over time or among stocks. A similar relationship can be calculated for groups of stocks, like the S&P 500;

Interest rates. The dollars of interest income received per $100 of investment.

ARE THE ECONOMY AND INVESTMENTS RELATED?

At this point, would a better understanding of the economy help make better investment decision possible? Are the economy and investment decisions related? If so, how?

Movements in the economy, in corporate profits, and in stock prices are related. The economy and interest rates are also connected. The following figures provide examples of relationships between economic information and the movement of stock prices and interest rates.

The figures cover a long period of time—from 1950, just after World War II, to 1997. This 48-year period was different from the years prior to World War II in terms of economic growth rates and cyclical fluctuations. It also encompassed the Korean and Vietnam wars, two oil shocks that led to bursts of very high inflation, a recent period of moderate growth and low inflation, and population shifts that changed the allocation of scarce economic resources. This longer-term viewpoint should provide the needed perspective to evaluate the transitory developments and the external shocks that often heavily influence investment decisions.

The Economy and Corporate Profits

Figure 1.1 compares *gross domestic product (GDP)*, the broadest measure of the output of goods and services in the United States, with the *corporate profits* generated from that output. These two measures will be examined in more detail in Chapters 2 and 10, but for now we just want to demonstrate that the movements of the economy and of profits are related. GDP is expressed in current dollars—reflecting both movements in physical output and changes in prices. The measure of corporate profits used here is called *operating profits* or *economic profits*. These profit numbers are an estimate of all corporate profits in the economy before state and federal taxes. They are adjusted to eliminate the effects on profits of fluctuations in the value of the inventories corporations carry on their books. These profit numbers also are adjusted to show the depreciation of corporate plant and equipment to reflect current rather than historical costs. Thus, this profit measure is the one most directly related to current output.

A word about the method of presentation in Figure 1.1. GDP is measured by the scale on the left side of the figure. This scale is

Figure 1.1 Gross Domestic Product vs. Corporate Profits, 1950–1997

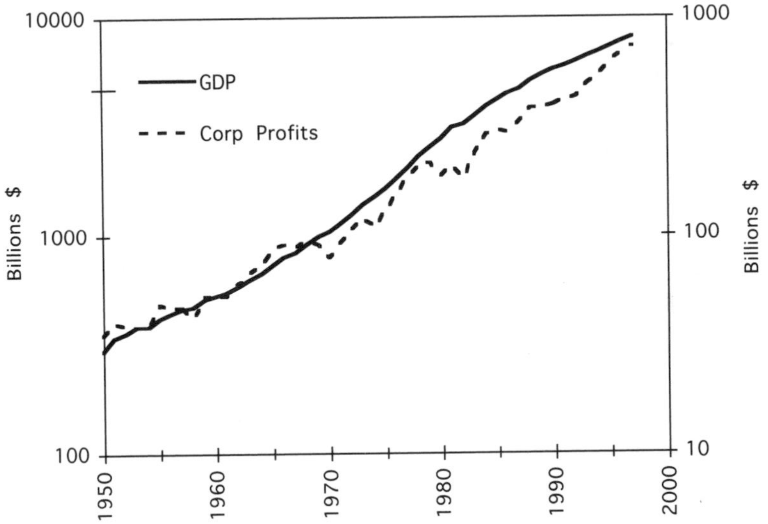

Source: STAT-USA NIPA Historical estimates, SCB, June 1998,
Table 1, p. D-2 and Table 1.14, p. D-5

ten times the right scale, which is used to measure operating profits. These dual scales are used to bring the lines on the figure closer together so that they can be compared more easily. The vertical axes of the figure are set so that vertical distances on the chart show equal *percentage* changes rather than equal dollar changes. Note, for example, on the left scale, the distance from 100 to 1,000 (an increase of 900) is equal to the distance from 1,000 to 10,000 (an increase of 9,000). However, both distances represent a 900 percent increase. Such a figure, called a *semi-log chart,* permits better comparisons of variables that differ widely in amount.

Several observations can be made about the data on this figure. First, the economy and profits appear to be related; they both have a broad upward sweep. However, the trend of profits was not so steep as that of the economy prior to 1993, suggesting that the profit share of output did not keep pace with overall economic growth. Part of the reason for this difference was the rising share of employee compensation, especially fringe benefits, that grew as a percent of total output. The second reason was the increase in indebtedness of U.S. corporations, resulting in interest costs that claimed an increasing share of corporate output. But in the period since 1993 the profit share increased relative to the increase in GDP and the share for employee compensation and interest shrank— indicating, in part at least, corporate response to slower profit growth by cost cutting, debt repayment, and increased efficiency in production that improved employee productivity.

Another difference is clearly evident. Profits fluctuate a good deal more than the economy as a whole (remember that equal vertical distances on the figure represent equal percentage changes). These fluctuations are due to periodic fluctuations in the economy called *business cycles*. Business cycles are an economic phenomenon that affect different sectors of the economy in varying ways (more about business cycles in Chapter 9). The point made here is that business cycles affect profits, and anyone interested in profits needs a better understanding of cyclical fluctuations in the economy.

STOCK EARNINGS AND PRICES

Figure 1.2 examines the relationship between corporate profits or earnings and the prices of the stocks of the companies that generated those earnings. (The economic profits for all corporations shown in Figure 1.1 and the earnings per share for the stocks in the Standard & Poor's 500 stock index shown in Figure 1.2 have had generally similar fluctuations over time. The Standard & Poor's index is comprised of 500 large, successful corporations; this index is used in order to compare earnings and stock prices of the same companies.) The scales of the figure have been constructed so that the price scale on the left side is ten times the earnings scale on the right side.

Several factors are evident in this figure. Although prices have been more volatile than earnings, both have trended upward in a similar manner to growth in the economy. The position of the price line above and below the earnings line not only indicates that prices are more volatile, but that they also move in broad patterns around the earnings line, sometimes higher and sometimes lower. Stock prices are fundamentally related to earnings, but the prices that investors are willing to pay for these earnings change from time to time.

Figure 1.2 S&P Earnings and Prices, 1950–1997

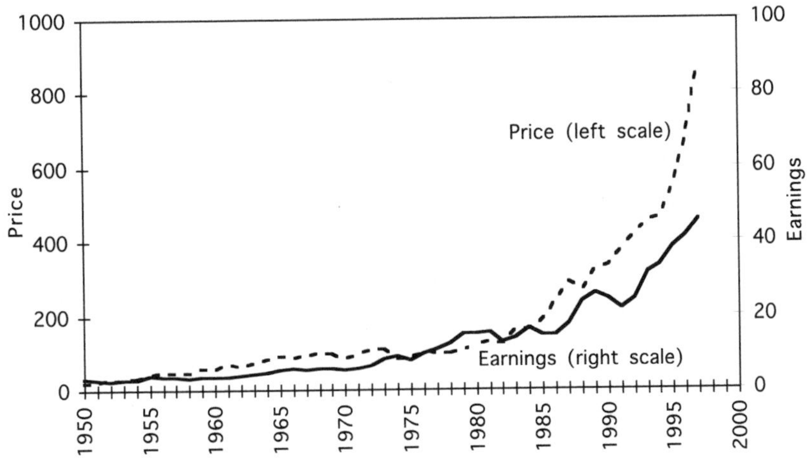

Source: Price: ERP, 1998, p. 390; Earnings: *S&P Trade and Statistics Manual*

The Price/Earnings Ratio

The relationship between prices and earnings is shown more clearly by the solid line on Figure 1.3. Data for the solid line were computed by dividing the annual earnings of the S&P 500 stock index by the average price each year, resulting in what investors call the *price/earnings ratio,* shown on the scale at the left of the chart.

Several distinct patterns are found in this ratio. Prices moved from a low of about 7 times earnings in 1950 to a peak of more than 21 times in 1961. Except for that one year, the ratio fluctuated between about 14.5 times to just under 19 times between 1959 and 1972. The decline thereafter was sharp, and the ratio moved between 7 to 11 times until 1984. Since then the ratio has moved upward and by the end of 1997 was near the peak reached in 1962. The average P/E ratio for the entire 1950 to 1997 period was about 14.5 times.

Why has this ratio, which represents the value thousands of investors have placed on corporate earnings, fluctuated this way? Although a number of explanations can be advanced, one simple

Figure 1.3 Stock P/E Ratios and Inflation, 1950–1997

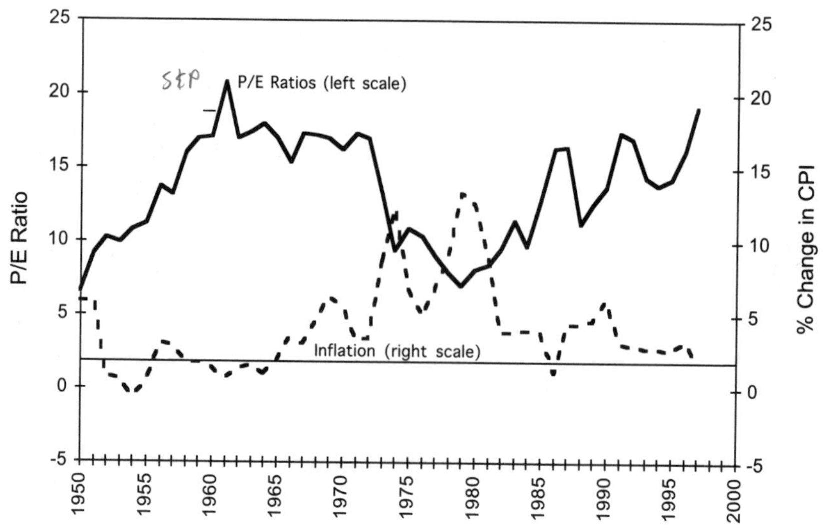

Source: Inflation: ERP, 1998, Table B-63, p. 353; P/E computed from data for Figure 1.2

relationship is significant. The dotted line on the figure shows the annual change in the *consumer price index (CPI)*—one method often used to measure inflation. The inflation rate averaged less than 2 percent from 1950 to 1963, which was a period of rising P/E ratios and thus rising valuation of earnings by investors. The costs of the Vietnam War and the two oil price shocks in the 1970s led to a surge in inflation, slower growth in corporate earnings, and a sharp downward revision in P/E ratios. The recession and deflation that began in 1982 drove inflation rates under 4 percent, and the recent low inflation environment sent inflation under a 3 percent rate. This development, along with economic expansion and rising profits, had a salutary effect on stock price multiples, sending them up again.

In summary, growth and cyclical fluctuations in the economy affect corporate profits, and the inflation rate has a strong influence on the valuation investors place on those earnings. Knowledge of what makes the economy move and the causes of and changes in inflation rates can help to explain broad movements in stock prices as well as assist in making better investment decisions.

INTEREST RATES

The importance of interest rate movements in making invest-ment decisions was mentioned earlier in this chapter. Figure 1.4 provides a long-term view of the movement of both short- and long-term *interest rates* for the 1950 to 1997 period. (Interest rates are expressed as a percent, computed by the dollars of interest received per $100 of investment. The value of the investment is ordinarily expressed in terms of its market price.) Short rates are measured by the yield on 30-day U.S. Treasury bills. Many short-term rates, like those on bank certificates of deposit (CDs) and savings accounts, are directly related to the Treasury bill rate; they are a part of the holdings of many money-market mutual funds. Long-term rates are represented by yields of high-grade corporate bonds. This infor-mation is prepared regularly by Moody's Investors Service.

Two interesting characteristics of interest rates may be observed from this figure. The first is that short rates have been more volatile than long rates. In fact, an analysis of the monthly movements in short-term interest rates would reveal that short-term rates have relatively large movements that conform to cycli-cal fluctuations in the economy. Turning points in long rates lag

Figure 1.4 Short- and Long-Term Interest Rates, 1950–1997

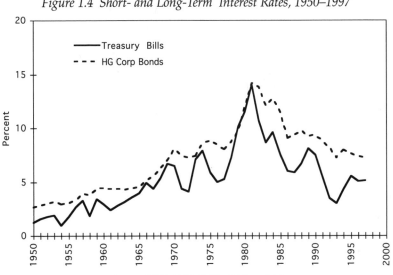

Source: ERP, 1998, Table B-73, p. 366

behind short-rate turns and have smaller amplitudes. Moreover, near cyclical business-cycle peaks, short rates tend to exceed long rates, resulting in a so-called inverted yield curve, which will be discussed in Chapter 8. Presumably these movements reflect different supply and demand forces affecting these securities, and these forces are related to the economic conditions prevailing in these particular years.

The second characteristic is the trends of both short and long rates during this period. Both rates trended upward from 1950 to 1981 but fell thereafter. A possible explanation of these trends is the same force that affected stock P/E ratios. Figure 1.5 plots the fluctuations in the Treasury bill rate (the solid line) against the annual changes in the consumer price index (the dotted line). As a generalization, the bill rate has fluctuated almost consistently with the annual inflation rate, running slightly above it in the earlier years, and below it in periods of high inflation. Since 1981, however, the bill rate has run considerably above the inflation rate. This latter phenomenon suggests either investors in recent years have demanded a higher return above inflation than in earlier periods or they anticipate high inflation rates in the future. In any event,

Figure 1.5 Interest Rates and Inflation, 1950–1997

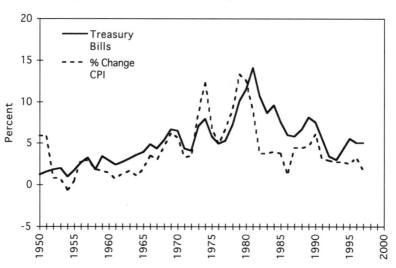

Source: Bills: ERP, 1998, Table B-73, p. 366; Inflation: Table B-62, p. 352

knowledge of the stage of the business cycle and the prospects for inflation can be important in evaluating interest rate prospects.

SUMMARY

Knowing how to interpret fluctuations in the economy is important. All investment decisions are impacted by changes in the economy—including those that don't involve buying and selling stocks.

Movements in corporate profits are related to movements in the economy. Stock prices are consequently affected by profit movements and the price that investors are willing to pay for these profits. This relationship is reflected in the P/E ratio; the P/E ratio is influenced by changes in inflation rates. Interest rates are also related to fluctuations in the economy, and trends in interest rates are related to trends in inflation rates.

Thus, economics and investments are intertwined. A better understanding of the economy will lead to a better understanding of the major influences on investment returns. It will also reduce the influence on your business and investment decisions of the minor or extraneous factors that loom large in newspaper headlines.

CHAPTER 2

What Is GDP Anyway?

Understanding the economy involves unraveling a confusing flood of statistics and conflicting opinions of economists interpreting these statistics. This chapter attempts to sort out the statistical confusion first; the confusing economists are dealt with later.

The easiest way to explain the economy is to start with the "Big Picture" and examine the broadest measure of economic activity available, or gross domestic product (GDP). GDP measures output as the sum of final expenditures—consumer spending, private investment, net exports, and government consumption and investment. The other side of this output is gross domestic income (GDI), which measures output as the sum of the costs incurred and the incomes earned in the production of GDP.

In concept, GDP and GDI numbers should be the same. They differ because their components are estimated using largely independent and less-than-perfect source data. The Bureau of Economic

Analysis (BEA) of the U.S. Department of Commerce considers GDP as the more reliable measure of output because the source data are considered more accurate. The difference between GDP and GDI is called the "statistical discrepancy" and is recorded in the national income and product accounts (NIPAs) as an income component to reconcile the two approaches.

After discussing the dual concept of GDP, the economy can then be analyzed in terms of each of the major components of GDP: the consumer, business, government, and international sectors. Under each of these four divisions, other statistical data will be discussed that, in addition to GDP and its parts, provide useful insights into each sector. Hopefully, a more comprehensible picture of the operation of the economy will emerge.

Among the terms introduced in this chapter are:

Gross domestic product.[1] A measure that estimates the output of goods and services produced by labor and property located in the United States and also the income generated by that output of goods and services;

Final sales. That portion of GDP that is taken by the ultimate user. Final sales are made to consumers, government, and foreigners as well as business spending for plant and equipment and residential housing sales and maintenance;

Changes in business inventories. The additions to or reductions in business holdings of inventories. When these changes in inventories are combined with final sales, the result is total GDP;

---

[1] Some readers may be more familiar with the term *gross national product* (GNP), which was used for many years until December 1991, when the Bureau of Economic Analysis (BEA) of the U.S. Department of Commerce substituted gross domestic product (GDP) as the principal measure of aggregate economic activity. The purpose of this change was to make U.S. measures more comparable with international measures. The difference between the two measures is that GNP covers the goods and services produced by labor and property supplied by U.S. residents; the labor and property can be located anywhere in the world. GDP, by contrast, covers goods and services produced by labor and property located just in the United States; the suppliers (workers or owners of property) may be U.S. residents or residents of the rest of the world. The difference between the two measures has been less than 1 percent since 1985. The main item affected is the exclusion from GDP of the receipts of corporate profits from abroad (because they are not earned in the United States). But GDP includes business profits earned by foreign-owned businesses in the United States. The reverse is true in computing GNP.

Income side of GDP. Includes employee compensation and the interest paid by business (less the interest it receives), indirect business tax and nontax liability, plus corporate profits, incomes of proprietorships and partnerships, and rental income of persons.

WHAT IS GDP?

GDP is a part of the national income and product accounts (NIPA) prepared and distributed by the federal government. The process is similar to a corporation keeping books with income and balance sheet accounts reflecting the health of the corporation. However, GDP accounts are much broader in scope; they are designed to show the production, distribution, and use of the nation's output of goods and services. A full set of the national accounts includes about 140 tables of statistical information with several thousand items, and much of the information is of interest primarily to those who specialize in a particular area.

This chapter will cover only the major parts of the GDP accounts and will explain how the limited GDP data reported in the press or on TV can be interpreted to understand the status of the economy.

Definitions

GDP can be measured in two ways:

How the output of goods and services in any particular time period is apportioned among various users of the output; or

How the income generated by that output of goods and services is distributed.

The measurement of the domestic output of goods and services reflects *final sales* to domestic purchasers only; sales at intermediate stages of production are excluded.[2] If the *changes in business inventories*

---

[2] The purpose of this exclusion is to avoid multiple counting. For example, iron ore is used to make steel, which is used to make bicycles. If the iron ore is counted when it is first mined, again as a part of the content of the steel and then again as a part of the steel in the bicycle, it would be counted several times. The price of the bicycle when it is finally sold includes the value of the iron ore and the other materials used in manufacture as well as the value added at each stage of production.

(either additions or reductions) are added to final sales, we get total GDP or output.

THE OUTPUT SIDE OF GDP

Final sales of domestic product are made to four sectors:

1. Sales to consumers;
2. Sales representing gross fixed investment, that is, plant and equipment spending by business plus new residential housing sales;
3. Sales to government, defined as government consumption expenditures (including compensation of government employees) and government gross investment (essentially purchases of military and nonmilitary structures and equipment);
4. Sales to foreigners, that is, exports less imports of goods and services. By definition, imports are of foreign rather than domestic production; therefore they are subtracted to get a measure of the production attributable to the United States.

In addition to final sales, one other element must be included—the addition to or the reduction of business inventories, which either add to or subtract from output in a particular period. Note that inventories are valued at current replacement cost, not the value that businesses carry inventories on their book. (See the discussion in Chapter 10 on the inventory valuation adjustment in corporate profits.)

Table 2.1 shows GDP in 1997 and how it was taken off the market by these sectors. As the table indicates, the consumer takes the largest portion of the nation's output, more than two-thirds. Government takes the next largest slice, about 18 percent. Business fixed investment (structures as well as machinery and equipment) and business accumulation (or reduction) of inventories follow with about 10 percent. The residential investment—the value of on-site construction of single-family homes, multiple dwellings and of mobile homes (4 percent) follows. (The figure does not represent sales to homebuyers but rather outlays for construction of new housing units during the period being measured. It also represents outlays for home improvements, about one-third of total outlays.) Finally, net exports are a negative sum because in the United States in 1997, domestic consumption of goods and services imported was greater than goods and services exported.

Table 2.1   How GDP Was Taken Off the Market—1997

	Billions of $	Percent
Total GDP	8079.9	100.0
Personal consumption expenditures	5485.8	67.9
Residential fixed investment	327.2	4.1
Nonresidential fixed investment	846.9	10.5
Change in business inventories	68.4	0.8
Government consumption expenditures and gross investment	1452.7	18.0
Net exports	–101.1	–1.3

Source: SCB, June 1998, Table 1.1, p. D-2

One other note about the way GDP is reported. Each month the reports show GDP and its components at *seasonally adjusted annual rates*. Seasonal adjustment is a statistical technique that makes allowances for seasonal patterns in activity caused by weather or predictable surges due to events such as Christmas or Easter shopping. Showing the figures at annual rates indicates the degree of change for a whole year if the change in a particular quarter continued for a year at that rate. This way of presenting the information makes it possible to compare the data at seasonally adjusted annual rates for a particular quarter with that for an entire year.

Data for GDP are reported in two ways. The first reflects prices that prevailed during the reporting period. This information is referred to as *current dollar* or *nominal* GDP, and it is used when comparing total output with other current dollar numbers, such as corporate profits, as illustrated in Figure 1.1.

For other analytical purposes, it is helpful to segregate GDP changes into those caused by changes in prices and those caused by changes in physical output. The latter measure is called *real* or *inflation-adjusted* GDP. Prior to 1996, real GDP was calculated as the sum of the detailed real components after dividing the components by appropriate price indexes for a particular year, e.g., 1987.

The GDP price deflator was then derived as the ratio of current dollar output to the sum of the real detailed estimate.

However, as the calculations were moved further away from the base year, distortions inevitably occurred. An outstanding example involves computers, where prices fell sharply while computer purchases soared. By using 1987 prices as a divisor in estimating this surging physical volume instead of the lower prices actually prevailing, the contribution of computers to real output became more and more overstated over time. Expanding this problem to other products, using prices fixed in a particular year to restate output in real terms in other time periods causes distortions to accrue the further away you get from the base year. In addition, whenever a shift in the base year occurred, a noticeable change in past growth rates also occurred.

To get around this problem, the Commerce Department introduced a statistical procedure called *chain weighting*. Measures of real output and prices in adjourning periods are averaged (using a geometric mean) and then "chained" (multiplied) together to form a time series that allows for the shifts in relative prices and in the composition of output over time. The result is a type of index that uses weights appropriate for each time period. Dollar estimates are then calculated from these indexes.

A disadvantage is that, when stated in terms of 1992 chained dollars, the GDP components are not precisely additive, especially for periods far away from the base period. However, the percent changes calculated using the chain output index are correct even though the dollar estimates are not additive. But this is an issue more for statisticians; for ordinary near-term business analysis, the new chain-weighted indexes are more useful than the prior procedure.[3]

Figure 2.1 shows GDP in both current dollars (the dashed line) and in chained 1992 dollars (the solid line) annually from 1950 through 1996. The data are plotted on a semi–logarithmic scale, so that equal percentage changes are comparable rather than equal dollar changes. During this 1950–97 period, nominal GDP increased at about a 7.3 percent annual rate, while real GDP increased at about a 3.3 percent rate.

---

[3] For an excellent and detailed discussion, see J. Steven Landefeld and Robert P. Parker, "BEA's Chain Indexes, Time Series and Measures of Long-Term Economic Growth," *Survey of Current Business*, Volume 77, Number 5, May 1997, pp. 58–68.

Figure 2.1
Gross Domestic Product in Current and Chained (1992) Dollars, 1950–1997

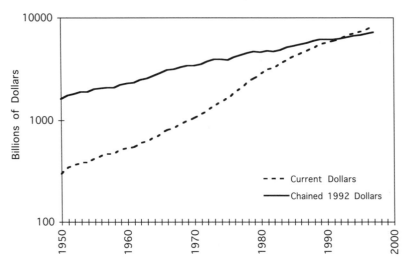

Source: SCB, June 1998, Tables 1.1 and 1.2, p. D-2

THE INCOME SIDE OF THE NATION'S OUTPUT

Another way of looking at the nation's output is to consider it as the sum of incomes generated in producing it. Table 2.2 indicates the distribution of the nation's output in 1997. However, in order to present a complete picture of income distribution, allowance must be made for income received *from* the rest of the world net of payments *to* the rest of the world. This computation is shown at the top of the table. The purpose of these adjustments is to reach gross national product (GNP) to get to the goods and services produced by labor and property supplied by U.S. residents for which they receive income. (See footnote 1 on page 14.)

The second step is to adjust GNP for the consumption of fixed capital during the period being measured. (*Gross* national product is the output of an economic unit in a specific period of time and excludes components produced in a different period of time. Therefore, only that portion of fixed capital, mostly depreciation of plant and equipment, that is used up in production in the specific time period should be deducted to get *net* national product.)

The next step is to deduct indirect taxes charged as a business expense (sales, excise, and property taxes), because these payments reflect costs transferred from business to governmental units. A few minor adjustments are made that account for less than 1 percent of GNP. They include business transfer payments (mostly business charitable deductions and consumer bad debts) and a statistical discrepancy to absorb the unexplained differences between the income and product side of accounts. The resulting figure is called *national income,* which is then distributed between the costs of production and profits.

Table 2.2 shows the income distribution of GNP in 1997. As the table indicates, the national income distributed after these adjustments to GNP is more than 80 percent of total GNP. Almost 60 percent is employee compensation, which is composed of:

Wages and salaries, both in the private sector and also salaries of employees of government and government enterprises;

Supplements to wages and salaries, including employee contributions to social insurance. (In 1997, these supplementary payments represented more than 12 percent of total employee compensation.)

The second production cost, net interest, reflects the interest paid by business as a part of its operations, less interest received.

The profits figure has two components: corporate profits and proprietors' income from farm and nonfarm business. These components receive about 10 and 7 percent of GNP, respectively. These profits are before income taxes.

The final payment, rental income to persons, represents rent from farm and nonfarm residential as well as nonresidential properties; it also includes royalties reported on individual income tax returns. This payment accounts for less than 2 percent of national income.

REVISIONS

A complete record of every economic transaction that takes place in the United States does not exist. In addition, information becomes available at different times, often with a considerable time lag. Therefore, the numbers for GDP and its components (and for most economic statistics, for that matter) are estimates, the reliability of which generally improves over time. The GDP data provided by the government are a compromise between the need for prompt information and the desire for accuracy. Some data are more reliable than others; for example, the dollar value of new car sales is more accurate than the dollars spent on motor vehicle repair, washing, parking, and rental. Some data are little more than educated guesses (e.g., the estimated rent of owner-occupied dwellings). Consequently, the accuracy of the numbers should not be taken too literally and certainly not believed to the last decimal place!

Table 2.2   Income Distribution of the Nation's Output—1997

	Billions of Dollars	Percent
Gross Domestic Product	8079.9	100.0
Plus: Receipts of factor income from rest of world	262.2	3.2
Less: Payments of factor income to rest of world	282.0	3.5
Equals: *Gross National Product*	8060.1	99.8
Less: Consumption of fixed capital	867.9	10.7
Equals: *Net National Product*	7192.2	89.0
Less: Indirect business taxes	619.4	7.7
Statistical discrepancy	–86.0	–1.1
Plus: Other adjustments	–9.1	–0.1
Equals: *National Income*	6649.7	82.3
Distributed as follows:		
Production costs:		
Employee compensation	4703.6	58.2
Net interest received by business	448.7	5.6
Profits:		
Corporate profits	805.0	10.0
Proprietorships and partnerships	544.5	6.7
Rental income of persons	147.9	1.8

Source: SCB, June 1997, Tables 1.9 and 1.14, pp. D-4 and D-5

Quarterly GDP estimates are published each month, generally between the 26th and the 31st day of the month. The first estimate for a particular quarter—the *advance estimate*—is published in the first month of the following quarter; for example, the first estimate of the first quarter is published at the end of April. The second estimate, the *preliminary estimate,* is published a month later, and the third or *final estimate* is published in the third month of the succeeding quarter.

Each July, the data for the previous three years are revised based on more complete information and on data available only on an annual basis. Finally, every five years or so a complete overhaul is done to include information from the periodic surveys the government makes of the economy. Even with a statistical reporting system considered one of the best in the world, it should not be surprising that revisions in where the economy *was* are partly responsible for the difficulties economists encounter in estimating where the economy *is going.*

BUSINESS ANALYSIS

Unfortunately, the quarterly reports of GDP published in the press and on television hardly provide the depth and wealth of information the full releases contain. Usually, only a brief comment on the quarter-to-quarter change in real GDP is reported, perhaps accompanied by a comment on the change in prices during that period.

However, even this brief information has some analytical value, especially if successive estimates are tracked for a particular quarter to determine whether the economy seems to be getting stronger or weaker. For example, the initial report of the quarterly change in GDP for the fourth quarter of 1987 (the big stock market crash occurred in October) was an increase of 4.2 percent at an annual rate, quite a bit better than had been expected. And in the next two months, the estimate was revised to show gains of 4.5 and 4.8 percent, respectively, indicating that the market crash did not paralyze the economy as many had feared. (As a matter of fact, the most recent revisions of GDP now show estimated growth at an estimated rate of 6.0 percent for the fourth quarter of 1987!)

Another very important factor to remember in interpreting economic reports is not attaching too much significance to quarter-to-quarter or month-to-month changes. Movements over several years should be reviewed in order to get an impression of the general direction of the series being examined.

As an example, Figure 2.2 shows the quarterly percent change in inflation-adjusted GDP from the first quarter of 1986 to the first quarter of 1998. The period prior to early 1990 was one of fairly steady growth, followed by a cyclical downturn that extended from the third quarter of 1990 through the first quarter of 1991. Quarterly growth continued thereafter for the second longest expansion since the end of World War II, although the quarter-to-quarter changes were more erratic. If only because of this length, the components of growth discussed in later chapters of this book will be carefully scrutinized in the months ahead to look for signs of an inevitable contraction.

Figure 2.2   Change in Real GDP, IQ 1986–IQ 1998
Quarterly Change at Seasonally Adjusted Annual Rates

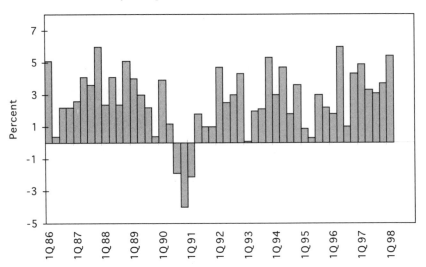

Source: SCB, May 1997, Table 2A, pp. 16–17; June 1998, Table 8.1, p. D-24

The demand components of the quarterly GDP estimates are usually provided in the business section of the daily newspapers, and an examination of the changes can provide clues to the cyclical position of the economy. The details of these components will be considered in Chapters 4, 5, 6, and 7.

SUMMARY

This chapter described GDP, the broadest measure of economic activity in the economy. This measure is comprised of two parts: the product side and the income side. GDP is also reported in current prices and adjusted for price changes to provide a measure of the physical volume of output (as discussed in Chapter 3).

Quarterly details of GDP at an annual rate are made available each month. The advance estimate is available toward the end of the month following the close of the quarter. A revised estimate is published a month later, followed by the final estimate in the third month. A complete revision covering the previous three years usually is published each July.

For business analysis, the primary focus should be on the output or product side, which is available earlier than is the income information. Tracking the quarterly percentage changes as well as the revisions should be reviewed in the perspective of several years of changes. Analysis of the components of demand can provide clues to the future cyclical path of the economy.

CHAPTER 3

Measuring Price Changes

In Chapter 2, some of the problems in calculating current dollar and constant dollar measures of output were discussed, as well as the impact of price changes when estimating physical output. This chapter will provide a more comprehensive discussion of measuring price changes.

Price indexes serve a more important function than just adjusting current dollar GDP. One of the key issues facing the United States in the years ahead is the outlook for inflation. *Inflation* is a slippery word, meaning different things to different people. However, the most commonly accepted definition is a period of accelerating price increases. Why are price changes important, and how are they measured?

This chapter will cover three types of price indexes that have been developed for measuring price changes in the GDP accounts.

In addition, two other measures of prices that are more widely known and used than those in the GDP accounts are discussed.

As part of the regular reports of gross domestic product in the national income and product accounts, three particular measures of prices are important:

- *GDP implicit price deflator*—an index that is the broadest measure of prices in the economy, reflecting an estimate of prices prevailing in a particular period (calendar year or quarter), weighted by the composition of GDP in that period. These prices are derived from federal government surveys.

- *GDP chain-type index*—an index of the prices in a particular period (e.g., a calendar year or quarter), using a base year (currently 1992) and calculating prices forward and backward from that base year by averaging the weights in two adjacent years.

- *Price index for gross domestic purchases*—a measure of the prices paid for goods and services purchased by U.S. residents during a particular period. This index also is a chain-type price index.

The other indexes are as follows:

Consumer price index—reflects the prices a typical consumer pays for a fixed-market basket of consumer goods and services.

Producer price indexes—prices received by domestic producers of commodities at three stages of processing—crude materials, intermediate materials, and finished goods.

WHY ARE PRICE CHANGES IMPORTANT?

Price changes, especially price increases, are important for several reasons. Rising (or falling) prices introduce inequities into the economy. The ability to offset rising prices varies; for example, those receiving periodic payments in a specific number of dollars are hurt if their payments are not indexed to inflation. These include private pension fund recipients or persons who own securities where the income payments are fixed, such as bonds or savings accounts or certificates of deposit. In a period of rising prices, the purchasing power of the fixed amounts they receive is eroded. The inequities within the economy are magnified if other fixed payments are adjusted for inflation through law (as in the case of social security payments) or contract (as in the case of cost-of-living adjustments in labor contracts).

In addition to the inequities that arise when prices change, a relationship exists over time between prices and wages. The dotted line on Figure 3.1 shows the annual changes of the consumer price index less food and fuel prices from 1958 through 1997. (Food and fuel prices are subtracted because they are so volatile, depending on the weather in the case of food and on the whims of foreign oil producers, in the case of fuel. The index less food and fuel prices is often referred to as the *core inflation rate*.) The solid line indicates the annual changes in average hourly earnings in nonagricultural industries. Although the correspondence is not precise, clearly in the period of generally rising prices from 1965 to 1980 compensation tracked the price rises, and increases in compensation slowed when prices declined after 1980.

Figure 3.1 Prices and Wages, 1958–1997

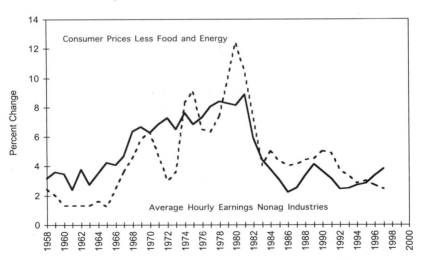

Source: ERP, 1998, Earnings Table B-47, p. 336; CPI Table B-63, p. 353

Although wages may lag behind price changes, wages inevitably go up as prices go up, because labor attempts to maintain its share of national income. The lags in adjustment add to the distortions in the economy in the short run. In addition, higher labor costs add to pressures for higher prices, setting a vicious cycle in motion.

Even the fear of inflation is so worrisome that it has become a major concern of the U.S. monetary authority, the Federal Reserve (Fed). Consequently, signs of inflation usually result in tighter monetary policy, causing higher interest rates. Because of this emphasis on price changes, it may be helpful to understand the measures available to monitor prices, so that they can both be followed, understood, and interpreted.

As expected, the broadest measures of price changes are associated with the broadest measure of economic activity, the GDP. In addition, several other price measures are available, some of which are probably better known than the GDP price measures. We shall examine all of them in the remainder of this chapter.

GDP PRICE MEASURES

Estimates are made of GDP in both *current* or *nominal* and in *price-adjusted terms,* so that changes associated with physical volume can be separated from changes associated with prices. To accomplish this separation, several price measures are used.

Implicit price deflators reflect both changes in prices and changes in the composition of output. They are derived by dividing nominal GDP by real GDP; this is done for total GDP and its components. Because they are not based on prices directly observed but are derived from estimates of real and nominal GDP quantities, they are called "implicit" price indexes. In addition, these indexes reflect changes in both prices and physical amounts, so they are not a measure of pure price change. Therefore, they are not useful as measures of price changes only.

A second measure used prior to 1996 was a *fixed-weight index of prices,* in which nominal output was divided by prices in a base year. The difficulty in using this measure was that the price weights of the GDP components and their aggregates were frozen in that base year. Changes in the composition of the outputs or in prices as the measuring period moved backward or forward in time resulted in prices that were not indicative of actual component prices in time periods other than the base year; these distortions increased over time.

Thus, *chain-weighted prices* are now used, which are averages of prices in adjourning periods. For example, the 1992–93 percent change in real GDP uses prices in 1992 and 1993 as weights. Similarly, the 1992–93 percent change in prices uses quantities for 1992 and 1993 as weights. These changes are averaged (using a geometric rather than an arithmetic mean) and then are moved forward and backward in time, forming chained indexes of prices of GDP and its components that use weights appropriate for each period.

The GDP chain-type price indexes reflect prices of GDP and its components, including prices for exports and imports. A further refinement reflects *prices paid for gross domestic purchases*, i.e., prices paid for goods and services purchased by U.S. residents during a particular period. This index is becoming the most widely used of the GDP price measures; its only weakness is that it is reported for calendar quarters rather than months and is revised as later data become available. The consumer price index and the producer price indexes are based on monthly surveys and thus provide more current information. The consumer price index is rarely revised. The producer price index is subject to revision for four months after it is released. Revisions to the comprehensive index, the producer price index for finished goods, tend to be minor, although at times larger revisions are reported for producer price indexes for particular commodities.

THE CONSUMER PRICE INDEX

The price index most familiar to the average consumer and investor is the *consumer price index (CPI)*. This index is the one used to adjust social security payments as well as labor and other contracts with a cost-of-living adjustment. The index is supposed to reflect the changes in the prices the typical consumer pays over time for a fixed market basket of consumer goods and services. The CPI for all urban consumers represents spending patterns for about 87 percent of the noninstitutional population. The index is based on prices for food, clothing, shelter and fuels, transportation fares, charges for doctors' and dentists' services, drugs, and other goods and services that people buy for day-to-day living.[1]

Prices are collected in 87 urban areas across the country from about 60,000 housing units and 21,000 retail establishments. Prices of food, fuels, and a few other items are collected every month in all 91 locations. Prices of all other commodities and services are collected every month in the three largest geographic areas and every other month in other areas.

Figure 3.2 provides a breakdown of the CPI in December 1997. Housing costs are the largest component of the index. The 30 percent shown in the pie chart for shelter includes rents or home-owners' equivalent of rent, household insurance, and maintenance and repairs. Other household costs are fuel and utilities (5 percent) and house furnishing, housekeeping supplies and services (5 percent). All told, household costs account for 40 percent of total consumer expenditures. In addition, food and beverages account for 16 percent of consumer expenditures, apparel and upkeep account for 5 percent, transportation for 17 percent, medical care for 6 percent, recreation for 6 percent, education and communication for 6 percent, and other goods and services for 4 percent.

What Does the CPI Measure?

The CPI is a measure of price change for a fixed market basket of goods and services of constant quantity and quality purchased for consumption. The CPI should not be considered a cost-of-living index, because the weights of the items included remain fixed between major revisions and do not reflect interim shifts in consumer spending patterns. As consumers change their purchasing patterns, the CPI samples and weights are updated periodically to reflect these changes. In addition, other improvements have been made outside of the revision framework, such as adjustments for changes in the quality of new cars, a shift in the cost of owner-occupied housing to rental equivalent, and a quality adjustment for apparel prices.

---

[1] This index is technically called CPI-U. Another index, CPI-W, is also issued. It represents urban wage and clerical workers employed in blue-collar occupations. It accounts for a smaller (only 32 percent) of the noninstitutional population, and it is not used so much as the CPI-U index.

Figure 3.2 *Components of Consumer Price Index, December 1997*

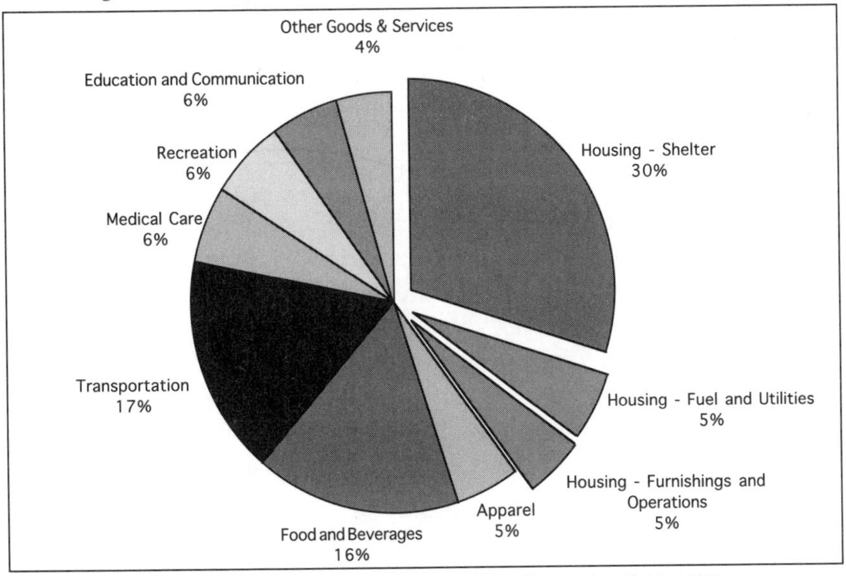

Source: Bureau of Labor Statistics, CPI release, April 14, 1998

    The Bureau of Labor Statistics (BLS) does a major overhaul of the index about every ten years, and the most recent will be completed within the six-year period ending with the year 2000. Included in the overhaul is an updating of the content of the "market basket" of goods and services, the prices of which are included in the CPI. The current revision is identified as the 1998 CPI revision, because the market basket revisions were shifted effective with the January 1998 report.

The Major Changes in the January 1998 Revision

The major changes in the recent revision include the following:

- Movements in the index beginning in January 1998 are based on 1993–95 consumer expenditure patterns, instead of the 1982–84 patterns that were used from January 1987. However, the numerical reference base will remain the same, with 1982–84 = 100. BLS decided not to change the reference base, because historical data are less accurate after rebasing; rebased index values are smaller and precision is lost in rounding. In addition, users who are viewing indexes over long periods must convert old numbers to the new base.

- The geographic sample selection was revised based on the 1990 decennial census, with thirty-six new sampling units added to the fifty-one that were continued, in order to reflect current demographics more accurately.

- The market basket of goods and services was updated, with a new group, education and communications, added to the prior seven groups: apparel, medical care, transportation, food and beverages, housing, recreation, and other goods and services. Personal computers and telephone services (including cellular phones) are included in education and communications and no longer included in housing entertainment (now called recreation) and other goods and services.

- The medical care component has been dramatically revised to reflect the changes in the delivery of hospital services, reimbursement methods, and payment sources for hospital visits. Pricing now will reflect a shift from pricing individual items (such as a unit of blood) to pricing combined sets of goods and services provided on selected patient bills. (Hospital services amount to about one-quarter of the total medical component of the CPI.)

- In January 1999, the housing portion of the CPI revision will shift to a new estimating method for homeowner shelter costs and use a new housing unit sample based on the 1990 decennial census. Within the housing component, the rental equivalent of owner-occupied dwellings comprises 20 percent of the total CPI, rental of a primary residence 7 percent, lodging away from home 2 percent, and the remainder reflects prices of fuel, utilities, and household furnishings and operations.

- In early 1999, a shift from sample rotation to item category rotation using telephone point-of-survey data collection will lead to faster data turnaround and more up-to-date information on the distribution of consumer spending. In addition, in January 1999 a technical change will be made in the formula for calculating the basic components of the CPI.

These new changes will improve the quality of the CPI and make it more reflective of current conditions. The net effect will be to make the index a few tenths of a percentage point lower than it otherwise would have been. These changes are a part of the on-going efforts of all government statistical agencies to improve the promptness and accuracy of their reports on the workings of the economy.

How Accurate Is the CPI?

In recent years, controversy has swirled around the accuracy of the computations of the CPI. The issue is significant because it affects the annual so-called "cost-of-living" adjustment in social security payments (as well as many in private contracts). Reducing the amount of the social security adjustments because they overstate increases in the cost of living could have a significant impact on the federal budget deficit as well as on the personal budgets of many retired persons.

At the outset, the CPI is not a good measure of the changes in the cost of living. A cost-of-living index would be one that measures the change in the cost of purchasing goods and services that would enable the purchases to obtain a fixed level of well-being. The CPI rather is an index that reflects the prices of a fixed market basket of goods established by consumer spending patterns in the base years 1982–84.

In carrying the prices of this fixed basket forward, several problems arise, and in June 1995 Congress appointed a commission, the Boskin Commission, to report on the issue. In 1996, the Commission issued a report that estimated the CPI overstated the increase in the CPI by 0.8 to 1.6 percent a year, with a point estimate of 1.1 percent a year. The causes of this overstatement were identified as follows:

1. *Substitution bias.* This bias occurs at two levels: a lower-level shift when spending patterns change, e.g., a shift from apples to oranges or from one type of apple to another, or a shift from beef to chicken. This bias is estimated to result in an overstatement in the CPI of about 0.5 percent a year.

2. Other sources of bias that account for the remaining 0.6 percent include inadequate adjustment for quality changes in the goods and services people buy, improper accounting

for the value to consumers of newly available goods, and deficiencies in the way the CPI treats differences in the prices charged at different retail outlets.

Needless to say, the Bureau of Labor Statistics is addressing these issues as best it can within the limited funding of statistical programs by Congress, and modifications will be made to the index as considered appropriate. However, the production of a true cost-of-living index probably is many years away.

Consumer Prices in Perspective Over Time

Figure 3.3 provides a perspective of the annual changes in consumer prices for most of the time since World War II, the 47-year period from 1950 through 1997. For this entire period, the average annual price increase was 4.1 percent. However, in this case, the average conceals some very interesting differences. The average annual increase from 1950 to 1965 was a low 1.9 percent. The Vietnam War effects on the economy caused prices to more than double for the 1966 to 1972 period. Two oil price shocks sent prices soaring in the 1973 to 1981 period, when the average annual price increase was more than 9 percent, with several years well above

Figure 3.3 Consumer Price Index, 1950–1997

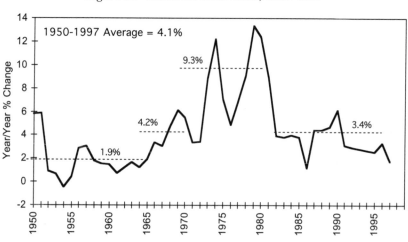

Source: ERP, 1998, Table B-63, p. 353

that level. The business contractions of 1980 and 1981 to 1982 as well as the restrictive monetary policies of that period caused prices to fall considerably, so that in 1982 to 1997 price increases averaged 3.2 percent, and more recently have been running below that average. As for the future, the long-term outlook for inflation as well as the economy will be considered in Chapter 9.

Figure 3.3 provides a background against which monthly price reports can be evaluated. However, regular press reports on consumer prices usually focus on the month-to-month price changes—and these numbers may seem deceptively small. After all, a monthly gain of 0.3 or 0.4 percent may not seem like much. A more useful piece of information usually included in most press reports is the percentage rise in prices over the past 12 months, which then can be compared with the annual changes in Figure 3.3.

But even this additional information may not provide an appropriate perspective. Year-to-year changes as shown in Figure 3.3 do not reflect the cumulative effects of price increases over a longer period of time. Figure 3.4 illustrates this point. An average annual inflation rate of 4.2 percent may not seem like a lot, but the devastating effect on the value of the currency is shown by the fact that a $1 in 1950 had lost more than 85 percent of its purchasing power by 1997 and was worth about fifteen cents!

Figure 3.4 Purchasing Power of a 1950 Dollar

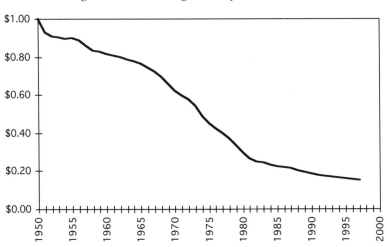

Source: Same as Figure 3.3, computations by author

PRODUCER PRICE INDEXES

A third group of price indexes reflects prices of products only, not services. These indexes reflect prices received by domestic producers of commodities at all stages of processing. The base reference period in the index is 1982 prices set to equal 100. About 32,000 commodities and 80,000 price quotations are obtained each month.

Actually, price indexes are prepared for three separate stages of production: crude materials for further processing; intermediate materials, supplies, and components; and finished goods. The finished goods index is the one usually picked up and reported in the press. In this index, consumer goods represent about 76 percent of the weight of the total index (24 percentage points are foods) and capital equipment 24 percent of the total. In addition to the three basic indexes, separate computations are made for prices at various stages of processing excluding food and energy components.

Not surprisingly, the producer price indexes are more volatile than either the CPI or the GDP implicit price deflator. Figure 3.5 compares the year-to-year fluctuations in these three indexes for the period 1950 to 1997. As indicated in the figure, the dotted line representing the producer price index is the most volatile, followed by the consumer price index.

Figure 3.5 CPI vs. PPI vs. GNP Deflator
Year-to-Year Percent Change, 1950–1997

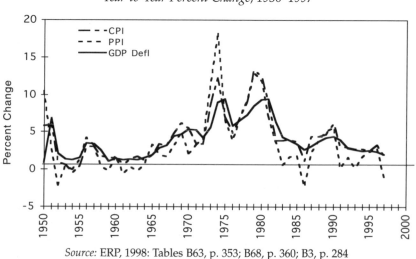

Source: ERP, 1998: Tables B63, p. 353; B68, p. 360; B3, p. 284

WHICH INDEX IS BEST?

As is the case in most indexes, no one index is "best"; it depends on what you want to measure. The index of prices paid for gross domestic purchases, included in the GDP reports, is the broadest measure and best reflects the movements of prices in a dynamic economy. The defects in this index are that it is issued only quarterly and is subject to frequent revisions.

The CPI is a monthly index and is prepared by sampling, so that month-to-month revisions do not occur. However, the index becomes less meaningful as purchasing patterns change or quality improvements occur; for example, higher prices for better products. Revisions in the composition of the index are made only about every ten years, so they can get out of date in reflecting buying patterns of the consumer.

The CPI also differs from the price indexes for personal consumption expenditures in the GDP accounts. The CPI represents prices of a fixed market basket of goods, reflecting the purchases in various geographical areas in a certain base period. Personal consumption expenditure prices used in the GDP accounts are estimates of the prices of those amounts of goods and services taken off the market by all consumers in a particular quarter or year.

The producer price indexes are used more by economists as foreshadowing indicators of commodity prices that will later affect goods prices in the CPI. These indexes are also used by manufacturers to track prices of their products as well as their raw materials and intermediate components. Given the growing importance of services in the economy, measuring only goods prices has limited usefulness to the average consumer or investor. However, service prices are now included and coverage is expanding in crude and intermediate goods indexes.

SUMMARY

This chapter described the three price indexes that are issued as a part of the regular GDP reports: the implicit price deflator, the chain price index, and the index of prices paid for gross domestic purchases. In addition, the consumer price index and the producer price indexes were discussed. Although the CPI is probably the best known, no one index is "best"; it depends on what is being measured or what index will give you the information you need.

CHAPTER 4

Tracking the Consumer

In this and the next three chapters the various GDP components are reviewed in more detail, providing additional background and historical perspective. Several other economic reports, which are helpful in following the performance of a particular sector, are also discussed.

This chapter is about the consumer. Many of the statistics reported regularly in the financial press deal with consumer income, spending, and saving. Such emphasis is appropriate, because the consumer is one of the most important players on the economic scene. Personal income is significant because it is the source of both spending and saving in the economy. Personal consumption accounts for about two-thirds of GDP, and changes in consumer spending can have a significant effect on business conditions; personal saving is a significant portion of total saving in the economy.

A review of the regular statistical reports that economists track to follow the movement of consumer income, spending, and saving is provided in this chapter. Some of the reports that cover personal income are:

Personal income. A monthly report that reflects the two sources of this income—current production (e.g., wages and salaries, other labor income, personal interest, dividend and rental income, partnership and proprietors income) and transfer payments from business and government to persons (e.g., payments from a corporate health plan or social security payments);

Monthly employment report. Provides information on the sources of personal income. A sample survey of households gives information on the size of the labor force and data on employment and unemployment. A survey of payroll reports gives information on payroll employment; the change in jobs in service, manufacturing, and related industries; and weekly and hourly earnings.

Personal spending by consumers is tracked by these reports:

Personal consumption expenditures. Reported monthly, indicating consumer spending for durable goods, nondurable goods, and services;

Automobile sales. Reported monthly, the earliest and clearest indication of this important part of consumer durable spending;

Retail sales. Available monthly before the personal consumption report, reflecting spending for durable and nondurable goods. Because of the volatile nature of this report, it is difficult to interpret; other measures of consumer spending are more useful;

Housing starts and building permits. Reported monthly, indicating future trends in residential consumption expenditures.

Consumer saving and borrowing are measured as follows:

Personal saving. Reported monthly, a part of the income and expenditure report and essentially the difference between income and spending. However, personal saving is only a part of total sources of saving. Undistributed corporate profits, depreciation, state and local government surpluses, and funds from abroad are also included in the total sources of saving;

Consumer borrowing. Available monthly, measured by consumer installment data. However, month-to-month changes of credit outstanding or credit related to income are of little assistance in short-term business analysis.

Another way to follow whether the consumer will spend or save is to ask about consumer attitudes toward the economy and plans for the future.

Consumer attitudes. Tracked by sample surveys that ask questions of consumers about general business conditions, job availability, and buying intentions.

PERSONAL INCOME

Trends in personal income foreshadow changes in spending. In Table 2.3, the income side of GDP was described, moving from GDP to national income and then the distribution of this income among production costs and profits. Recall that the components of national income are:

Employee compensation, including wages and salaries, and employer contributions to employee benefit funds;

Net interest received by business;

Corporate profits;

Rental income of persons;

Income of proprietorships and partnerships.

If corporate profits and net interest received by business are subtracted from national income, the remainder is income from current production that goes to persons. However, a few other adjustments must be made in order to get to personal income. These are shown in Table 4.1, which shows the full relationship between national income and personal income.

Table 4.1   Relationship of National Income and Personal Income—1997

		Billions of Dollars
National Income		6649.7
Less:	Corporate profits	805.0
	Net interest received by business	448.7
	Contributions for social insurance	732.1
Plus:	Personal interest income	768.6
	Personal dividend income	321.5
	Business transfer payments	27.1
	Government transfer payments to persons	1094.1
Personal Income		6873.9

Source: SCB, June 1998, Table 1.9, p. D-4

Personal income is derived from two sources—income from current production, and transfer payments from business and government. As the table indicates, one way of estimating personal income is to start with national income and subtract those payments not made to persons—corporate profits, net interest received by business, and the contributions both business and individuals make to the government for social insurance. Contributions to social insurance are subtracted because this amount represents income earned in any particular period (and thus is a part of national income) but not actually received.

Certain transfers made from business and government to individuals must then be added. These transfers include interest income and dividend income paid to individuals, and business transfer payments for such things as bad debts (the forgiveness of which is considered income to consumers). Government transfer payments include benefits such as social security payments, health benefits, unemployment insurance, veterans benefits, and retirement benefits for government employees.

Figure 4.1 indicates the significance of each of the components of personal income to the total; the data are for the calendar year 1997. Wages and salaries are the largest component, accounting for

56 percent of total personal income. Another 6 percent is accounted for by other labor income, consisting of employer payments to private pension funds and welfare funds, such as health and life insurance and workers' compensation. Personal interest income is the second largest component at 11 percent, and transfer payments from business and government is third at 12 percent. Proprietors and partnership income accounts for 8 percent; dividends paid to persons accounts for 5 percent. Rental income received by persons accounts for about 2 percent of personal income.

The Department of Commerce releases data on personal income in the third or fourth week of each month to cover the information for the prior month. Personal income data are also included as a part of the monthly reports provided by the Commerce Department on the quarterly movements in GDP.

Figure 4.1   Sources of Personal Income—1997

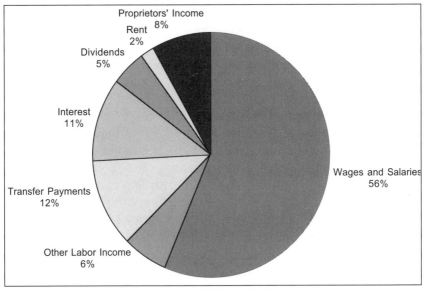

Source: SCB, June 1998, Table 2.1, p. D-6

Monthly Employment Report

Because the monthly income report comes out late in the following month, another economic report issued earlier in the month is examined more closely; it provides the first indication of future changes in personal income and is keenly followed by most

business analysts as the first major clue to the economy's performance in the prior month. The monthly employment report covers
the employment and unemployment situation, especially the part
indicating the number of employees on nonagricultural payrolls.
This information usually is released by the Bureau of Labor
Statistics on the first Friday of each month, covering information
for the previous month.

Unfortunately, only part of the information in the monthly
report is presented by the news media. Two key items are the percent of the labor force unemployed and the number of jobs created
(or lost) in a particular month. However, the full significance of the
report is not often discussed. Therefore, it is worthwhile to examine some of the background and the essential features of the
monthly release.

The Household Survey. Two basic methods are used to
assemble the data in the monthly employment report. The first
method provides information on households and is gathered in a
monthly survey of a sample of households scientifically designed
to represent the civilian noninstitutional population. Inmates of
institutions and persons under 16 years of age are excluded when
computing the employment and unemployment statistics. Data on
members of the armed forces in the United States are obtained
from the Department of Defense and added to the estimate of the
civilian labor force to obtain the size of the total labor force.

Each month about 50,000 households are visited for an inter-
view; three-quarters of the household sample is common from one
month to the next and half of the sample is common with the same
month a year ago. The purpose of the interviews is to obtain information about the employment status of each member of the household 16 years of age and older.

In the household surveys, employed persons are those who,
during the survey week (the week that includes the 12th of the
month), worked as paid employees or in their own business, or
were temporarily absent from their jobs because of illness, bad
weather, vacation, labor-management disputes, or personal reasons. Unemployed persons are those who were available for work,
and had made specific efforts to find employment some time during the prior four weeks but had no employment during the survey
week. (This definition is especially significant when comparing the

unemployment rate in the United States with that of other countries, where unemployment is defined as a person actually collecting unemployment insurance.)

From the surveys and the information from the Department of Defense, the following data are computed:

Size of the civilian and the total labor force;

Number of persons employed and unemployed;

Duration of unemployment;

Number of job seekers;

Unemployment rates by various categories, such as sex, race, and age.

The Establishment Data.   The second source of employment information is based on payroll reports that provide current information on wage and salary employment as well as hours and earnings in individual nonagricultural establishments, categorized by industry and geographic location. Employment data refer to persons on payrolls who receive pay for any part of the pay period that includes the 12th of the month. Excluded are people who are on layoff, on leave without pay, or on strike during the entire period.

The number of establishments included in the report varies by industry. In order to ensure adequate coverage, more establishments are covered in industries with smaller size establishments. About 390,000 establishments are covered each month, which employ more than one-third of total workers in the United States.

The information in the establishment reports permits computation of:

Number of people on payrolls for production and related workers in manufacturing and mining;

Construction workers in construction;

Nonsupervisory employees in private service-producing industries.

Other information provided includes:

Increases or decreases in jobs in service, manufacturing, and related industries;

Average weekly hours per employee;

Average hourly earnings;

Average weekly earnings.

From all of this information, economists pay the most attention to the total change in employees on nonagricultural payrolls. The data for the months in 1987 to 1998 are shown in Figure 4.2. Monthly changes are indicated by the dotted line on the figure. Monthly changes fluctuate widely; to smooth the data and make it easier to interpret, a three-month moving average of monthly changes has been computed, shown by the solid black line. One further adjustment has been to remove from the data the number of census workers that were added to the labor force between January and May 1990 and then subsequently eliminated from June through the end of the year. Their inclusion would make the numbers even more volatile and would not reveal underlying trends of employment.

Figure 4.2   Change in Employees on Nonagricultural Payrolls, 1987–1998

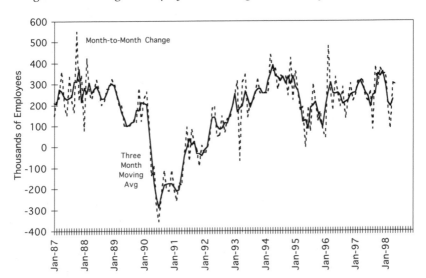

Source: BLS Employment and Earnings, historical data file

A review of the figure indicates the importance of several years of data. Beginning in 1989, job increases definitely shifted to a level lower than that of the previous two years, and the significant drop in job gains in 1990 is evident. This perspective provided early indications of a definite slowing in the U.S. economy in the latter part of 1990. Job growth slowed again in 1995 although it was essentially positive. Since then, growth has been steady at a relatively good level.

Unfortunately, the monthly information on changes in payroll employment is often revised and the revisions may seem large. However, the changes are a very small percent of the total number of jobs. For example, a monthly change of as much as 100,000 jobs is a change of less than 0.1 percent on a job base of 126 million. When reviewing job changes, the initial report should be viewed with some degree of skepticism until revised data are reported in the next two months.

Other Employment and Unemployment Data. The number that gets the most attention in the media is the monthly unemployment rate, probably because of its political sensitivity. Not surprisingly, unemployment rises in business-cycle contractions and falls in business expansions. However, *some* unemployment is inevitable, so-called frictional unemployment caused by people changing jobs, moving from one place to another, deciding to enter the labor force when another member of the family becomes unemployed, and so on. An acceptable level of frictional unemployment is more of a political than an economic issue. However, most economists would now accept the idea that rates much below 5 percent for all practical purposes represent "full" employment in the United States, and this level prevailed since mid-1997.

A problem in interpreting the unemployment rate is the difficulty in measuring unemployment in the summer months, with the entry and exit of many students into and out of the labor force. Attempts are made to adjust for this seasonal phenomenon, but the number of summer job seekers varies so much from year to year that large variations in the unemployment rate during these months are not unusual.

The monthly employment report does contain some helpful bits of information. The employment report is a good indicator of the change that will occur in the monthly industrial production index reported by the Federal Reserve about the 15th of each month. Many of the components of the industrial production index are estimated based on man-hour production data rather than the output of physical units. An increase in payroll employment and hours worked usually indicates an increase in industrial production.

Another helpful bit of information in the monthly employment report is contained in the average hourly earnings data. By comparing month-to-month or year-to-year changes over a period of time, some feeling of the rate of change in wages can be obtained. As seen in Table 2.3, wages are a very important component of production costs. Wages rising faster than prices foreshadows future price increases. As indicated in Figure 3.1, changes in consumer prices, excluding food and energy and changes in compensation, have tracked each other rather well.

PERSONAL INCOME AND CONSUMPTION EXPENDITURES

A report on personal consumption expenditures (PCE) accompanies the monthly report of personal income. Plotting these two series in a figure would result in two lines that move steadily upward. Therefore, as in the case of nonagricultural payroll employment, the month-to-month changes have been plotted instead. Figure 4.3 plots these changes in monthly personal income and personal consumption expenditures from 1992 to 1998.

As the figure shows, the lines move up and down erratically, making it hard to discern underlying trends. Unusual spikes in personal income are caused by payments not compensated for by seasonal adjustments, e.g., extra large year-end bonuses, cost-of-living adjustments to social security and government retiree payments, natural disasters that may affect rental income, or irregular farm subsidy payments.

Information on personal income and consumption is of some value in following trends over a period of months. However, the availability of the data late in the month makes it a less useful indicator of current business conditions. The wealth of detail in the report is more useful to analysts of particular areas of the economy. Some of this detail is discussed on the following page.

Personal consumption expenditures are divided into durable goods (goods expected to last three years or more), nondurable goods, and services. Table 4.2 compares PCE in 1950 with those in 1997. In viewing the data, keep in mind that PCE increased about 28 times during this period; GDP increased slightly less.

Of more interest is the shifting composition of PCE. Durable goods purchases fell somewhat: 16 percent of PCE in 1950 and 12 percent in 1997. However, nondurable goods purchases decreased from 51 to 29 percent, while services spending grew from 33 to 59 percent.

The shifts within the components are also interesting. Table 4.3 indicates the shift in durable goods spending. Over the 1950 to 1997 period, durable spending increased about 21 times, less than the increase in total PCE. Within durable goods spending, both motor vehicles and parts, and furniture and household equipment spending, fell from about 45 to 40 percent of the total. Purchases shifted to durables spending on other items, including sports equipment, boats, computing equipment, durable toys, jewelry, and watches.

Figure 4.3   Monthly Percent Change in Personal Income and Personal Consumption Expenditures, 1992–1998

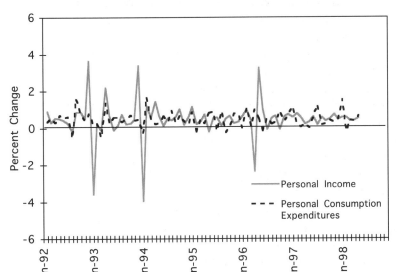

Source: SCB, August 1997, Table 2.9, p. 62; June 1998, Tables B.1 and B.2, p. D-27

Table 4.2
Distribution of Personal Consumption Expenditures (Billions of Dollars)

	1950	%	1997	%
Durable goods	30.8	16.0	659.3	12.0
Nondurable goods	98.2	51.0	1592.0	29.0
Services	63.7	33.0	3234.5	59.0
Total	192.7	100.0	5485.8	100.0

Source: STAT-USA, NIPA Historical estimates

Table 4.3
Distribution of PCE—Durables (Billions of Dollars)

	1950	%	1997	%
Motor vehicles	13.7	44.6	263.4	40.0
Furniture and HH Equipment	13.7	44.6	267.4	40.5
Other	3.3	10.8	128.5	19.5
Total durables	30.7	100.0	659.3	100.0

Source: STAT-USA, NIPA Historical estimates

Table 4.4 shows the changes in spending for nondurables. Total spending for nondurables grew about 16 times during the 1950 to 1997 period. Most of the large components of spending decreased: food from 55 to 49 percent; clothing from 20 to 17 percent; fuel oil and coal from 3 to less than 1 percent. Gasoline and oil spending rose slightly from 6 to 8 percent. The decreases reflected increased "other" spending for nondurables, including toilet articles, drug preparations, semidurable house furnishings, nondurable toys, and sport supplies.

Table 4.5 indicates the shift in PCE for services. This segment increased more than 51 times from 1950 to 1997, compared to a rise in GDP of 27 times. The change in the composition of services spending is even more interesting. The percent of service expenditures for housing, household operations, and transportation decreased slightly, but the percent of service expenditures for medical care expanded dramatically—from 11 to 26 percent. "Other" expenditures held their percent of the total; these expenditures included items such as personal care, recreation, personal business costs, religious and welfare activities, and private education. Services spending fluctuates less in business cycles than spending for durables. The increased portion of consumer spending for services, especially for such important items as medical care, has provided greater stability to overall consumer spending. This greater stability has tempered the severity of business downturns.

Table 4.4
Distribution of PCE—Nondurables (Billions of Dollars)

	1950	%	1997	%
Food	53.9	54.9	776.4	48.8
Clothing and shoes	19.6	20.0	277.3	17.4
Gasoline and oil	5.5	5.6	124.6	7.8
Fuel oil and coal	3.4	3.5	10.8	0.7
Other	15.8	16.1	402.8	25.3
Total nondurables	98.2	100.0	1592.0	100.0

Source: STAT-USA, NIPA Historical estimates

Table 4.5
Distribution of PCE—Services (Billions of Dollars)

	1950	%	1997	%
Housing	21.7	34.1	826.5	25.6
Household operation	9.5	14.9	327.8	10.1
Transportation	6.2	9.7	236.3	7.3
Medical care	7.2	11.3	854.2	26.4
Other	19.1	30.0	989.7	30.6
Total services	63.7	100.0	3234.5	100.0

Source: STAT-USA, NIPA Historical estimates

AUTOMOBILE SALES

Although the smallest of the three areas of consumer spending, the series watched most carefully is spending for durables, because purchase of these items are postponable and therefore fluctuate cyclically. About 40 percent of durable spending is for automobiles and parts. Because of its importance in both the cyclical part of personal spending and the automobile industry in the economy as a whole, automobile sales are a carefully watched statistic that reflects the spending mood of the consumer and indicates possible future increases or decreases in production.

Information on automobile sales has two major advantages relative to other economic information. In the first place, they are available early; sales are reported about five business days after the last day of the month. Second, unlike many statistics, the numbers are not subject to later revisions, so that the first report can be relied on as accurate.

One caution should be kept in mind in interpreting the data. Sales are often reported in the news media compared with sales for the similar period of the previous year—not particularly useful when you are looking for trends over recent months.

One way of tracking automobile sales is shown in Figure 4.4. Domestic car sales, light truck sales (which include minivans and sport utility vehicles as well as a small number of imported light trucks), and imported car sales are shown monthly at seasonally adjusted annual rates. Light truck sales have been gaining steadily in popularity and now roughly equal domestic car sales. This gain has been mostly at the expense of imported car sales—overseas auto producers missed the shift in tastes of U.S. consumers to light trucks and sport utility vehicles.

A disadvantage in following monthly motor vehicle sales data is that the information is not available all at one time. Most manufacturers report their prior month's sales on the first working day of the month, one reports on the third working day, and truck sales generally are available several days after the auto sales figures. The seasonally adjusted rate of sales is usually estimated and reported by some analysts or the media before the total seasonally adjusted figures are reported by the Commerce Department, and at times these reports are not accurate. It is better to wait for the

Figure 4.4   U.S. Motor Vehicle Sales, 1992–1998

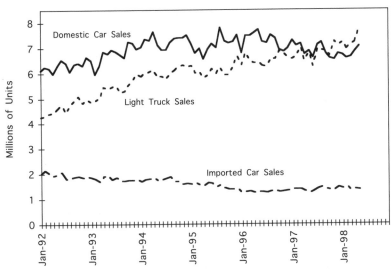

Source: STAT-USA, NIPA Auto and Truck Sales and Production

Commerce Department data, which are available to subscribers to Stat-USA, usually in the second week of the month. (See Chapters 11 and 12 for a discussion of sources of economic information.)

RETAIL SALES

Another report available about midmonth—and therefore available before the report on personal consumption—is retail sales. These sales are accounted for by a broad variety of stores, as illustrated in Figure 4.5. About 41 percent of retail sales are accounted for by sales of durable goods. Auto and parts stores account for 23 percent of total retail sales and about 59 percent of durable goods sales by retail stores. Because durable goods sales are more volatile than total retail sales, and auto and parts are such a significant part of durable goods sales, fluctuations in domestic auto sales figures can provide a good clue to the subsequent retail sales number. Food store sales represent about 17 percent of retail

Figure 4.5   Composition of Retail Sales—1997

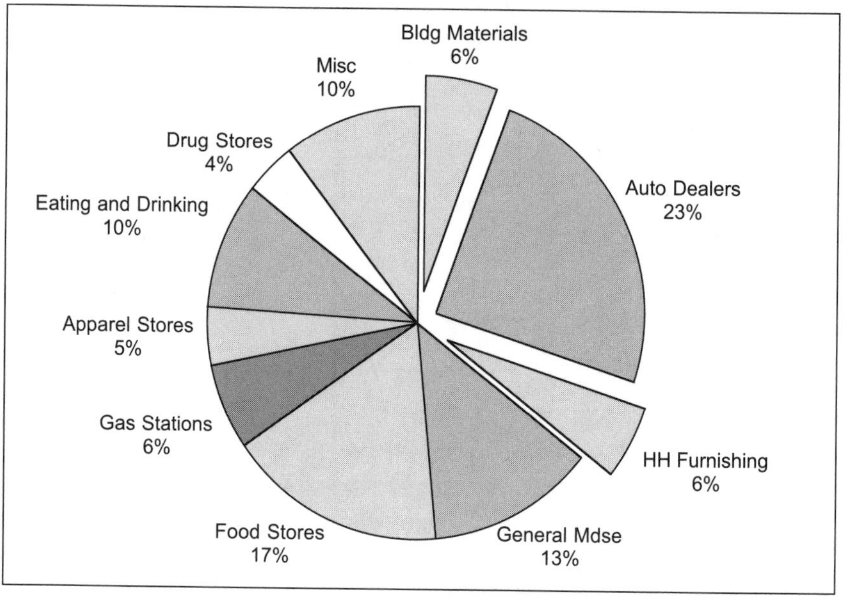

Source: Bureau of Census, Monthly Retail Sales by Kinds of Business, 1997

sales; eating and drinking establishments another 10 percent. Department stores, more accurately described as general merchandising stores, account for just 13 percent of total retail sales. Thus, when the news media report the sales results of the major retail stores about a week before retail sales are available, the report is not necessarily a good indicator of total retail trade. Other smaller samples of weekly and monthly retail sales made by private organizations are less reliable indicators of consumer spending patterns—and of retail sales results as well.

The pattern of monthly change in retail sales is illustrated on Figure 4.6, which plots this information for the months of 1987 to 1998 on a year-over-year percent change basis to smooth out big monthly fluctuations. As the figure illustrates, the changes are erratic, so that drawing conclusions from one or two months' data is hardly warranted. The difficulties in interpreting monthly retail figures favor using automobile sales and consumer confidence measures as better indicators of near-term consumer spending trends.

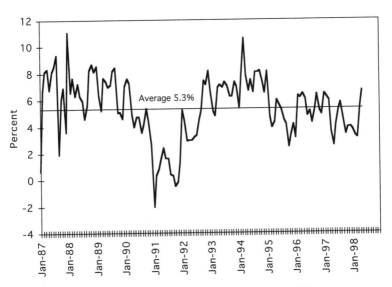

Figure 4.6 *Retail Sales, 1987–1998*
Year-Over-Year Percent Change

Source: Bureau of Census, Retail Sales historical data

CONSTRUCTION

Other monthly statistics that reflect large consumer commitments are the reports on the dollar value of residential construction as well as housing starts and permits, especially for single-family units. Total construction expenditures, exceeding $600 billion a year, are of considerable economic significance. Private construction accounts for about 77 percent of total construction expenditures; public construction accounts for the other 23 percent. New residential construction accounts for about 56 percent of private construction.

The dollar value of construction and its components are available about two months after the reported month. For example, October data are reported in early December. However, it is not especially useful in evaluating the current economic scene, because it is one of the late statistics available and is often revised.

Residential investment is also reported as a part of the quarterly GDP accounts. One of the components of GDP is fixed investment, which includes private residential as well as nonresidential investment. (Government investment is included in the government consumption expenditures and gross investment section of the GDP accounts.) Nonresidential investment will be discussed in Chapter 5, which is devoted to the business sector.

Residential investment in the GDP accounts is divided into single-family homes (about half of total residential investment), multifamily homes (about 7 percent); the remainder is accounted for by additions and alterations, mobile homes, hotels, dormitories, nursing homes, and brokerage commissions on sales. Residential construction is one of the more volatile areas of investment. It averaged 4.7 percent of GDP in the past 48 years, ranging from a low of 3.2 percent in 1991 to a high of 7.0 percent in 1950. Because the data on residential investment in the GDP accounts are available only quarterly and are usually revised, they are not given so much attention in the analysis of current business conditions as other monthly series that report on residential construction.

Residential investment decisions may initially be made by builders and contractors, but ultimately individuals make these decisions. Consequently, residential construction is affected in the long term by the growth in the number of households and their desire for a home, and in the short term by mortgage interest rates and the growth in family income.

A long-term view of residential fixed investment is shown in Figure 4.7, which plots residential fixed investment as a percent of GDP from 1950 to 1997. Two facts stand out: the downtrend from 1950 to 1967 and the increased volatility from 1970 to 1997. Residential building in the years immediately after World War II was influenced by the surge in home ownership as families moved to the suburbs. The 1970s reflected the next surge in home ownership as the baby boomers of the postwar era entered the home-buying age. During this time, real interest rates also were relatively low. High real and nominal interest rates caused home ownership to slip in the 1980s. Since 1990, home ownership has been stimulated by a surge of legal immigrants who want to own their own homes and an expansion in the older age groups who have the largest percent of home ownership. In addition, a shift to larger size and better quality homes, as well as an increase in remodeling expenditures, have added to the growth of spending in this area.

Looking ahead, housing is likely to be a sustaining force in economic growth, fostered by favorable household growth, further aging of the population, and replacement or remodeling of existing homes.

Residential construction near term is usually tracked by monthly data on housing starts, divided into single and multifamily units. Each single-family house and each separate apartment within an apartment building are counted as one housing start. The measure includes both privately and publicly owned housing. Data are collected by the Census Bureau and are available during the third week of the month following the reported month. The data are seasonally adjusted and reported at annual rates.

Another series reported at the same time is building permits, or new construction authorizations currently granted to builders by local government bodies. The Bureau of the Census obtains the data by a mail survey of local building permit officials. The permit data account for almost 90 percent of total housing starts. The relationship between permits and starts may not be too close, because the time between obtaining a permit and starting the house may vary.

Figure 4.7   Residential Investment as a Percent of GDP, 1950–1997

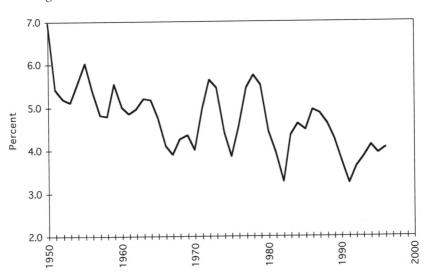

Source: STAT-USA, NIPA Historical estimates

Figure 4.8 provides a useful way of following starts and permits. The data are plotted monthly for the 1987 to 1997 period for starts and from January 1994 for permits. (Comparable earlier data for permits are not available.) Permit activity roughly leads starts, as seen in the figure.

One factor to keep in mind in reviewing housing data is to remember that the data are at seasonally adjusted annual rates. Because housing is affected significantly by weather, few starts are actually made in many sections of the country in the winter months. Should winter weather be unusually mild, a small increase in the actual unadjusted number of housing starts can be translated into a big surge when the figures are seasonally adjusted—a factor clearly evident in the winter of 1989 to 1990.

Figure 4.8   Housing Starts and Permits, 1987–1998
Monthly at Seasonally Adjusted Annual Rates

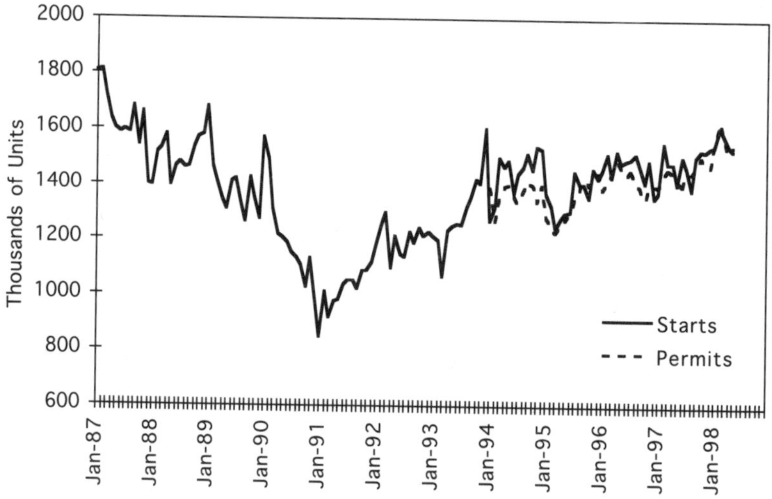

Source: Bureau of Census, Historical data series

CONSUMER SAVING

In addition to a current income stream, the consumer can obtain funds for consumption from either past saving or borrowing. Month-to-month changes in these two factors are not especially significant in determining future consumer spending, but trends over several years in the saving rate and borrowing can be informative. This section discusses consumer saving; borrowing is discussed in the next section.

Information on the consumer saving rate is available monthly as a part of the report on personal income and spending; it is also available monthly as a part of the estimates contained in the quarterly national income and product account release. Table 4.6 shows the relationship between personal income and personal saving.

As the consumer becomes more concerned about the future, saving is likely to increase; the opposite is also true. However, this measure is not very precise. As Table 4.6 illustrates, the amount of saving is a residual derived by subtracting estimated personal consumption and personal tax payments from personal income, and as a residual, it reflects all of the errors (some of them offsetting) in the figures used to derive it.

In addition, large segments of consumer spending are estimates rather than calculated directly. For example, in the case of owner-occupied homes, an estimate is made of the rental value of the dwellings less all of the costs associated with owning the dwelling, including mortgage interest. The personal saving figure does not take into account the effects of capital gains and losses, such as an increase or decrease in the value of residential real estate or the change in the value of stock holdings after a sharp market rise or drop. It also does not reflect the creation of financial credit by the banking system and

Table 4.6
Personal Income and Personal Saving—1997 (Billions of Dollars)

Personal income	6873.9
Less: Personal tax and nontax payments	998.7
Equals: Disposable personal income	5885.2
Less: Personal consumption expenditures	5485.8
Interest paid by persons	154.8
Personal transfer payments to rest of world	17.9
Equals: Personal saving	226.7
Personal saving as a percent of disposable personal income	3.9%

Source: SCB, June 1998, Table 2.1, p. D-6

the Federal Reserve, which can expand consumer purchasing power. Consequently, small monthly shifts in the saving number should not be given too much weight, although a trend downward or upward over a year or more is of considerable significance.

Even though these measures are imprecise, why is tracking saving important? For individuals, savings are important because some funds should be set aside for family emergencies or for longer term family objectives. For the country as a whole, saving is viewed differently, as indicated in the following relationships:

Total *output* of the economy generates income equal to the value of that output;

And *income* minus *consumption* equals *saving;*

But *output* minus *consumption* equals *investment;*

Consequently, *saving* equals *investment.*

The larger the saving in a society, the greater the sum available for investment. The greater the investment, the greater the potential for productivity gains of its work force, leading to a more prosperous country as a whole. Consequently, following the long-term trends of saving measures can provide useful clues to the future performance of the economy.

Figure 4.9 plots the annual personal saving rate in the United States for the years 1950 to 1997. For 1950 to 1997, this saving rate averaged 7.2 percent of disposable personal income. It reached a postwar peak of 9.5 percent in 1973–74, and fell to a low point of 3.9 percent in 1997.

Considerable attention has been paid to the drop in the U.S. saving rate, focusing primarily on why it has been so low since 1985. Most of the argument has been that the low rates are the result of faulty measurement. For example, the Commerce series does not reflect realized capital gains, the net additions to the social security trust funds (discussed further in Chapter 7), or the equity buildup in owner-occupied dwellings. In addition, the unrealized profits that have accrued in many individual equity portfolios in the past several years of booming stock prices certainly have increased individuals' feeling of enhanced net worth not captured in the Commerce series. In any event, other measures of saving tell a different story.

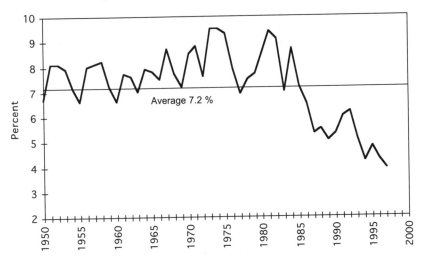

Figure 4.9
Personal Saving as a Percent of Disposable Personal Income, 1950–1997

Source: STAT-USA, NIPA Historical estimates

Other Savings Measures

Personal saving can be measured in other ways. The Federal Reserve, for example, prepares a quarterly estimate of personal saving that includes as a part of saving consumer durable goods purchases, government insurance credits, and capital gains. This saving rate has also trended downward since the mid-1970s, but in 1997 it was 7.1 percent, versus 3.9 percent in the Commerce estimate of the saving rate.

The saving measures mentioned thus far are measures only of personal saving. Undistributed profits of corporate business as well as depreciation credits of corporate and noncorporate business (roughly the same as private consumption of fixed capital in Commerce reports) are a form of saving and should be included when estimating national saving. State and local governments have been running an annual surplus of funds in excess of expenditures and capital consumption allowances, which adds to the saving stream. Of importance also is the net flow of funds from abroad. Saving is used for gross private domestic investment (both by business and for residential construction) and also for gross government investment—federal, state, and local. In addition, saving covers the federal deficit in excess of the allowance for the consumption of fixed capital.

These relationships are shown in Table 4.7 for the years 1992 and 1997. The year 1992 was selected for comparison to 1997, the most recent year for which data are available, because that was the year when the federal budget deficit peaked out. Several interesting points are shown in the table. Private consumption of fixed capital is the largest source of saving, with personal saving next. State and local governments have been a steady supplier of saving. Foreign borrowing has been an increasing source of funds, both in dollars and as a percent of total. Of greatest significance, however, is the shift of the federal deficit to a surplus (to be discussed further in Chapter 7), which has made more funds available for private investment. The importance of the federal government as a net consumer of saving cannot be overemphasized.

Table 4.7   Sources and Uses of Saving—1992 vs. 1997

	1992		1997	
Sources of Saving	*Billions of Dollars*	*Percent*	*Billions of Dollars*	*Percent*
Personal saving (Commerce definition)	285.6	24.4	226.7	14.6
Undistributed corporate profits	115.5	9.9	219.5	14.1
Private consumption of fixed capital	585.4	50.0	716.8	46.1
State and local government surpluses	148.6	12.7	187.3	12.0
Net foreign	50.5	4.3	160.2	10.3
Wage accruals less disbursements	−15.8	−1.4	1.2	0.1
Federal government surplus	—	—	42.8	2.8
Total	1169.8	100.0	1554.5	100.0
Uses of Saving				
Gross private domestic investment	790.5	67.6	1242.5	19.9
Gross government investment	209.2	17.9	226.0	14.5
Federal deficit less consumption of fixed capital	215.0	18.4	—	—
Statistical discrepancy	−44.9	−3.8	86.0	5.5
Total	1169.8	100.0	1554.5	100.0

Source: STAT-USA, NIPA Historical estimates

CONSUMER BORROWING

Information about consumer borrowing is provided monthly by the Federal Reserve Board about six weeks after the month to which the data refer. This series on consumer installment credit covers most short- to intermediate-term credit extended to individuals that is scheduled to be repaid in two or more installments. The major categories of credit are automobile credit (about one-third of the total), and revolving credit, for example, credit cards and check credit plans (about 43 percent). Other loans, such as mobile homes, home improvement, vans and pickup trucks, and student loans, are reported in an additional category. The figures represent the amount outstanding at the end of each month and reflect the net effect of extensions and repayments.

Figure 4.10 shows consumer installment as a percent of personal income monthly since January 1992. The broad upsweep of credit relative to income is evident from 1993 through mid-1996,

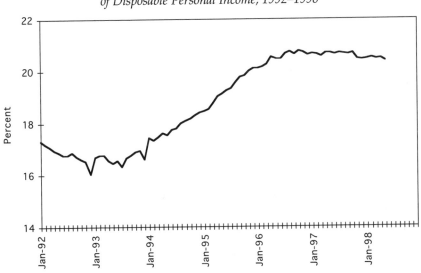

Figure 4.10   Consumer Installment Credit as a Percent of Disposable Personal Income, 1992–1998

Source: FRB G.19 Report, historical files; STAT-USA, NIPA Historical estimates

when it leveled off. Outstanding consumer credit typically expands and contracts as the economy expands and contracts, so that it accentuates the cyclical nature of consumer spending, especially for durables. Consumer borrowing is now near record levels. However, many consumers use revolving credit as a convenience, paying off their outstanding debt on a regular basis; revolving credit as a percent of total credit has increased considerably in recent years. Therefore, for this reason and because this ratio does not reflect the asset position of the indebted consumers, interpretation of the level of debt to income is difficult. Moreover, because the data are released late and the month-to-month changes are of limited significance, the consumer credit data are not critical for short-term business analysis.

CONSUMER ATTITUDES

Two other sources of information on the consumer are surveys of consumer attitudes, compiled by The Conference Board, a nonprofit private research organization in New York, and the Survey Research Center of the University of Michigan in Ann Arbor. The Conference Board survey results are available in the first week of the month for the survey taken the prior month; the results usually are reported in the financial press, especially in *The Wall Street Journal*. The Michigan survey results are made available only to subscribers. However, a summary of the results usually are reported in the financial press.

The Conference Board consumer confidence index reflects consumer attitudes about the general business situation and job availability. The Board also publishes an index of consumer expectations, in which consumers express their opinions on the outlook for business, jobs, and their own financial situation. The data are converted to an index (with 1985 used as a base index), but the significance is in the rise and fall of the index rather than any particular level. Figure 4.11 plots the confidence index monthly from 1987 to 1998. In the spring of 1998, the index was at record levels. Consumer confidence measures, when used with other economic data, provide useful indicators of future economic activity.

Figure 4.11   Consumer Confidence Index, 1987–1998

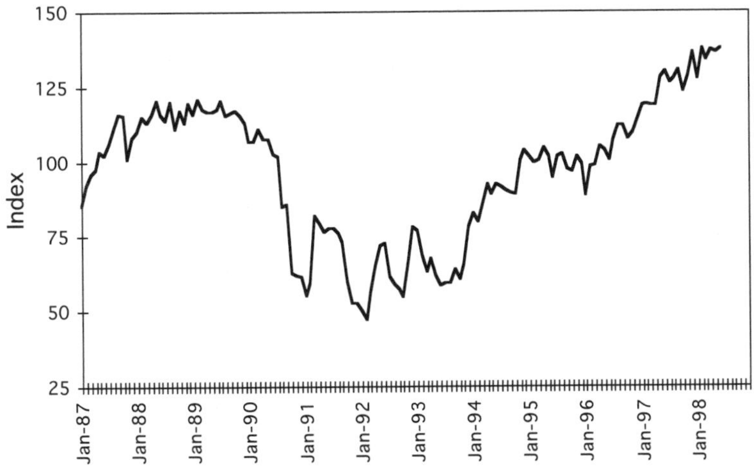

Source: The Conference Board Internet Service, used with permission

SUMMARY

Consumer spending accounts for the bulk of GDP. Consumer spending for durables, although the smallest percent of spending, is the most volatile and has the greatest cyclical significance. During the past 40 years, spending for services has risen from 33 to 59 percent of consumer spending, which has stabilized spending and lowered the cyclical vulnerability of the economy.

A wealth of data is available for analysis of the consumer sector. Some information is current, and movements in this information, for example, automobile sales, are very important in assessing the short-term outlook for the economy. Other information must be examined in a longer term perspective and is useful primarily in analyzing the condition of the economy, a condition that may persist for some time. In the following list those data most useful for short-term analysis are marked with an "*":

Early in the month:

The monthly employment report*

Automobile sales*

The dollar value of construction for two months previous

Midmonth:

Retail sales*

Housing starts*

Consumer confidence index*

Consumer price index*

Consumer credit for two months previous

Late in the month:

Personal income and personal consumption expenditures

The saving rate

Monitoring these reports—most importantly those marked—can provide meaningful information about this important sector of the economy.

CHAPTER 5

Following the Business Sector

This chapter initially considers those accounts of the GDP that deal with business investment: spending for plant and equipment, and additions to, or subtractions from, business inventories. The place of manufacturing in the economy and the statistics used to follow that sector will also be discussed.

Remember that the GDP accounts reflect only final demand, which is why personal consumption accounts for such a large part of GDP. Business activity is largely involved in producing or processing things, or providing services that will be consumed by others. As a result, the complex activities of business are not fully captured in the GDP accounts; only business investment is captured. Therefore, many other statistical series have to be reviewed to understand the contribution of business to the functioning of the economy.

The specific concepts considered in this chapter are:

Business capital investment, or plant and equipment spending, used for further production;

Fixed investment. The GDP accounts include private residential and nonresidential investment. Nonresidential investment is divided into structures and producers durable equipment. Residential investment is discussed in Chapter 4;

New orders for nondefense capital goods are useful predictors of future business spending plans. Other helpful measures are the monthly report on capacity utilization and quarterly information on corporate cash flow;

Changes in business inventories are important causes of business cycles. Inventory changes are a part of the GDP accounts and business sales and inventories are reported on a monthly basis;

Industrial production, reported monthly, is an important measure of manufacturing activity. Other early indicators of manufacturing are the monthly reports of the purchasing managers' index of activity and new orders for durable goods.

BUSINESS CAPITAL INVESTMENT

An important part of business activity is capital investment, or investment in the plant and equipment that will be used for further production. Although not a large percent of GDP, investment in capital goods is one of the critical forces influencing the growth and well-being of the economy. Capital goods production generates wages, adding to the demand for consumer goods, leading to more wages seeking more consumer goods, and so on. Capital goods output therefore has a multiplier effect on economic expansion.

Plant and equipment investment also affects productivity, or output per hour of goods and services, and thus the long-term growth rate at which the economy can expand. Moreover, investment in plant and equipment is made in large amounts. It usually bulges toward the end of a business expansion as output approaches capacity limits. Therefore, plant and equipment investment is a critical factor in determining the magnitude of the fluctuations and the duration of business cycles.[1]

Total *fixed investment* averaged about 16 percent of GDP during the past five decades, ranging from as low as 12.4 percent of GDP in 1991 to a high of 18.8 percent in 1978–79. Fixed investment is divided into *private residential* and *nonresidential* investment. It does not include government investment, which is included in government consumption expenditures and gross investment in the GDP accounts. Residential investment (discussed in Chapter 4), accounts for slightly less than 30 percent of total fixed investment; nonresidential investment accounts for the remainder. Nonresidential investment is divided into *structures* and *producers durable equipment (PDE)*.

Nonresidential Fixed Investment

Figure 5.1 plots total nonresidential fixed investment and its components as a percent of GDP for 1950 to 1997. The volatile nature of nonresidential fixed investment is evident. The rate of growth of GDP itself varies over time. Therefore, the changing percent of GDP accounted for by investment indicates that its volatility is greater than that of GDP. The other interesting factor is the rising trend in the percent of investment represented by PDE and the shrinking percent accounted for by structures. Buildings have become less important than what goes into them.

A clearer illustration of this divergence is shown in Table 5.1, which compares the distribution of nonresidential fixed investment in 1950 with that in 1997. As the table indicates, structures as a percent of the total decreased from 36 to 27 percent. The biggest gain was in information processing equipment (office, computing, and accounting machinery; communication equipment; instruments; and photocopy and related equipment), which rose from 7 to 25 percent. Computers and related equipment, which were not even reported separately in 1950, are now about 40 percent of the information processing equipment segment.

---

[1] Many people might consider purchases of consumer durable goods such as automobiles, furniture, and appliances as investment. However, by convention such purchases are treated in the national accounts as consumption rather than investment. These durable goods purchases were discussed in greater detail in Chapter 4.

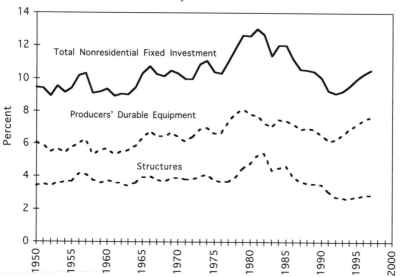

Figure 5.1   Nonresidential Fixed Income Investment
as Percent of GDP, 1950–1997

Source: STAT-USA, NIPA Historical estimates

Table 5.1
Nonresidential Fixed Investment Distribution, 1950 vs. 1997
(Billions of Dollars)

	1950	%	1997	%
Information processing	1.8	6.5	212.3	25.1
Industrial equipment	4.4	15.9	134.8	15.9
Transportation equipment	6.4	23.1	150.0	17.7
Other equipment	5.1	18.4	119.5	14.1
Total producers durable equipment	17.7	63.9	616.7	72.8
Structures	10.0	36.1	230.2	27.2
Total	27.7	100.0	846.9	100.0

Source: STAT-USA, NIPA Historical estimates

BUSINESS INVESTMENT EXPECTATIONS

The broadest series tracking business investment is the component of GDP called nonresidential fixed investment, which is reported as a part of the data in the monthly reports on quarterly GDP. These data, like all GDP components, are reported in current dollars and constant dollars; but other series are more useful in anticipating future movements in business fixed investment.

Nondefense Capital Goods Orders

A monthly series used to track present and future business investment is new orders, shipments, and unfilled orders (backlogs) for nondefense capital goods. This information is part of the monthly report on total manufacturers' new orders, sales, inventories, and backlogs. Nondefense capital goods orders must be evaluated carefully—from time to time they can be distorted by aircraft orders, which can be very large and very volatile dollar items.

Figure 5.2 shows the pattern of new orders for nondefense capital goods by month from January 1987 into 1998. The volatile nature of new orders is clearly evident, due primarily to big aircraft new orders in certain months. The downward trend in orders from 1990 through 1993 is an interesting contrast with the series excluding aircraft orders, which has been in an uptrend since 1997.

Determinants of Business Investment

Business investment decisions are usually influenced by two factors:

The cost of capital; and

The expected return on investment.

The cost of capital, which is critical in determining the return on investment, in turn is influenced by:

The level of interest rates; and

Tax law changes.

Figure 5.2   New Orders for Nondefense Capital Goods and Nondefense Capital Goods ex Aircraft, 1987–1998

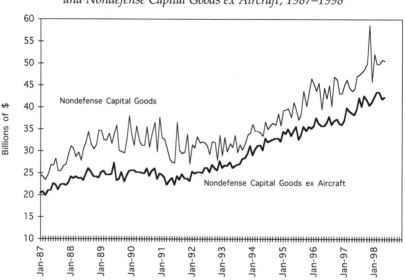

Source: Bureau of Census, Historical data series

Interest rates will be discussed in Chapter 8. With respect to tax law changes, Congress has from time to time changed tax laws to encourage business investment. One way is to reduce the corporate tax rate, which encourages investment by lowering the so-called hurdle rate, the rate of return below which capital investments are not considered profitable.[2]

Another method of encouraging investment is to permit accelerated depreciation of capital equipment. By increasing the dollar amount of depreciation of assets in any one year, more corporate income is exempt from taxes because depreciation is a deduction from income before computing corporate income taxes. Thus higher depreciation means more income exempt from taxes, lowering the effective tax rate. Although depreciation charges do not represent a cash outlay, reducing tax payments presumably makes available additional funds to the corporation that could be used for investment.

---

[2] This rate varies from company to company and from industry to industry, depending on such factors as cost of capital, risk, competition, tax rates, and so on.

Measuring Capacity Utilization

In addition to watching tax law changes, an important influence on future business fixed investment is the relationship of output to capacity.

Why is *capacity utilization* important? As demand increases, rising utilization rates may require use of less efficient plant and will increase labor costs due to overtime and second shifts. These rising costs can cause price increases. Prolonged high utilization rates lead to increased business spending for plant and equipment. Measures of capacity utilization are used as indicators of business cycle turning points. Finally, capacity utilization measures are useful in estimating war mobilization capabilities.

Some Definitions. Most of us have an intuitive feeling that capacity is the maximum physical output that a plant can produce—that feeling is correct if we are talking about an engineering or war mobilization concept. However, operating "flat out" cannot be continued indefinitely. It assumes that no shortages of labor and materials impede production, that higher production costs such as overtime are not considered, and that downtime for maintenance and repairs is minimized. The concept of capacity becomes more elusive when we consider not just an individual plant but expand the concept to the capacity of a firm, an industry, or an economic sector (for example, manufacturing).

A different approach to capacity considers cost of production. Economists use two cost concepts: *average or unit cost* and *marginal cost.* Average cost is obtained by dividing the total cost of production by the current level of output. Marginal cost is the additional cost a firm incurs in producing one more unit of output. As the rate of output increases, average cost initially falls as fixed or overhead costs are spread over more units of production. However, at some point the fixed costs begin to rise (e.g., as machinery or labor is used more intensively). At that point, the cost of producing one more unit, or marginal cost, exceeds average cost, and average costs begin to rise. Consequently, an economic concept of capacity is the point where average costs are lowest, that is, where marginal costs and average costs are equal. Beyond that point, average costs begin to increase and future plant investment must be considered because the output is not being produced at the most efficient rate.

Some consideration of these factors underlies any corporation's answer to what its production capacity is.

How Is Capacity Utilization Measured? Two government agencies provide measures of capacity utilization. The first is an annual survey conducted by the Bureau of the Census; the second is prepared monthly by the Federal Reserve Board.

The Bureau of the Census conducts a survey in the fourth quarter of each year that covers about 17,000 manufacturing establishments in 458 manufacturing industries. The survey compares the market value of goods produced with (1) the value of products that could have been produced if the plant were operating at full capacity in the fourth quarter, and (2) the value of products that could have been produced if required in a national emergency. The actual value of production in the fourth quarter is then compared with production capability under the two assumptions.

Full production capability makes the following assumptions: (1) only machinery and equipment in place and ready to operate will be utilized; (2) normal downtime, maintenance, repair, and cleanup; (3) the number of shifts, hours of plant operation, and overtime pay that can be sustained under normal conditions; (4) the availability of labor, materials, and utilities are not limiting factors; and (5) a product mix typically representative of fourth-quarter production.

National emergency production, which should be greater than or equal to the value of production at full production capability, is the maximum production the plant could sustain for one year or more. The assumptions include: (1) full use of machinery and equipment in place, with minimal downtime as well as multishift operations; (2) operating seven days a week and twenty-four hours a day less minimal downtime; (3) overtime pay, full availability of labor, materials, utilities, etc.; (4) all output can be sold; (5) product mix can change; (6) services can be contracted outside the plant if necessary.

The Federal Reserve Board provides a monthly report on capacity utilization, or output divided by capacity. This series provides information on total industry capacity, divided into manufacturing, mining, and utility sectors. Although focus is on total operating rates, 50 manufacturing components, 18 mining components, and 2 utility components are also covered.

The Federal Reserve itself conducts no surveys of capacity, or utilization. It uses data from surveys of utilization rates made by other organizations, such as the Bureau of the Census, and various trade associations. Presumably, the survey respondent has some knowledge and data available to estimate the necessary assumptions. Capacity can then be measured by dividing output by the utilization rate. (If the capacity utilization rate is equal to output divided by capacity, then capacity can be computed by dividing output by the utilization rate.)

The Federal Reserve, in its estimation of monthly capacity, starts with these survey results, checks them against production indexes, and estimates the industry additions to capital stock, industry estimates of physical capacity, and businesses' estimates of changes in capacity. The Federal Reserve then prepares estimates of monthly capacity levels. To obtain operating rates, the Federal Reserve's monthly production index for certain industries as well as total manufacturing, mining, and utility sectors are divided by the appropriate capacity indexes to get utilization rates.

Limitations of the Data. Several limitations of the data must be mentioned. The Census survey is only available annually, and continuity is always threatened by inadequate funding. It is also computed on a plant basis and therefore does not take into account bottlenecks or problems at a company, industry, or sector level. It is based on a market value rather than a physical volume basis. In addition, the respondent may or may not be knowledgeable in interpreting the questions, or the answers may not be representative of the industry or sector because of nonresponse. Consistency over time is difficult to achieve. Trends over longer periods of time are more informative than month-to-month changes.

Figure 5.3 indicates the total industry monthly operating rate for the 1987 to 1998 period, as reported by the Federal Reserve. In addition, the high of the index in 1988–89 of 85.3 percent and the 1982 low of 71.1 percent are shown.

Typically, operating rates much above approximately 85 percent have signaled potential pressures on prices as more costly facilities are brought into production and factories move into overtime. In 1996 and into 1998, operating rates were below this level, reflecting the spending for equipment to improve efficiency made during that period.

Figure 5.3   Total Industry Capacity Utilization, 1987–1998

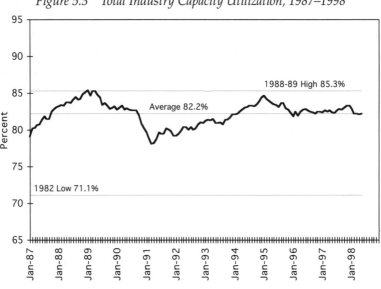

Source: FRB, Historical data bank

CORPORATE CASH FLOW

In addition to operating rates as a foreshadowing indicator of business spending plans, *corporate cash flow* can also affect trends in spending. Cash flow consists of corporate profits after taxes plus depreciation. Depreciation allowances, as mentioned earlier, are a permitted business expense deducted before taxes; they are not cash outlays.

Cash flow is reported after two adjustments are made. The first excludes *inventory profits*, which are not considered coming from current production.[3] The second adjustment estimates depreciation of plant and equipment on a current replacement cost basis rather than on a historic or original cost basis (the way most companies keep their books). The reason for these adjustments is to get a more

---

[3] Inventory profits occur in a period of rising prices when inventory purchased earlier at less-than-prevailing prices is used in production and the company uses a first in/first out (FIFO) method of inventory valuation. The cost of production is understated and artificially inflates profits, because the inventory used up will have to be replaced at a higher cost. Because these profits are illusory, they are not considered a part of the cash flow of corporations to offset fixed investment.

accurate estimate of cash flow in an economic sense rather than in a conventional accounting sense. Corporate cash flow is regularly reported as a part of the quarterly GDP reports on corporate profits.

A further adjustment is made to these figures when they are reported. Considerable research has revealed that corporate directors consider the maintenance of a regular dividend rate or payout rate of corporate earnings more important than capital expenditures. Consequently, a significant figure to watch is *net* cash flow, which is the sum of undistributed profits (i.e., profits after dividend distributions) and capital consumption allowances adjusted to a replacement cost basis.

Figure 5.4 compares this corporate net cash flow with nonresidential fixed investment for the years 1950 to 1997. As the figure indicates, internally generated cash flow has not equaled nonresidential fixed investment in any of these years. The differences are accounted for by corporate external financing, by fixed investment of noncorporate entities that is included in the investment expenditures, or by corporate managers viewing net cash flow in an accounting and not an economic sense.

Figure 5.4   Nonresidential Fixed Income Investment vs. Corporate Net Cash Flow, 1950–1997

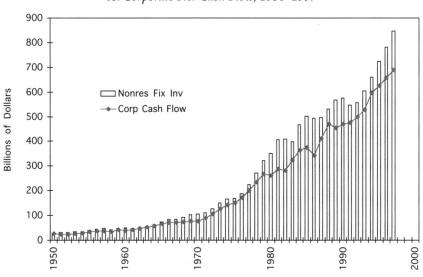

Source: STAT-USA, NIPA Historical estimates

During this period, corporate cash flow accounted for about 83 percent of nonresidential fixed investment. For 1991–97, however, it averaged 86.6 percent, probably acting as a stimulant to business fixed-investment spending during that period.

BUSINESS INVENTORIES

The second form of business investment is reflected in the data on business inventories—their changes, their level in relationship to sales, and their relationship to cycles in business activity.

Inventory Cycles

An oversimplified and exaggerated example may illustrate the significance of inventories in causing cycles in business activity. Assume a company has a fairly steady demand of 100 units a month for a product that it manufactures. In order to meet this demand, the company produces 100 units a month and keeps 100 units in inventory in various stages of fabrication. The company's inventory-to-sales ratio therefore is 1, one month's supply, which the company has found by experience to be a satisfactory level.

Now assume that demand picks up to 150 units a month. The 100 units in inventory are now only two-thirds of a month's supply, so that production must be increased to 200 a month (150 units to meet the higher level of demand and another 50 units to restore the inventory-to-sales ratio to 1 again). In short, production has to be doubled on a 50-percent increase in demand. Of course, the reverse is true; if demand fell to 50 units, inventories on hand would represent two months' supply, so that production would have to be cut back sharply to accommodate the lowered level of demand and to reduce a now bloated level of inventories. The correction process is further exaggerated because of the uncertainty before managers can determine whether the latest increase or decrease in demand is temporary or more permanent. Consequently, action to increase or decrease production is delayed and then overcorrected.

This effect of inventories on production, which does not occur in service industries that do not make a product, explains the greater volatility in output of companies that produce goods and why inventory cycles are the most frequent (although not the only) causes of cycles in economic activity.

Measuring GDP Inventory Change

Economists follow two separate statistical series to monitor business inventories. One is contained in the quarterly reports of GDP, which reflects quarter-to-quarter *changes* in business inventories at seasonally adjusted annual rates. The second measure is a monthly series covering total business (i.e., manufacturing, wholesale trade, and retail trade) sales and inventories.

The manner of reporting these two series differs. In the quarterly GDP release, the change in inventories is reported. If more goods are produced than are consumed, the excess is reported as an increase in business inventories and is included in the GDP total as a part of the product during that period. However, if more inventory is consumed than produced, it reflects a reduction in output for the period. Similarly, if the rate of increase in inventories slackens from one quarter to the next, it causes a slowing in the economy's rate of increase. However, the opposite is true if inventory building accelerates.

In the GDP inventory data, the Commerce Department seeks to measure the value of inventory changes expressed in current dollars for a particular reporting period and also in constant chained 1992 dollars. Consequently, some adjustment is required because businesses have various ways of reporting the value of their inventories. Most companies value inventory on a FIFO basis, i.e., the cost of the oldest inventory on hand is used in accounting for the cost of goods sold. As a result, when prices are rising, inventories held in stock would rise in value even if no change occurred in the physical volume, because the lower cost inventory has been replaced by higher cost inventory.

However, in the GDP accounts, when the data are expressed in current dollars rather than constant dollars, the intent is to report the physical change in inventories, valued in prices that prevailed during a particular period. The constant dollar series reflects the change in the physical volume of inventories. Therefore, the Commerce Department adjusts the values of business inventories reported to them to the values required in the national income accounts. This adjustment also becomes a measure of inventory profit on the income side of the accounts, which will be considered again when measuring corporate profits.

Figures 5.5 and 5.6 indicate two different ways of looking at business inventory changes in the GDP accounts. Figure 5.5 shows the quarterly change in business inventories from 1960 through 1998. The volatility is evident, indicating why changes in inventories cause most of the fluctuations in business activity. The periods when inventories were actually liquidated (1960, 1975, 1980, 1982–83, and 1990–91) were all years of cyclical contraction. The only period of inventory contraction not accompanied by a cyclical downturn was the second half of 1986.

Figure 5.6 indicates the quarter-to-quarter percent changes (at annual rates) in GDP including and excluding the change in business inventories. This figure is similar to Figure 2.1, with one addition. The white bar represents the quarterly percentage change in GDP. The black bar reflects the quarterly percentage change excluding the change in business inventories, so that it reflects the change in final sales or final demand only. The difference between the two, of course, reflects the change in inventories. Some of the

Figure 5.5   Change in Business Inventories, IQ 1960–IQ 1998
(Billions of Chained 1992 Dollars at Seasonally Adjusted Annual Rates)

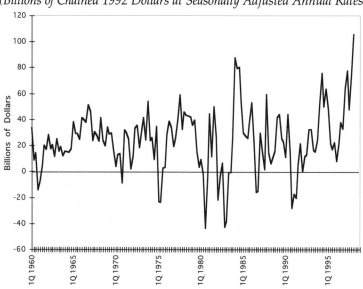

Source: STAT-USA, NIPA Historical estimates

quarterly changes are similar, but others are different. The final sales changes are considered a better indicator of underlying demand in the economy and therefore are watched just as carefully as the changes in total GDP.

Business Sales and Inventories

The second way inventories are reported is in the vast array of information released monthly by the Commerce Department on business sales and inventories. These series cover about 70 percent of all inventories held in the economy; inventories excluded are primarily agricultural and those found in the construction industry. The information is released about 45 days after the end of the month to which it refers. Unlike the GDP inventory figures, these figures are not corrected for any appreciation or depreciation that may have occurred because of changing prices, so that inventory profits and losses are reflected in the totals.

If monthly percent changes in both sales and inventories are plotted, the data fluctuate considerably. Nevertheless, monthly

Figure 5.6
Change in GDP and Final Sales, IQ 1990–IQ 1998
(Quarterly at Seasonally Adjusted Annual Rates)

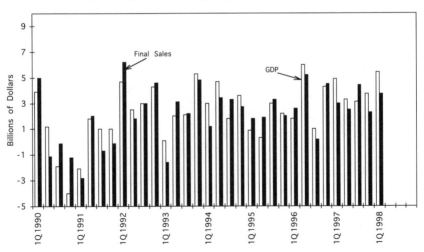

Source: STAT-USA, NIPA Historical estimates

changes are the usual method of communicating this information
in the financial press; needless to say, a one-month change in this
series should not be given too much weight. In Figure 5.7, the
monthly data have been smoothed out by taking a three-month
moving average of percentage changes and plotting them. The
data are still erratic; nevertheless, it appears that inventory
changes are greater in the months after a rise in sales, a not unex-
pected development. However, it is difficult from this type of chart
to determine whether inventories are excessive or not.

A more useful way of appraising the level of inventories is to
examine the ratio of inventories to sales, which provides an idea of
how many months inventories would last at current sales rates if
inventories were not replaced. Figure 5.8 presents this information
for total business, manufacturing, and retail levels for the period
1987 to 1998. The ratio for total business appears to have trended
downward from early 1991, indicating no significant buildup of
inventories during that period. Retail inventory-to-sales ratios
increased from early 1994 to early 1996 but declined thereafter.
Recent levels do not suggest an excess inventory problem.

Figure 5.7   Change in Business Sales and Inventories, 1987–1998
Three-Month Moving Average

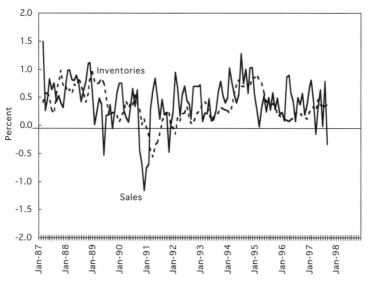

Source: Bureau of Census, Historical data base

Figure 5.8
Inventory to Sales Ratios—Business, Manufacturing, and Retail, 1987–1998

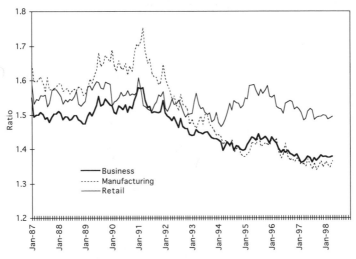

Source: Bureau of Census, Historical data base

MANUFACTURING

Concern is often expressed about the "decline" in U.S. manufacturing and the unwholesome change from a production to a service economy. However, the goods-producing sector of the economy contributes about the same percent of total output now as it did three or four decades ago—about 37 percent of GDP expressed in constant dollars. The shrinking has occurred on the input side, not the output side. Due to rising productivity, manufacturing employment has never exceeded the peak of about 21 million workers reached in 1979. Employment in the nonmanufacturing industries has exceeded manufacturing employment since late in the nineteenth century.

Manufacturing is still at the core of our industrial economy, where the efficient production of goods-needed permits the growth of other sectors, including services. Manufacturing is also important because some 58 percent of exports and 69 percent of imports are classified as goods. Moreover, as indicated earlier, fluctuations in inventories of goods are an important cause of cycles in business activity.

Industrial Production

Statistics on manufacturing are followed carefully as a clue to the future path of the economy. One of the most carefully watched series is the monthly industrial production index prepared and released by the Federal Reserve Board. This index measures the physical output of manufacturing, mining, and utilities, relating them to a base year of 1992. In the index, manufacturing industries account for approximately 86 percent of the weight, with mining and utilities accounting for 6 and 8 percent, respectively. The index is also divided by major markets, such as consumer durable and nondurable goods, business and other equipment, and intermediate products and materials. Several special breakdowns are also prepared. The largest part of the index is based on production of actual items, another part on electric consumption of producing industries, and the balance on production work hours in producing industries.

Figure 5.9 presents the monthly changes in the industrial production index from 1987 into 1998 (dotted line). A three-month moving average (solid line) is plotted because of the considerable volatility in the month-to-month changes. If manufacturing were also plotted, it would track the total index very well. The upward trend of the index from mid-1996 indicates the strength of the economy through the end of 1997.

Figure 5.9   Monthly Percent Change in Industrial Production, 1987–1998

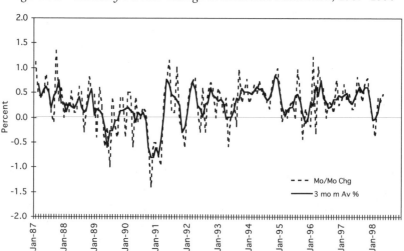

Source: FRB, Historical data file

Purchasing Managers' Index

Another index with a particularly good forecasting record for both manufacturing and the total economy that is available early each month is contained in the *Report on Business* issued by the National Association of Purchasing Management (NAPM), Tempe, Arizona. The report is widely reported in the financial press.

The participants are about 300 members of the association, and they are selected to parallel closely each manufacturing industry's contribution to GDP. Responses from each member are given equal weight, regardless of company size. Each participant is asked to compare this month's activity with that of the previous month with respect to production, new orders, prices, inventories, supplier deliveries, employment, and exports and imports—up, down, or no change. From these replies, a composite index is prepared showing the prevailing direction and the scope of change. The index may fluctuate between 0 and 100 percent, with an index of 50 percent showing no change. An index reading below 50 percent indicates contraction in the manufacturing sector of the economy. Research on historical relationships between replies and general business conditions reveals that a reading below 43.8 percent is a sign of a general economic contraction.

Figure 5.10 presents the monthly readings in the index from January 1987 through mid-1998. Although still above the 50 level that indicates manufacturing expansion, the index peaked in mid-1997. The NAPM in June 1998 introduced a new index covering nonmanufacturing business that is constructed similarly to the manufacturing index. It is plotted on Figure 5.10 as the dashed line. More experience with this index will be necessary to evaluate it as a business analysis tool.

Durable Goods New Orders

About one week after the industrial production index is released, the Department of Commerce issues an estimate of the dollar value of new orders for durable goods for the previous month. This series is watched because it has been a leading indicator of business-cycle turning points at both peaks and troughs. New orders are important because they provide a forecast of future manufacturing activity. Unfortunately, this first approximation

Figure 5.10   Purchasing Managers' Indexes, 1987–1998

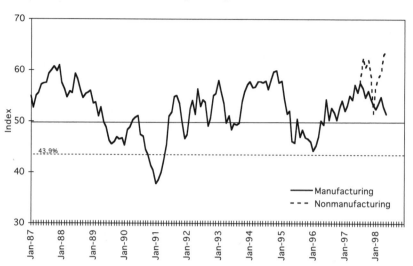

Source: NAPM, Historical data series

is just a rough measure and is frequently revised when manufacturing new orders, sales, and inventory data are released about a week later. Moreover, the series is volatile, making it difficult to determine trends.

Figure 5.11 plots durable goods new orders monthly from 1987 to 1998. Some of the volatility can be removed by subtracting aircraft new orders, as shown by the solid line on the figure.

SUMMARY

The essentials of following business fixed investment, business sales and inventories, and the manufacturing component of the business sector were discussed in this chapter. Although it accounts for a smaller percent of GDP than does the consumer, the business sector gets a greater degree of analytical attention. Cyclical movements in the business sector are considerably greater than in other areas of the economy. Anticipating these movements can provide clues to future changes in employment, payrolls, retail sales, interest rates, and stock prices.

Figure 5.11
Durable Goods New Orders and DGNO ex Aircraft Orders, 1987–1998

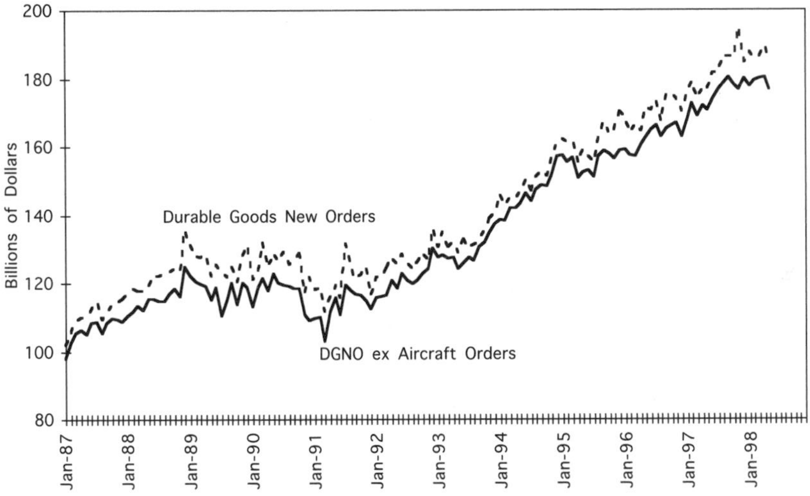

Source: Bureau of Census, Historical data base

Some of the data for analyzing the business sector are monthly and current. Other data are available less frequently but are also of significance. The following list provides the monthly and quarterly series discussed in this chapter. The most timely data for short-term business analysis are marked with an "*":

Business Fixed Investment:

Nonresidential fixed investment (monthly as a part of the quarterly GDP report);

Capacity utilization (mid-month for previous month)*;

Nondefense capital goods, new orders and shipments, inventories, and backlogs (end of month for previous month, updated about ten days later)*;

Business cash flow (available as a part of the second and third monthly estimates of quarterly GDP and its components).

Business Inventories:

Business sales and inventories and their components (monthly about six weeks after the end of the reported month)*;

Change in business inventories (monthly as a part of the report on quarterly GDP).

Manufacturing:

Purchasing managers' report (monthly at beginning of month)*;

Industrial production (monthly at mid-month)*;

Durable goods new orders (monthly toward the end of the month, updated about ten days later)*.

CHAPTER 6

The World Overseas

American economic relations with the rest of the world have received a lot of attention in recent years. The United States has increasingly become a part of the world economy. The trade deficit, foreign ownership of U. S. companies and real estate, and calls for protectionist legislation in Congress make the headlines. News is transmitted instantly. Money can move just as quickly, and investments are made daily—on a national as well as on a global basis.

This chapter will cover only the part of U.S. international relationships that deals with the performance of the U.S. economy in foreign trade, foreign investment, and the dollar in international exchange markets. The major concepts discussed are:

Balance of payments. The measure of the flow of goods, services income, and unilateral transfers between the United States and countries overseas, as well as the flow of funds back and forth to pay for them;

Balance on current account. That portion of the balance of payments that measures the flows of goods, services income, and unilateral transfers;

Net exports of goods and services. That part of the quarterly GDP reports that measures the exports and imports of goods, services income, and investment income;

Merchandise trade. The flow of exports and imports of goods and services and the only part of the balance of payments reported monthly;

Offsetting capital flows. Reported as *increases* or *decreases* in U.S. assets abroad and in foreign assets in the United States. The *value* of these assets in the United States and abroad is also reported;

Direct investments in the United States and abroad. Investment in industrial plants, commercial and residential property, and other physical assets.

Dollar in international trade. This trade is denominated primarily in dollars. The exchange value of the dollar can be measured directly against other currencies and also by an index weighted by the average world trade of ten major trading countries. The effects of the dollar's exchange movements on trade and investment as well as on monetary policy of the U.S. and foreign central banks are discussed because of their importance in foreign trade.

BALANCE OF PAYMENTS

Exports and imports of goods account for approximately half of the dollars in U.S. international transactions. However, other transactions also cause funds to flow between the United States and countries overseas. Some funds flow abroad unilaterally, such as U.S. grants, pensions paid to Americans living overseas, or remittances and gifts sent abroad by U.S. residents or to U.S. residents from abroad. Investment income, fees, royalties, and military transactions flow both ways. Finally, U.S. capital investments are made abroad and foreign investments are made in the United States; these assets ultimately result in income flows back and forth.

When overseas obligations of the United States are matched against foreign obligations to the United States, a surplus or deficit exists. This surplus or deficit is balanced out in the case of a surplus by the United States investing or loaning funds overseas; if a deficit exists, it is offset by foreign loans or investments in the United States. The measure of these flows of goods and services between the United States and overseas is reflected in the *balance of payments accounts*.

The balance of payments accounts provide two kinds of information. The first reflects foreign trade in goods, services income, and unilateral transfers. The second reflects the money and capital flows used to finance trade, transfers, and grants. Theoretically the two should match, but because of inadequate statistical data a "statistical discrepancy" is used to make up the difference. The balance of payments data are issued quarterly by the Department of Commerce about 75 days after the end of the quarter to which they refer. They usually are published in the April, June, September, and December issues of the Department of Commerce monthly publication, *Survey of Current Business.*

Components

The components of the balance of payments is summarized in the following list.

Exports of goods, services, and income, consisting of three parts:

Goods;

Services, including travel costs, royalties, and other private services;

Income received from U.S. assets owned abroad.

Imports of goods, services, and income, which has three parts:

Goods;

Services, including direct defense expenditures overseas, travel costs, royalties, and other private services;

Income payments from foreign assets owned in the United States.

Unilateral transfers, net, including transfers, or flows of funds, into and out of the United States:

U.S. government grants, pensions, and other government transfers;

Private remittances and other private transfers.

The capital flows that offset these three components are as follows:

Net increase or decrease in U.S. assets abroad, reflected by changes in:

U.S. official reserve assets, including gold, special drawing rights, and the reserve position in the International Monetary Fund (IFM) plus foreign currency holdings;

Other U.S. government assets held abroad, including loans to foreign nations, capital contributions to international organizations except the IMF, and other holdings of foreign currencies;

U.S. private assets held abroad, including direct investment, foreign security holdings, and claims on foreigners.

Net increase or decrease in foreign assets in the United States' reflected by changes in:

Foreign official (government or government entities) assets owned in the United States, including foreign holdings of U.S. government securities, corporate debt and equity securities, and of state and local governments;

Other foreign assets, including U.S. government as well as private securities, and direct investment in U.S. assets;

Other liabilities to foreigners.

The quarterly report on the balance of payments has a wealth of information on U.S. international transactions, much of which is of a specialized nature. For the purposes of tracking the U.S. business picture, however, focus should be concentrated on the three major summary reports that are usually communicated in one way or another in the financial press:

Balance on current account. A quarterly report that includes exports and imports of goods, services, and income, plus net unilateral transfers;

Net exports of goods and services. Reported as a part of the quarterly GDP accounts;

Balance on trade in goods and services. The only component of the balance of payments report available monthly.

BALANCE ON CURRENT ACCOUNT

The report on the balance on current account reflects the net difference between exports and imports of goods, services, and income, combined with the net difference between unilateral transfers that occur between the United States and the rest of the world.

Figure 6.1 plots this information for the 1980 to 1997 period. The segment of each bar above the zero line reflects that part of the current account where the United States received more than it sent overseas. The amount below the zero line represents a deficit for the United States.

Figure 6.1   U.S. Balance on Current Account, 1980–1997

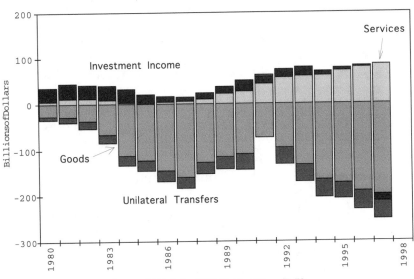

Source: SCB, July 1998, Table F.2, p. D-52

The United States last had a surplus on current account in 1981; since then the current account has been in deficit, which grew until 1987, shrunk again until 1991, and then increased again. The small deficit in 1991 was caused in part by payments to the United States from our allies to help defray the cost of the Gulf War. The deficit in 1996 was more than $148 billion, and in 1997 it was $166 billion, and, thanks to the Asian crisis, it will be much larger in 1998. As the figure indicates, the deficit has been caused by increasing deficits in goods, swelling unilateral transfers, and shrinking net investment income, which has not been offset by rising services income.

NET EXPORTS OF GOODS AND SERVICES

Net exports of goods and services are reported as one of the parts of the quarterly GDP reports; they are given in both current and constant dollars. The information includes not only trade in goods, but also services income and investment income; unilateral transfers are excluded. This series is monitored because it is an inclusive measure of current external economic transactions that affect the U.S. economy.

Figure 6.2 on page 96 places exports and imports in current dollars into perspective by relating them to GDP for the 1950 to 1997 period. The net export line at the bottom of the figure generally fluctuated around zero percent of GDP up to the mid-1970s. Until then, net exports fluctuated so little and were so modest in size relative to the whole economy that they received little attention in business forecasts.

Two developments changed that focus. Beginning in the early 1970s, exports and imports, taken separately, increased as a percent of GDP. Part of the increase in imports was caused by higher prices for oil imports, and part by the increasing demand in the U.S. for automotive vehicles, appliances, and electronic equipment made overseas. U.S. exports also became a larger part of national output, although the growth did not become significant until U.S. corporations became more competitive worldwide from the mid-1980s forward.

Figure 6.3 on page 96 shows on a monthly seasonally adjusted basis exports and imports of goods and services from January 1992;

the gap between the dotted lines and the solid lines reflects the deficits in goods and the surplus in services. The net trade balance is plotted in Figure 6.4. These monthly figures, released by the Department of Commerce about 45 days after the end of the month to which they refer, are probably the most carefully watched of the total balance of payments statistics.[1] The month-to-month changes in the goods data are erratic and large, while the services component movements are relatively steady. When trying to evaluate the figures, it is best to examine the data over a longer period and not concentrate on month-to-month changes.

The largest items in services are travel and other transportation costs as well as income payments on foreign assets in the U.S. or U.S. assets held abroad. The positive balance on services has been fairly steady but the negative balance on goods has been increasing. This growing imbalance can be seen more clearly in Figure 6.4, which reflects a growing trade deficit in goods and services that hovered around $10 million a month in 1996 and 1997, rising to about $14 billion a month in the spring of 1998. An evaluation of the prospects of the trade deficit can be estimated more accurately after a review of the components of exports and imports as well as a review of the major U.S. trading partners.

Table 6.1 on page 99 contrasts the major categories of U.S. goods exports in 1970 and 1997. During that period, U.S. goods exports grew more than 16 times in current dollars, while total GDP grew only about 8 times. The most significant shift during this period was the declining share of agricultural exports, which fell from 17 percent to 7 percent of the total. Capital goods and automotive products are the largest component of U.S. exports, increasing from 44 to 54 percent of the total. Aircraft and parts and electronic equipment products are a good part of these exports.

Table 6.2 on page 99 indicates that, during 1970 to 1997, imports grew about 22 times, causing the growing deficit in goods and services trade. Capital goods and automotive products increased from 24 percent to 45 percent of the total during that period, while petroleum products imports increased from 7 to 8 percent.

---

[1] Business inventory statistics for all of the months of the quarter are not available until shortly before the second estimate of the quarterly GDP data, and full net export information is not available until shortly before the third estimate. The changes in these two volatile areas account for most of the revisions between the first and the final estimates of GDP for a particular quarter.

Figure 6.2   *Exports and Imports as a Percent of GDP, 1950–1997*

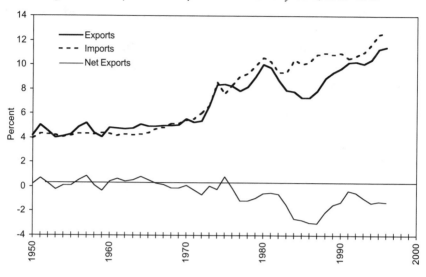

Source: STAT-USA, NIPA Historical estimates

Figure 6.3
U.S. International Trade in Goods and Services, 1992–1998

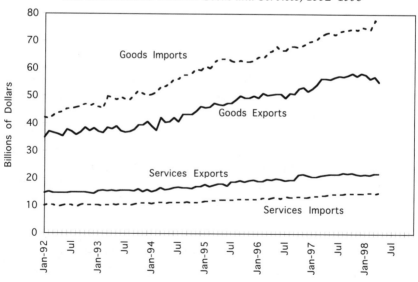

Source: Bureau of Census, Historical data series

Figure 6.4 U.S. Trade Balance in Goods and Services, 1992–1998

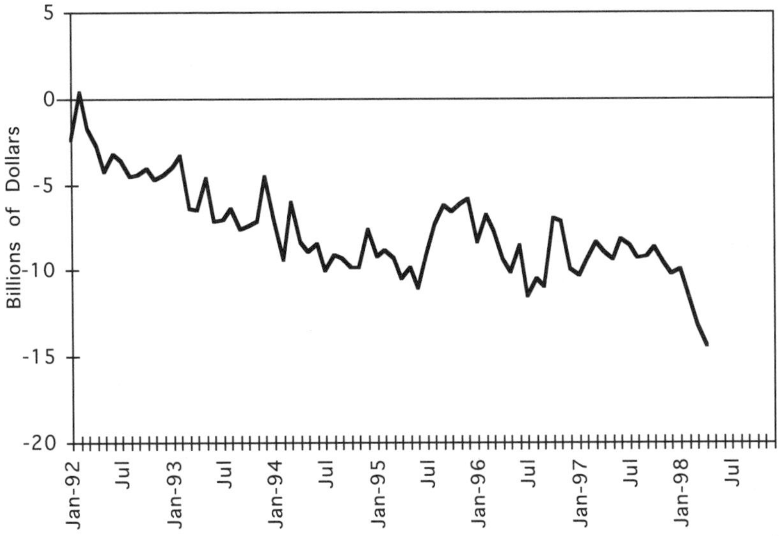

Source: Bureau of Census, Historical data series

Reviewing our major trading partners, during 1997 exports to Canada were 22 percent of total U.S. exports, Western Europe about 23 percent, Mexico 10 percent, other South and Central American countries 9 percent, Japan about 10 percent, and the newly industrialized countries of Asia (Hong Kong, Korea, Singapore, and Taiwan) about 11 percent. The largest importers to the United States were Canada (19 percent of total imports), Japan (14 percent), all of Western Europe (20 percent), Mexico (10 percent), and the newly industrialized countries of Asia (10 percent). Imports from China have been growing and in 1997 were 7 percent of total imports. In short, the largest export markets for the United States were the Western hemisphere and Western Europe, while the bulk of U.S. imports came from Asia and the Western hemisphere.

What is the outlook for the U.S. trade balance in the years immediately ahead? That depends on several factors. Several years ago, U.S. goods were not considered competitive in price and quality, but this generalization is no longer true as U.S. corporations have significantly improved their competitiveness. In some areas, such as aircraft and certain computer products, the United States is an undisputed leader in the field. In automotive products, U.S.-

made vehicles, especially light trucks and sport utility vehicles, have become popular domestically and have offset the competition of imported cars. U.S. exports have been growing, especially in high-tech areas, and are fully competitive in quality.

Price competitiveness is another matter. Certain imported products, such as shoes and some apparel, can be manufactured more cheaply abroad, and imports of these products have increased. In other areas, the trade outlook depends on the exchange value of the dollar, discussed later in this chapter. Briefly, a rising dollar relative to other currencies curtails U.S. exports by making them more expensive overseas, and imports, by contrast, become less expensive. The dollar moved up relative to the currencies of our major trading partners in 1997, and the financial crises in Asia in the latter part of the year and into 1998 were accompanied by severe devaluations of their currencies. The result is a sharp drop in the prices of their exports and a major effort to increase exports in an effort to stimulate their depressed economies. Therefore, U.S. exports to Asia are likely to fall and imports from there accelerate.

Another factor influencing the outlook for the U.S. trade and services balance is the extent to which trade negotiations with other trading partners can reduce tariff and nontariff barriers that constrain trade. This process is better than enacting protectionist legislation, which can only lead to retaliatory legislation abroad and lower foreign trade generally. The present process of patient negotiations with each country or through international trade organizations, to change trade practices and reduce trade barriers, is more likely to contribute to an improvement in the U.S. trade deficit.

In the latter part of 1997, Congress refused to extend the President's so-called "fast track" negotiation authority. This process requires that Congress, although still with final authority on any trade treaty, must vote on the entire agreement without adding amendments to an agreement already negotiated. With all agreements now subject to further changes when they come before the Congress, many nations will be reluctant to enter into negotiations with the United States. Consequently, the ability to negotiate elimination of trade barriers and tariffs will be constrained.

A combination of these factors will curtail U.S. trade expansion and will increase imports. Therefore, the outlook for an improvement in the U.S. trade position is not promising, and the trade deficit will have to be offset by other means, including borrowing abroad.

Table 6.1   U.S. Goods Exports, 1970 vs. 1997 (Billions of Dollars)

	1970	%	1997	%
Agricultural products	7.4	17.4	51.4	7.6
Industrial supplies and materials	12.3	28.9	158.1	23.3
Capital goods ex auto	14.7	34.6	294.1	43.4
Automotive	3.9	9.2	73.4	10.8
Other	4.3	10.1	101.3	14.9
Total	42.5	100.0	678.3	100.0

Source: SCB, April 1998, Table E, p. 60

Table 6.2   U.S. Goods Imports, 1970 vs. 1997 (Billions of Dollars)

	1970	%	1997	%
Petroleum products	2.9	7.3	72.1	8.2
Industrial supplies and materials	12.4	31.1	145.3	16.6
Capital goods ex auto	4.0	10.0	254.2	29.0
Automotive	5.5	13.8	140.7	16.0
Other	15.1	37.8	264.9	30.2
Total	39.9	100.0	877.2	100.0

Source: SCB, April 1998, Table E, p. 60

OFFSETTING CAPITAL FLOWS

Increases or decreases in U.S. assets abroad and of foreign assets in the United States are the means of financing the foreign trade in goods and services as well as unilateral transfers. Figure 6.5 shows the annual increases (denominated in dollars) in U.S. assets abroad and in foreign assets in the United States from 1960 through 1997. The year-to-year increase in U.S. assets abroad kept pace with the year-to-year increase of foreign assets in the United States until 1982. The deterioration in the U.S. current account after 1982, as shown in Figure 6.1, resulted in a significant rate of

increase in foreign assets in the United States, while the growth of
U.S. assets abroad did not keep pace.

A more dramatic illustration of this change is shown in Figure
6.6, indicating the value expressed in dollars of U.S. assets abroad
compared with the value of foreign assets held in the United States.
The value of foreign assets in the United States has exceeded U.S.
asset holdings abroad since 1989. These assets include U.S. Treasury
and other securities as well as direct investments. The Commerce
Department reports these totals in current cost as well as market
value; the data plotted on the chart are at market value. The sharp
increases in recent years reflect not just the flow of investment funds
into and out of the United States, but also the significant appreciation in stock prices both in the United States and abroad.

One other measure is worth considering. Figure 6.7 compares
the dollar value of U.S. direct investments abroad with foreign
direct investments in the United States. These figures also are plotted at market value. *Direct investments* reflect investment in industrial plants, commercial and residential property, as well as other
physical assets. It is worth mentioning that in 1996 direct investments represented about 36 percent of U.S. assets held overseas
but 25 percent of foreign assets held in the United States.

Figure 6.5   Asset Flows from and to the United States, 1960–1997

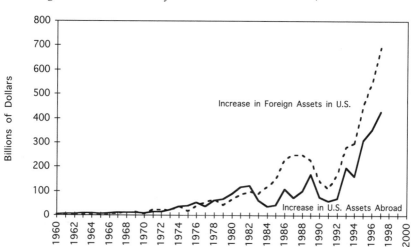

Source: ERP, 1998, Table B-103, p. 399; *Economic Indicators*, May 1998, p. 37

Figure 6.6   U.S. International Investment Position, 1982–1996

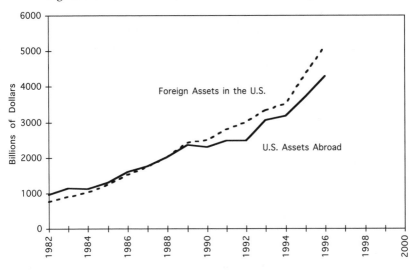

Source: SCB, July 1997, Table 3, p. 33

Figure 6.7   Foreign vs. U.S. Direct Investment, 1982–1996

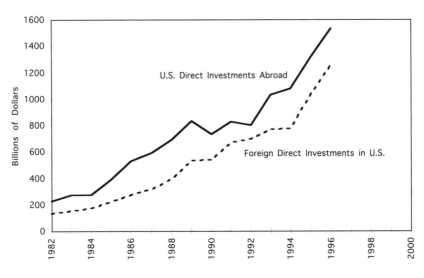

Source: SCB, July 1997, Table 3, p. 33

The total amount of foreign direct investment in the United States was about $630 billion in 1996, on an historical cost basis. Of this, 65 percent was accounted for by European countries. The United Kingdom accounted for 23 percent, the Netherlands 12 percent, Germany 10 percent, and other European countries the remainder. The second largest country in direct investment after the United Kingdom was Japan, with 19 percent of total direct investment. These data are reported annually in great detail by the Department of Commerce and published in the *Survey of Current Business.*

FOREIGN INVESTMENTS

What has caused foreign investment and ownership of assets in the United States to grow? The primary cause is the significant increase in the United States trade deficit, which put a large amount of dollars in foreign hands. Foreigners, having more and more dollars, have invested a large portion of these dollars in the United States. Such action is especially likely if foreigners see a stable economy, low inflation, and better returns than are available in their own countries. These trends will continue until the U.S. trade deficit is reduced significantly or U.S. investment becomes relatively less attractive.

Is foreign investment in the United States sufficiently large to give overseas investors significant market power in the U.S. economy? Several studies have concluded that no great threat is seen from the size of current holdings. Any measure of superiority foreign-owned companies have comes more from their competitive advantages than their ownership. Moreover, the United States has antitrust laws and other regulations that prevent unfair competition, which are equally applicable to firms owned by overseas investors.

Foreign ownership has contributed to U.S. employment, technology, capital flows, and a more competitive environment, all of which have been good for this country. It should be remembered that the United States was a debtor nation until the turn of the century, and investment from overseas prior to that time contributed a great deal to the early economic development of the United States. Subsequent U.S. investment abroad has helped develop economies overseas, and has reaped benefits through investment income from this free flow of capital worldwide.

Restrictions on capital flows, such as trade restrictions, are not reasonable solutions to the challenge of foreign ownership or investment. Such moves invite retaliation and further restrictions on trade and capital flows, and ultimately can only harm the economies of the countries that participate. (One exception where foreign ownership should be restricted, however, is the defense area, where national interests should mandate domestic control of U.S. companies.)

Foreign ownership is not an isolated problem but rather part of many problems involved in an intertwined, complex international world. As part of that interdependence, the views of foreign investors, central banks, and governments regarding U.S. political and economic policies are now very important. The flow of investment funds from abroad indicates that thus far the evaluation is more positive than negative. Should this flow of funds slow or stop, the funds now provided from overseas will have to be raised in the United States. Higher interest rates would result from increased competition for funds. In the long term, a lower U.S. standard of living could result as we pay interest and dividends on, as well as repay the principal of, our overseas debt.

THE DOLLAR

An issue closely related to international trade is the value of the U.S. dollar in foreign exchange. Why, since 1971, when exchange rates were free to fluctuate, have the dollar's movements become increasingly important to the U.S. consumer and of major importance to the U.S. investor?

International trade is denominated primarily in U.S. dollars (crude oil is a good example). Direct foreign investment in the United States requires dollars. Overseas portfolio investments are made in dollar-denominated securities by central banks and other institutional investors. Large dollar-denominated capital markets exist overseas. Therefore, fluctuations in the dollar have international repercussions.

The dollar, as do most major currencies, trades relatively freely in foreign exchange markets, its value rising and falling with the demand and supply provided by buyers and sellers. Increasing dollar fluctuations distort the terms of international trade, so that central banks at times intervene in these markets, but their purchases and sales are designed only to stabilize currency markets.

In the past 25 years, a significant amount of dollars has flowed abroad, changing the United States from a creditor to the world's largest debtor nation. One reason for the flow was the very substantial increase in the price of crude oil, beginning in 1973. This increase transferred a significant portion of wealth into the hands of the oil-producing countries. Overseas lending by U.S. banks caused an additional accumulation of dollars in foreign hands. Also, as pointed out earlier, the American consumer developed a strong taste for foreign goods, resulting in a growing trade deficit. Finally, and by no means the least important, large federal budget deficits led to fears of inflation, and the Federal Reserve instituted a tight monetary policy that ultimately broke the back of inflation while sending interest rates to record highs. These higher rates attracted funds to the United States from overseas.

Foreigners were willing to hold and add to their dollar holdings, thus bidding up the dollar's value relative to other currencies. Comparable U.S. assets were selling at prices lower than prices elsewhere. Foreign investment, both in real assets and securities, was attracted to the United States because interest rates were higher than those available at home. The demand for dollars drove its value up relative to other currencies until 1985. At that point, foreign concern about the U.S. budget deficit, trade deficit, and political fights over the budget deficit started a decline in the dollar's value; by the end of 1987 the dollar was down almost 50 percent against major currencies. The dollar has moved in a moderately narrow-range until mid-1998, when the Asian crisis caused the dollar to move higher.

The exchange rate of the dollar against most major currencies can be found in the financial section of most newspapers. The rates are usually reported in two ways:

The U.S. dollar equivalent of each unit of a foreign currency; and

The amount of a foreign currency that is equal to one U.S. dollar.

These exchange rates usually apply to rates for trading among banks in amounts of $1 million or more. Smaller transactions provide fewer units of foreign currency per dollar. In discussions of particular currencies, the British pound and the Canadian dollar are usually quoted in terms of how much is needed in U.S. dollars to buy a unit of that currency; for example, $1.67 is required to buy one pound. Other currencies are usually quoted in terms of the amount of their currency required to purchase a U.S. dollar; for example, 140 yen or 1.80 German marks are needed to buy one dollar.

Other methods are used to measure the value of the dollar relative to other currencies. Figure 6.8 plots the exchange value of the dollar against a group of other major currencies monthly from 1985 through mid-1998 in terms of an index number. The index is a weighted average exchange value of the U.S. dollar against the currencies of ten industrial countries. The weight for each of the countries is the 1972 to 1976 average world trade of that country divided by the average world trade of all ten countries combined.

Using this measure, the dollar fell from a peak in February 1985 to a low in January 1988. Since then, the dollar moved in a relatively narrow range until mid-1998. The rise since early 1995 reflects U.S. interest rates higher than those abroad, weakened economic recoveries overseas, and the financial crises in Asia toward the end of 1997.

Figure 6.8   Exchange Value of U.S. Dollar, 1985–1998

Source: FRB, Historical data bank

Effects of Dollar Movements

Movements in the foreign exchange value of the dollar have an effect on U.S. international trade, the U.S. economy, interest rates, and investments generally. Fluctuations in the value of the dollar in foreign exchange are caused by a complex mixture of actions by diverse participants with different objectives who may have different perceptions of the global political and economic environment.

What are the effects of the dollar *rising* relative to other currencies? (The effects are the opposite if the dollar is weak, as it was in 1990.) Essentially, a stronger dollar means that someone holding dollars gets more foreign currency per dollar when an exchange is made from dollars to that foreign currency. Clearly, U.S. travelers abroad benefit from a stronger dollar, but some of the broader economic implications are less obvious. Some of these implications are:

Importers who sell goods or services to the United States are paid in dollars and get more of their own currency in exchange. Therefore, they can afford to charge less in dollars for their goods or services, and can be more competitive relative to U.S. providers of similar goods and services. Consequently, imports rise in the U.S. balance of payments accounts. Demand for comparable domestic goods and services is discouraged, and price competition from imports reduces the ability of U.S. companies to increase prices, putting downward pressures on inflation. Slackening in the economy and downward price pressures may depress interest rates;

U.S. exporters selling their goods and services overseas are paid in foreign currencies and therefore get less dollars when their foreign currencies are exchanged into dollars. U.S. exports must therefore be priced higher or profit margins and profits will be lowered. Exports from the United States are discouraged, exports in the U.S. balance of payments are lower, and the domestic economy is slowed. Downward pressure on U.S. interest rates results because of this slackening in demand;

Foreign investors who hold U.S. investments get more of their domestic currency in income when they convert interest, dividends, and rent from dollars into their own domestic currency when the dollar is appreciating. The value of their U.S. investments also appreciates when translated into their domestic currency. Foreign investment in the United States is attractive, especially if the U.S. dollar is expected to continue to appreciate. Foreigners are willing to invest in the United States as long as they are not concerned about the safety of their investments and do not fear default. Because of the flow of funds to the United States from abroad, pressure on U.S. interest rates is downward;

Foreign investors who want to buy U.S. investments in a strong dollar market must pay more of their own currency to get dollars for the purchase. Therefore, investment in the United States is discouraged *unless* these investors believe that the dollar will continue to appreciate. If foreign investment is discouraged, funds for domestic uses must come from domestic sources, thus exercising upward pressures on interest rates;

U.S. investors who hold foreign investments receive less in dollars of income on their investments; in addition, the value of their overseas investments depreciates when translated into dollars. Investments outside the United States cost more when the dollar is strong and is therefore discouraged. The U.S. trade deficit increases as U.S. goods are less competitive, resulting in reduced income from abroad. However, investments in the United States are more attractive to U.S. corporations, and the greater funds available here puts downward pressures on interest rates;

Oil prices are denominated in dollars; therefore, dollar fluctuations have no effect on the cost of U.S. oil imports. However, other countries need more of their currencies if they buy the necessary dollars to purchase oil, diverting more resources to the purchase of oil and depressing their economies. (This effect has been somewhat modified by the development of barter deals between oil-producing and oil-consuming nations.) A stronger dollar helps oil-producing countries that can buy more foreign goods with the more valuable dollars they receive.

U. S. Monetary Policy

Monetary policy and the operations of the Federal Reserve will be discussed at greater length in Chapter 8. However, because movements of currencies in foreign exchange affect monetary policy, a few brief comments will be made here.

To understand the effects of a stronger dollar on monetary policy in the United States, the principal objectives of the Federal Reserve must be kept in mind:

Restrain inflation in the United States, suggesting that the Federal Reserve would favor a stronger dollar, increasing the competition from imports and exercising downward pressure on inflation and interest rates;

Encourage domestic economic growth, suggesting that the Federal Reserve would favor a weaker dollar, encouraging exports, discouraging imports, and stimulating domestic economic growth;

Maintain foreign investment interest in the United States in order to help finance both trade deficits and budget deficits. (Foreign investors now hold about 17 percent of outstanding federal debt and are significant buyers of new Treasury issues.) If foreign investment is not encouraged, more financing must be done internally, forcing U.S. interest rates up and discouraging U.S. economic growth. Therefore, a stronger dollar encourages foreign investment.

The Federal Reserve is faced with a difficult balancing act. To discourage inflation, the Federal Reserve would favor higher interest rates—but not so high as to discourage economic expansion. To encourage domestic economic growth, the Federal Reserve would like lower interest rates—but not so low as to encourage inflation. To attract foreign investment, the Federal Reserve would like higher interest rates—but not so high as to curtail domestic economic expansion. The choices are difficult, and policy emphasis shifts depending on what particular objective is most important at the time.

Foreign Central Bank Policies

Volatile currency movements are disruptive to international trade and financial transactions; central banks intervene from time to time in foreign exchange markets to dampen these currency fluctuations. However, the funds central banks can devote to currency stability are relatively small compared with the enormous volume of other transactions, so that underlying economic forces will ultimately set the direction of currency movements.

Foreign central banks cooperate with the Federal Reserve in interventions in foreign exchange markets, but their objectives in such cooperation are not necessarily the same. In addition to stabilizing currency fluctuations, foreign central banks have the following considerations in mind:

> Contain inflation and encourage economic growth in their own countries, especially by expanding exports, which are more important to the economies of many countries than they are for the United States. Helping the U.S. reduce its trade deficit is of secondary importance;

> Because foreign funds loaned to the United States to finance the U.S. trade deficit represent a capital outflow, foreign central banks are willing to help reduce the U.S. trade deficit only to the extent that is not inconsistent with their own domestic objectives;

> With respect to exchange rates, a strong dollar is generally preferable because it encourages exports to the United States and because the dollar is still the major reserve currency held by foreign central banks;

> U.S. interest rates higher than those in foreign countries encourage outflow of capital, which, unless a country has a very large balance of payments surplus, is not especially desirable;

> When foreign central banks are required to support the U.S. dollar by buying it in exchange markets, their purchases are paid for with their domestic currency, which increases supply and is therefore inflationary. Consequently, their willingness to continue dollar support is necessarily limited;

> The dollar is not the only currency that concerns foreign central banks; the currency relationships among all of their major trading partners are of concern. Therefore, actions may be taken that are directed at objectives other than just assisting the dollar. Nevertheless, the dollar is still the major currency in international transactions and therefore one that gets the majority of attention.

SUMMARY

This chapter discussed measures of the transactions of the United States with the rest of the world and fluctuations of the dollar in foreign exchange and the effects of these fluctuations on trade, investment, and monetary policy.

The detailed reports of the balance of payments are prepared and published by the Department of Commerce in its monthly publication *Survey of Current Business;* little of this detail is mentioned in the news media. The one part usually reported is the monthly data on U.S. international trade in goods and services; following the movements of exports, imports, and the net trade deficit will track about three-quarters of the dollars in U.S. international transactions. The data should be reviewed over a number of months because the figures are often revised significantly; the data initially reported for any month should be reviewed for revisions when subsequent months' data are reported.

The movement of the trade-weighted index is not normally covered in the news media, although it is available in the monthly *Federal Reserve Bulletin.* A simple way to track currency movements is to follow the dollar on a daily or weekly basis relative to its value compared with three major currencies: the British pound, the Japanese yen, and the German mark. (See Table 6.3.)

Table 6.3   High and Lows
U.S. Dollar vs. Major Foreign Currencies, 1985-1997

	Dollars per Pound	Yen per Dollar	Marks per Dollar
1985 high	1.0546	278.08	3.4375
1987 low	1.8870	121.10	1.5705
1989 high	1.5120	149.46	2.0340
1990 low	1.9830	124.33	1.4700
mid-1998 high	1.6713	146.15	1.8035

Source: Data from *The Wall Street Journal*

CHAPTER 7

Government and the Economy

Spending for goods and services by federal, state, and local governments now consumes about 18 percent of the nation's output. Therefore, trends and shifts in this spending are factors to be reckoned with in any analysis of business conditions. The role of the government is even greater because of the sums it transfers from one group of people to another as a part of its regular activities. Social security benefits, hospital and Medicare payments, unemployment insurance, veterans' benefits, and government pension payments are all part of what is called entitlements. *Entitlement* payments are made automatically to individuals who qualify and reflect the transfer of income or assets from one group to another in our society. Another government activity of economic significance is the effect of government borrowing in the financial markets.

Statistical data to measure government activity are not easily available, although political and social commentary can be found in abundance. This chapter will discuss the data regularly published on government activities. However, the bulk of the chapter will provide background material on spending, the deficit, the federal debt, and the critical issues of the future of social security and Medicare. This information may provide the reader with some perspective to interpret current reports and commentary in the media.

The important terms in this chapter are:

Government consumption expenditures and gross investment. That part the federal, state, and local governments take of the current output of the economy, or the GDP;

Federal, state, and local expenditures. The *total* amount of government outlays in a particular period. These differ from purchases of goods and services primarily because of *transfer payments.* These payments are not a part of current output but rather represent the transfer of income or wealth (e.g., social security payments and government pensions) from one group to another. Other items not included in purchases are interest on debt, grants, and subsidies;

Federal, state, and local receipts. The income received from various revenue sources, such as income and other types of taxes, social security payments, and unemployment insurance;

Federal deficits. The difference between federal government receipts and expenditures, which is financed by *federal debt,* borrowing both in the United States and abroad. Methods of issuing this debt have important consequences for economic activity;

The *federal budget.* The government's projection of annual receipts and expenditures, the difference being either a *surplus* or a *deficit.* The financing of deficit adds to the debt. The *national income and product accounts* (NIPA) provide more useful ways of tracking government spending than do budget numbers;

Social security. The system of providing retirement and disability benefits. Income exceeds payments at this time—the system is building a surplus placed in a government *trust fund* that, although not included in current calculations of the budget deficit, is a tempting target for other federal spending programs. The payment for nonhospital benefits under *Part B of Medicare* is significantly less than premiums received and is a growing drain on the federal treasury.

GOVERNMENT CONSUMPTION EXPENDITURES AND GROSS INVESTMENT

Prior to 1995, government spending and income were reported in the GDP accounts under the heading "government purchases of goods and services." This process lumped together government spending for current consumption as well as government spending for equipment and structures that might be expected to last for more than one year; all goods and services purchased by government were treated as if they were consumed in the period in which they were purchased. This treatment was different from the treatment of private investment spending. Beginning in 1996, however, the following reclassifications were made and the NIPA revised retroactively.

- Government expenditures for structures and equipment (such as highways, schools, motor vehicles, and computers) were reclassified as investment and shown in a new GDP component "gross government investment."

- The services of government-fixed assets, measured using depreciation, are added to "government consumption expenditures," a new GDP component.

- Depreciation on government-fixed assets is added to the "consumption of fixed capital" component on the income side of the GDP accounts (see Table 2.2) to spread the cost of government investment over the assets' service lives.

This new treatment, however, does not provide an estimate of the full value of the services of general government-fixed assets. These services, which are recorded as a current-account purchase, are measured using the convention that these services equal the estimate of general government cost of fixed capital. The net rate of return on general government-fixed assets is assumed to be zero; i.e., neither profit nor loss.

Information about consumption expenditures and gross investment for the federal, state, and local governments is provided each
month on a quarterly basis as a part of the regular estimates of the
GDP accounts. These expenditures account for about 18 percent of
total GDP. The federal government accounts for about 37 percent of
total government consumption expenditures and gross investment;
state and local spending account for the balance. National defense
expenditures account for about two-thirds of federal government
expenditures.

In order to provide some perspective of the dimensions of
government spending on the economy, Figure 7.1 plots federal,
state, and local spending as a percent of GDP annually from 1950
through 1997. The hump in federal spending from 1951 to 1954
reflects the cost of the Korean War, and the rise in the 1980s reflects
the costs of the Vietnam War, President Johnson's Great Society
programs, and the defense buildup of President Reagan. The
decline since 1990 reflects the efforts to bring the federal budget
into balance, which will be discussed later in this chapter. State
and local spending rose steadily as a percent of GDP from 1950
through the mid-1970s but has been relatively stable since.

*Figure 7.1   Government Consumption Expenditures
and Gross Investment as Percent of GDP, 1950–1997*

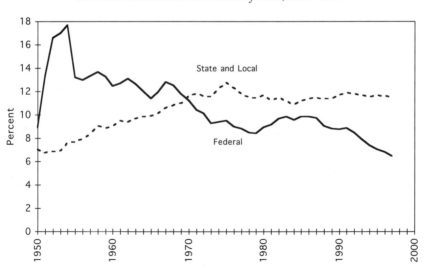

Source: SCB, August 1997, Table 1, p. 148; June 1998, Table 1.1, p. D-2

FEDERAL GOVERNMENT RECEIPTS AND EXPENDITURES

A detailed analysis of federal government receipts and expenditures is shown in Table 7.1 for 1997. The largest item of receipts is income taxes, which account for about 42 percent of total receipts. Contributions to social insurance, i.e., payroll taxes for social security,

Table 7.1
Federal Government Receipts and Expenditures—1997 (Billions of Dollars)

	Dollars	*Percent*
Receipts		
Personal tax and nontax receipts	686.7	43.3
Income taxes	666.8	42.0
Excise and gift taxes	17.5	1.1
Nontaxes	2.5	0.2
Corporate profits tax accruals	194.5	12.3
Federal Reserve banks	20.1	1.3
Other	174.4	11.0
Indirect business tax and nontax accruals	95.8	6.0
Excise taxes	56.4	3.6
Custom duties	19.2	1.2
Other	20.2	1.3
Contributions to social insurance	610.5	38.5
Total	1587.6	100.0
Current Expenditures		
Consumption expenditures	451.5	26.6
Defense	305.7	18.0
Transfer payments	763.5	45.0
Grants-in-aid to state and local governments	218.3	12.9
Net interest paid	227.1	13.4
Subsidies less current surplus of government enterprises	37.7	2.2
Total	1698.1	100.0
Current deficit, NIPA	−110.5	
Gross Investment	60.0	

Source: SCB, June 1998, Tables 3.2, p. D-8, and 3.7, p. D-9

hospital and Medicare, disability insurance and unemployment insurance, are the second largest source of receipts at 39 percent. Corporate taxes account for only 12 percent of receipts, and 10 percent of corporate tax accruals reflects the profits of the Federal Reserve banks that are returned to the Treasury.[1]

On the expenditure side, the largest item is transfer payments, i.e., social security, disability, hospital and Medicare, and government pensions. Consumption expenditures account for about 26 percent of current expenditures, of which defense is the largest part. Grants-in-aid to state and local governments and interest on the federal debt account for about 13 percent each. If current expenditures and gross investment are added, investment runs only about 3 percent of the total.

STATE AND LOCAL GOVERNMENT RECEIPTS AND EXPENDITURES

Table 7.2 shows state and local government receipts and expenditures as well as gross investment for 1997. One item of interest is that the state and local governments received federal grants-in-aid of $224 billion, which more than exceeded the current surplus, just as it was greater than the federal deficit, shown in Table 7.1. (This does not mean that the grants-in-aid *caused* the federal deficit or that these grants should be discontinued. It suggests that, without federal government help, state and local governments would either have to run a deficit or some state and local programs would have to be curtailed or canceled.)

On the receipt side, the major source of revenues was indirect business taxes and nontax accruals, which accounted for nearly half of receipts. Property taxes have been decreasing as a source of revenue and in 1997 accounted for less than 20 percent of the total. Income taxes are about 15 percent of total receipts; that area is a greater source of revenue for the federal government.

On the expenditure side, consumption expenditures make up about 80 percent of current expenditures and gross investment

---

[1] The Federal Reserve banks are included because their stock is owned by the nation's banks that are members of the system. However, after paying a 6 percent dividend to the stockholders, about 95 percent of the net earnings are paid into the U.S. Treasury.

combined. Education accounts for almost half of consumption expenditures and public safety for 14 percent. Expenditures for highways at 7 percent are slightly more than the 5 percent spent on welfare and social services.

Table 7.2
State and Local Government Receipts and Expenditures—1997
(Billions of Dollars)

	Dollars	%
Receipts		
Personal tax and nontax receipts	214.3	19.7
Income taxes	159.8	14.7
Excise and gift taxes	31.0	2.8
Nontaxes	23.5	2.2
Corporate profits tax accruals	37.6	3.4
Indirect business tax and nontax accruals	528.1	48.4
Sales taxes	257.4	23.6
Property taxes	208.8	19.1
Other	62.0	5.7
Contributions to social insurance	86.2	7.9
Federal grants-in-aid	224.2	20.6
Total	1090.4	100.0
Current Expenditures		
Consumption expenditures	762.9	77.6
Transfer payments to persons	311.8	31.7
Net interest paid	–65.2	–6.6
Less: Dividends received by government	14.6	1.5
Subsidies less current surplus of government enterprises	–12.2	–1.2
Total	982.6	100.0
Current surplus, NIPA	107.8	
Gross Investment	166.0	

Source: SCB, June 1998, Tables 3.3, p. D-8, and 3.7, p. D-9

THE FEDERAL BUDGET AND THE FEDERAL DEBT

The data in the previous sections have been on a national income and product account (NIPA) basis. These numbers are not the same as the more familiar federal budget figures reported in the press, although they are used by economists to track the government sector in the economy. The following section will deal with the budget figures, which at the outset should be distinguished from the NIPA figures. The differences are as follows:

- The federal budget figures are on a fiscal-year basis (now October 1 through September 30), while the NIPA figures are on a calendar-year basis. Using the NIPA figures enables easier comparisons with other economic data that are on a calendar-year basis.

- The NIPA figures include total receipts and expenditures. Thus they avoid the confusion created by "on-budget" and "off-budget" categories, which are used to segregate social security funds when computing the federal deficit.

- The quarterly NIPA figures are presented at seasonally adjusted annual rates, which are not done for the budget figures. Thus, the NIPA figures can be compared with other statistical measures of the economy that are reported seasonally adjusted.

- The NIPA figures now separate out current expenditures and investment; the budget figures do not. Some other minor differences reflect timing and coverage.[2]

Figure 7.2 presents the federal receipts, outlays, and the federal deficit for the fiscal years 1950 through the Congressional Budget Office's estimates for the years 1999–2008. Until 1974, the budget was roughly in balance. Thereafter, the annual deficit grew, reaching a record in 1992 of $290 billion. It has shrunk since, and shifted into surplus in 1999, aided by some efforts to curtail expenditures but mostly by the expansion in receipts due to the remarkable economic recovery and expansion of recent years and a big

---

[2] A reconciliation of receipts and expenditures in the NIPA and the federal budget figures for fiscal years 1992–96 are presented in Table 3.18B, SCB, October 1997, p. 11. Data for 1997 are not yet available in mid-1998.

Figure 7.2   Federal Budget Receipts, Outlays, and Deficit, 1950–2008 Estimated

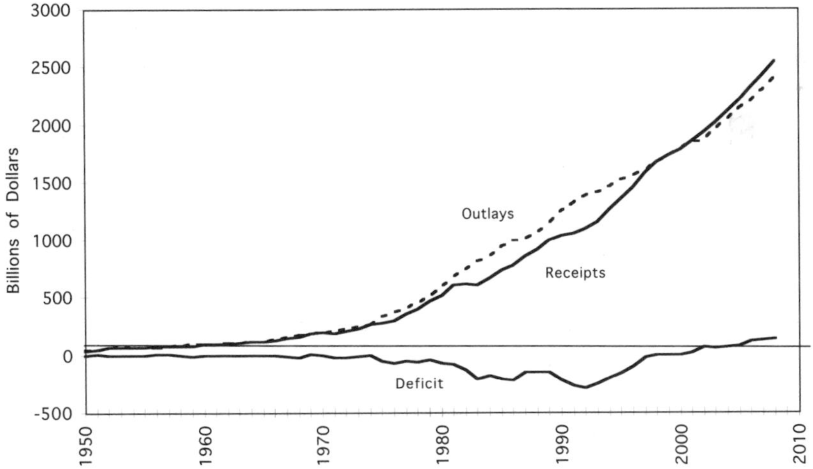

Source: Historical tables, *Budget of U.S. Government*, FY99; CBO,
Economic and Budget Outlook, January 1998

surge in tax collections. This chart reflects the movement into surplus and its continuance until 2008, according to estimates prepared in January 1998 by the Congressional Budget Office.

A somewhat different picture is reflected in Figure 7.3. In it, receipts and expenditures for social security (old age, survivors, and disability insurance) are taken out. Social security funds have been in excess of outlays since inception. Adding this surplus to the federal budget allows the budget numbers to appear in surplus beginning in 1999; if these income and expenditure items are excluded, the federal budget surplus disappears.

To put the budget deficit in some sort of prospective, compare it to the size of the economy. Figure 7.4 shows the budget surpluses and deficits as a percent of GDP for the years 1950 through the CBO estimate for 1998–2008. The low point was 1983, when the deficit reached 6 percent of GDP; even on an on-budget basis, it will be less than 1 percent of GDP early in the next century.[3]

---

[3] Comparing these numbers with some international standards of fiscal prudence, one of the criteria for a country's membership in the European Monetary Union set up by the Maastricht Treaty was that the government deficit for 1997 should be less than 3 percent of GDP; the United States would have met this criterion beginning in 1996 even on an on-budget basis.

*Figure 7.3   Federal On-Budget Receipts, Outlays,
and Deficit, 1950–2008 Estimated*

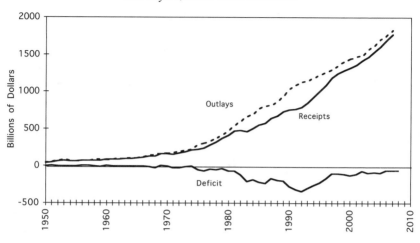

Source: Same as Figure 7.2

*Figure 7.4 Federal Deficits and On-Budget Deficits
as Percent of GDP, 1950–2008 Estimated*

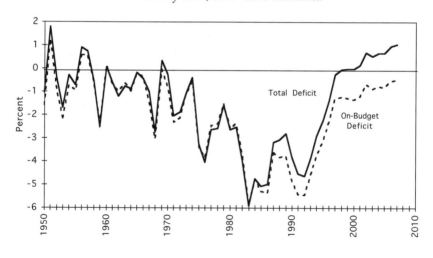

Source: Same as Figure 7.2

FEDERAL DEBT AND THE DEFICIT

The federal government has run a deficit for most years since 1950. When income is less than outgo, the difference has to be borrowed. As a result, the federal debt has been growing.

Figure 7.5 plots the federal debt in billions of dollars and Figure 7.6 shows debt as a percent of GDP. The lines on the chart plot both gross debt and debt held by the public. Debt held by the public includes individuals, private banks and insurance companies, the Federal Reserve banks, and foreign central banks. The difference between debt held by the public and gross debt is debt held in federal government trust accounts, i.e., civil service and military retirement accounts, social security and Medicare trust funds, and accounts like unemployment and highway trust funds. Of the two types of debt, the gross debt represents obligations that have to be met at some time in the future. However, the interest payments on debt held in trust funds is a bookkeeping entry, because the payments are from the U.S. Treasury to accounts held by the U.S. Treasury, so that interest payments on debt held by the

Figure 7.5   Federal Debt, 1950–2003 Estimated

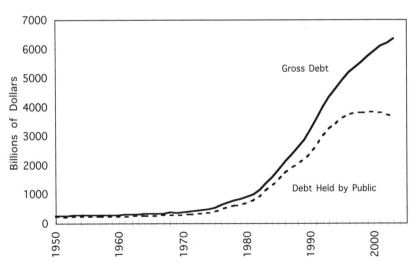

Source: Historical tables, *Budget of U.S. Government, FY99*, Table 7.1, p. 110

Figure 7.6   Federal Debt as Percent of GDP, 1950–2003 Estimated

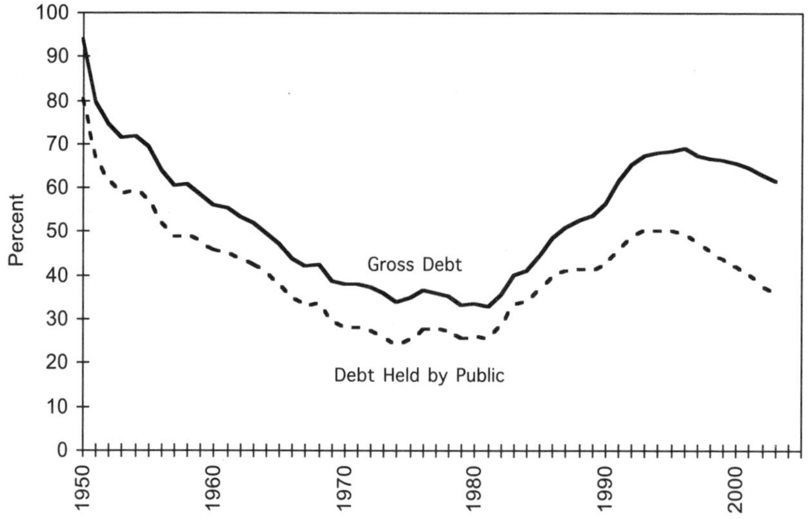

Source: Same as Figure 7.5

public represent obligations outside the federal government that must be met. As a percent of GDP, debt reached a low point in 1974 and has grown from about 32 percent for gross debt and 23 percent of debt in public hands to 66 percent and 47 percent, respectively, in 1997.

Some arguments have been advanced to minimize the size and importance of the federal debt. For example, only the debt held in public hands should be counted. Debt held by the government is an obligation the government owes to itself. However, these trust funds represent obligations that will have to be paid to someone at some future time. Another argument is that the debt is not much different from that of other major industrial nations. However, as a benchmark, one of the criteria for European countries to become members of the European Monetary Union is that gross debt be no more than 60 percent of GDP; in 1997 for the United States the amount was 66 percent, and it has exceeded 60 percent every year since 1991. It seems reasonable to say that the size of the debt is large and significant.

Financing the Federal Deficit

Financing the deficit is even more important than its size or growth. The federal debt makes major claims on the capital markets; it has also entailed borrowing overseas. Three major methods of financing the debt can be identified:

1. The first is either directly or indirectly out of the savings of individuals or corporations in the United States. If not purchased directly, government securities may be purchased indirectly through financial intermediaries such as banks, thrift institutions, and insurance companies. Funds used by the government are alternate uses of national savings; we, through our elected representatives, ultimately decide how these private savings are divided between the public and the private sector.

2. The second method is to obtain funds from abroad, which has become increasingly important. Foreign investors have been purchasing about 25 percent of new issues of U.S. government securities in recent years, and they now own about one-quarter of U.S. government debt. Consequently, their decisions to participate in regular Treasury financings, as well as their willingness to hold on to the securities they already own, can have a significant impact on U.S. security markets and interest rates. If they don't want U.S. securities, the funds will have to be raised in the United States somehow. The federal government has first claim on funds in the financial markets, because the money is needed to run the government and inability to raise money would result in political and economic chaos. If the government's needs increase, other borrowers will either have to pay higher interest rates or will have to go without.

3. The final source of financing is for the Federal Reserve System to purchase these securities. This process is potentially inflationary, because, in effect, the Federal Reserve takes the bonds into its own portfolio and pays for the securities by crediting the Treasury's checking account for the proceeds. As the Treasury spends this money, it adds to the supply of money available to purchase the same amount of goods and services.

Reducing the Deficit

If the federal debt is such a problem, what can be done about it? The obvious answer is to reduce or eliminate the annual deficit and slow or halt the growth of the federal debt. But that is easier said than done, as repeated struggles by the Congress and the Administration in recent years amply indicate. Most of the easy cuts have been made in the budget. It is difficult to get agreement on increasing taxes in order to raise any significant amount of revenue; higher personal income taxes would be necessary, a politically unpalatable solution. Reducing spending is almost as difficult, as an examination of current spending patterns will show.

Review Table 7.1 again. Interest on the federal debt is untouchable, and as the debt grows interest payments will increase as a percent of federal outlays. Defense spending has been cut from slightly under half of current expenditures in the mid-1960s to less than 20 percent now. Running the legislative, executive, and judicial branches of the government takes less than 2 percent of the budget. Pensions, veterans' benefits, and items such as unemployment compensation are set by current law and are unlikely to be altered. The major items remaining are payments for social security, disability benefits, and hospital and supplementary medical insurance. These are so large and so politically sensitive that they deserve some special discussion (see "How Does Social Security Work?" section). First, however, some comment is in order about the 1997 agreement to reduce the deficit and how the budget moved into surplus.

BALANCING THE FEDERAL BUDGET

In 1997, the outlook for the federal deficit was impacted by two major developments. The first was a significantly lower deficit in 1997 than had been expected at the beginning of the year. The Congressional Budget Office (CBO) was established by Congress in 1974 to advise Congress on fiscal policy and prepare projections of the federal budget. It is independent of the Office of Management and Budget (OMB), which does similar research for the executive branch of the government. In January 1997, CBO projected the deficit for the fiscal year 1997 at $124 billion. By January

1998, the CBO re-estimated the deficit at $22 billion, and the OMB forecast an even smaller number. The smaller deficit was attributed primarily to revenue larger than anticipated and to reduced spending, especially on assistance programs; the 1997 economy was considerably stronger than had been expected at the beginning of the year. The brighter economic outlook also improved the deficit projections for the years beyond 1997.

In a second development by midyear 1997, Congress had passed and the President had signed the Taxpayer Relief and Balanced Budget Acts of 1997, which were designed to put the budget in surplus by the year 2002. However the budget is expected to be in surplus in 1998 and beyond, primarily because of more optimistic economic assumptions. Tax revenue will be reduced by new tax credits for dependent children, a lower capital gains tax, lower estate and gift taxes, and expanded individual retirement accounts. However, these revenue losses are expected to be more than offset by capping discretionary outlays and reducing Medicare and Medicaid payments.

These two developments led many commentators to believe that the United States, after many years of struggle, finally is on the path for a permanently balanced budget. Should these expectations become a reality, it could have a significant impact on economic growth, monetary policy, and the financial markets.

The benefits of reaching a balanced budget are considerable:

- A balanced budget will reduce the claims of the government on the economy and the financial markets and significantly reduce inflationary prospects.

- Lower inflation means a decline in nominal interest rates because the gap between real rates and nominal rates will be smaller due to a lower inflation premium.

- Real interest rates are likely to be lower, because the volatility risk in the economy will decline as inflation is reduced.

- Lower demand for funds by the federal government should result in higher saving rates by individuals and businesses, increasing the flow of funds into the financial markets for the private sector.

- Increased saving means increased funds for investment. Higher business spending for capital investment should lead to greater economic growth, improved productivity, and higher profits. Lower interest rates also will help profits.

- Lower rates will reduce the need for capital inflows from abroad to help offset the federal deficit, thus lowering the current account deficit with the rest of the world.

- Interest payments on the federal debt would be lower because of lower borrowing costs, providing the opportunity for the government to reduce taxes or cut the outstanding debt.

- Formulating economic policy would be easier, because the Federal Reserve would not have to run so tight a monetary policy to keep inflation in check. Also, in the event of a recession, fiscal policy could once again become an available option.

- Lower federal deficits and debt would lead to greater financial stability.

As great as these benefits seem, a number of factors detract from the rosy picture:

- The dramatic lowering of the deficit in 1997 and 1998 may lead to overconfidence that the deficit problem has been resolved without having to make any policy changes. In fact, trial balloons for spending programs to take advantage of the reduced deficit were being floated at the end of 1997 and may well emerge as legislative proposals in 1998. The hard-won discipline that helped to reduce the deficit can easily be lost.

- The budget agreement is "back loaded," i.e., tax reductions come first and the expenditure cuts come toward the end of the five-year period. The political risk is always there that elected officials will not make the necessary spending cuts or will dilute them, so that the planned budget balance is not achieved. It will take some tough political decisions to assure that the budget agreement is carried out.

- The gravest risk is related to the aging of the "baby boomers." Beginning in 2008, the "baby boomers" of the post-World War II period will be reaching retirement age. In addition, people are also living longer today, so providing their benefits will cost more in the future. Moreover, the "baby boom" was followed by a "baby bust," so that labor force growth should shrink appreciably after 2010. As a result, the relationship of the retired population to the working population (whose payroll deductions in large part support the retired population's benefits) will shift dramatically, rising from 20 social security beneficiaries per 100 population in 1960 to 30 per 100 now, and to 50 per 100 in 2030. Figure 7.7 shows the percentage distribution of the population by age groups from 1950 to 2070. The right bar for each year indicates the growth of the over-65 age groups.

These developments will shrink the contributions to and accelerate the demands on the social security system as well as Medicare and Medicaid. Deficits could escalate sharply around 2010 unless these entitlements are addressed in the next few years, unpalatable as that may be from a political viewpoint.

Figure 7.7   Age Distribution of Population as a Percent of Total, 1950–2070

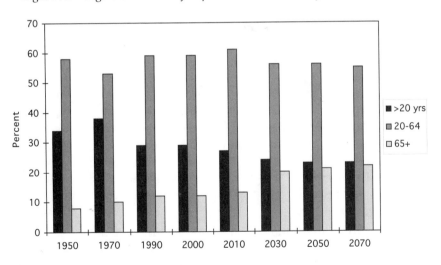

Source: CBO, *Long-Term Budgetary Pressures and Policy Options,*
May 1998, Table 1, p. xiv

The change in the fiscal picture of the federal government in 1997–98 has been dramatic. Instead of a dreary outlook of continuing deficits, the CBO now projects surpluses out to 2010—although the CBO stresses that their projections are admittedly precarious and a slight change in economic assumptions could easily shift a surplus into a deficit. If budget surpluses are used to increase spending or reduce taxes, the surplus also could disappear. Moreover, the basic problem of entitlements remains. If the economy continues on an expansionary track for the next few years, an opportunity will be presented to address the entitlement problems. Whether advantage is taken of this opportunity remains to be seen.

HOW DOES SOCIAL SECURITY WORK?

The social security trust fund is so large that it has its own rules; this major commitment of government to the public requires special discussion.

The social security system started in 1935 as a pension plan, with receipts to be held in trust for future beneficiaries just like in a corporate pension plan. However, the system quickly was changed to a pay-as-you-go basis, with current workers' contributions paying for benefits to retirees. Gradually, very little relationship existed between the dollar amount contributed by a worker and the benefits received. Benefits were gradually extended to many who had not contributed, and since 1972 benefits have been increased each year by the increase in the consumer price index. (This practice is in sharp contrast to the private pension system, where cost-of-living increases are made infrequently and usually voluntarily by the companies concerned.) Although often considered as providing retirement benefits, the system also provides benefits for survivors of deceased participants as well as for participants who become disabled.

Social security and a part of Medicare are funded by payroll taxes paid equally by the employer and the employee, with the 1998 rate 15.3 percent up to an earnings ceiling of $68,400 a year. As indicated on Table 7.1, social security taxes now generate almost as much revenue as individual income taxes.

The increases made in social security benefits plus the annual adjustment in payments for inflation almost bankrupted the system. However, in 1983 the Greenspan Commission recommended increasing contributions, taxing a portion of the benefits to some recipients and gradually extending the retirement age to 67. These changes made the system solvent, and are also building reserves to ensure payment of benefits to present as well as future participants.

What is the outlook for this trust fund? Figure 7.8 shows the income and outgo, together with the estimated surplus, as estimated by the Social Security Administration. The financial condition looks good out to 2002 at least. However, the 1997 report of the trustees of this fund, who include the secretaries of the treasury, labor, and health and human resources, indicate that, absent any legislative changes, the old age and survivors insurance (OASI) trust fund will peak out in 2012, the first year when outgo exceeds tax income. By 2031, trust fund assets will be exhausted. Of course, legislative changes will have to be made; running out of funds or even the appearance of doing so is politically unthinkable. Suggestions for curing the problem include lengthening the retirement age, shrinking the benefits (especially the size of the annual cost-of-living increase or the payments to higher-income individuals), or increasing the contributions made by employers and employees. These issues will have to be addressed early in the next century to ensure the viability of the system.

Figure 7.8   OASI and DI Income and Outgo, 1966–2003 Estimated

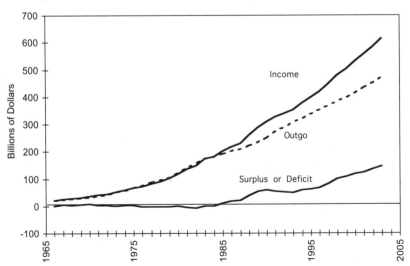

Source: Historical tables, *Budget of U.S. Government, FY99*, Table 13.1, p. 251 ff

Social Security and the Federal Budget

The problem of social security running out of money is even more complex. As social security payments are made into the U.S. Treasury, they are invested exclusively in nonmarketable debt issued by the Treasury; the funds are then spent by the Treasury for general government purposes. In effect, the money received is spent and replaced in the trust fund by a Treasury IOU to be paid at a future time.

Interest is paid on this nonmarketable debt in the trust fund. As the assets of the fund grow, interest paid by the Treasury also grows as a percent of total income. In 1990 interest as a percent of income was about 5 percent; it will grow to 12 percent in 2020 and diminish thereafter. Understand that these interest payments are, in effect, a bookkeeping entry, a "wash" as far as total government income and outgo is concerned. Interest payments are an on-budget expense for the Treasury and interest received is off-budget income. A more realistic measure of the social security surplus is the difference between the annual public contributions and the annual payments to beneficiaries, assuming no changes in current law. In 1996, this difference was estimated at $11 billion, by 2002 it is estimated to reach $30 billion. However, as mentioned earlier, by 2012 outgo exceeds tax income, and by 2031 trust funds assets are exhausted.

Thus, the social security trust fund is not some great pool of money available for beneficiary payments or for other programs. The current contributions from the public are spent by the government for general government purposes. The trust fund can be viewed as a segregated account on the government's books, reflecting the government's promise to pay future benefits as prescribed by law, by means of taxing or borrowing as funds are needed. The segregated trust fund makes clear the dimensions of this obligation and what will happen to this fund in the future under current law.

Proposals to use this trust fund for other purposes would merely transfer the IOUs to another program; future tax revenues or borrowing would still be required to pay for this alternative use. Proposals to reduce the social security payroll tax would just reduce Treasury receipts that are currently spent and reduce the growth of the pool of IOUs. The government's obligation to social security beneficiaries is set by current law and must be met (i.e., mandatory spending) unless the law is changed.

At some time early in the next century the government will face the problem of social security benefit payments exceeding the income from payroll deductions. Some additional ways to cover benefit payments will have to be devised or benefits will have to be reduced. It might be well to start to address this issue now rather than later under the pressure of a perceived depletion of the trust fund.[4]

Other Trust Funds

Three other major trust funds are worth a comment. The Disability Trust Fund (DI) and the Hospital Insurance Trust Fund (HI) are linked to social security payments. Whenever these funds incur a deficit, Congress adjusts the allocation between the funds and the Social Security Trust Funds to restore financial balance. In the 1997 report of the OASDI trustees, they commented that such action to restore the balance in DI and HI was necessary, and this probably will be done by Congress.

Figure 7.9 shows the income and outgo of the HI fund from 1966 through 2002. During most of that period, the fund ran a surplus and is projected to continue in surplus in the period ahead.

Medicare is a different matter. Medicare was introduced in 1966. It has two parts: hospitalization insurance (Part A) and supplementary medical insurance (Part B). Part B is financed about one-quarter from people eligible for benefits and the remainder from general tax revenues. And Medicare premiums are paid by all employees and employers, although the benefits are paid to those over 65 or with disabilities.

Figure 7.10 shows the financial condition of Medicare through 2002. The dotted line indicates the cash income (almost all premiums) and the top solid line the outgo. The gap between the two lines represents the contributions of the federal government, which in 1996 were estimated at $62 billion. The growing gap is an increasing drain on the Treasury. Of all of the funds, the Medicare gap is the most serious. Congress has addressed it in the past by decreasing the payments to hospitals and physicians, and premiums are increased each year as

---

[4] It has been proposed that the surplus of income over payments, instead of being invested in government securities, be lent to the private sector for investment. The interest income on the loans could assist in meeting future social security deficits. Such a development may make good sense economically but probably isn't politically feasible; it would be criticized as giving social security funds to corporations instead of using them to increase benefits.

well. But the costs of medical care continue to increase, and the retir-
ing "baby boomers" will place an increasing burden on costs as they
retire. Congress will have to address this politically charged issue
head on in the next few years, because limited opportunities remain
for further squeezes on payments to hospitals and doctors.

Figure 7.9   Hospital Insurance Income and Outgo, 1966–2003 Estimated

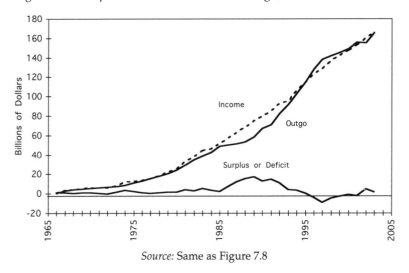

Source: Same as Figure 7.8

Figure 7.10   Medical Insurance Income and Outgo, 1967–2003 Estimated

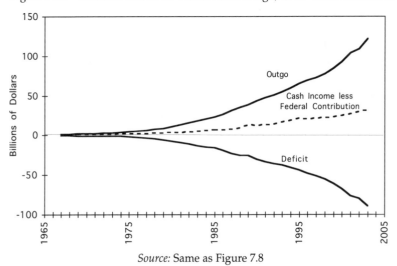

Source: Same as Figure 7.8

SUMMARY

Unlike the private sector, monthly statistics are not readily available to monitor the performance of the government sector. Information on government consumption expenditures and gross investment is published as a part of the quarterly GNP reports and may be mentioned in the financial section of some newspapers. Details of total spending can be found in the Department of Commerce's monthly publication, the *Survey of Current Business.*

Most information about actions of the government is of a more qualitative nature and is covered in the general news sections of newspapers and other media. The figures, tables, and discussion in this chapter are intended to provide information on government income, outgo, and debt, so that activities reported in the media can be understood and interpreted with a somewhat better perspective.

Controlling federal spending is difficult. However, the budget agreement in 1997 may reduce the size of the deficits in the next several years and slow the growth of the federal debt. A major long-term problem for the federal government is provision for payment of social security benefits as recipients grow and contributions from workers shrink. More immediate is the problem of Medicare, where three-quarters of the cost is not covered by payments from those who benefit.

CHAPTER 8

Interest Rates and Monetary Policy

In Chapter 1 interest rates were discussed briefly, indicating how movements in interest rates affect the decision-making process of the average person. The pattern of both short- and long-term interest rates from 1950 to 1997 was also reviewed, indicating how these rates were influenced by cyclical developments in the economy and changes in the inflation rate. Given this base of information, a closer look at interest rates can now be taken.

The day-to-day fluctuations in interest rates, like the day-to-day movements in the stock market, are generally random events that are impossible to predict. Over a period of time, however, the *trend* of interest rates does reflect the net results of certain forces pulling rates in different directions. Understanding and evaluating these forces

135

should help make a reasonable estimate of the future pattern of rates, which should assist in making investment decisions.

This chapter discusses the following items:

Factors affecting interest rates, including the path of the economy, inflation, the financing needs of the federal government, international forces, the difficulties faced by U.S. financial institutions and, most importantly, the activities of the Federal Reserve;

Federal Reserve System is important in its influence on interest rate movements (a part of this chapter is devoted to its purpose, organization, and operations). The Federal Reserve operates through its influence on *bank reserves;* these are defined and discussed. Setting *monetary policy* is reviewed, followed by techniques used in monitoring the central bank;

The *level and pattern of interest* rates are also discussed. The *yield curve* as well as the different shapes it takes at different times in the business cycle is explained. Interest rate patterns of bonds of different maturity and quality are considered. Suggestions concerning what the average individual can expect to accomplish in anticipating changes in interest rates are also examined.

WHAT ARE INTEREST RATES?

Interest rates arise because people who don't have money and want it must pay something to those who have money and are willing to lend it for a reward, called *interest.* The *interest rate* is the amount received related to the amount lent, usually expressed as a percent computed by dividing the dollars of interest received per hundred dollars lent.

A distinction should be made between specific interest rates and interest rates in general. *Specific interest rates* on a particular financial instrument or type of instrument (e.g., a mortgage or a bank certificate of deposit) reflect the time for which the money is lent, the risk that the loan may not be repaid, and the current supply of and demand for funds available for lending in the marketplace.

Some specific rates, such as those on Treasury or corporate bonds, are set daily in dealer markets by negotiations between buyers and sellers, and are called *market rates*. Other rates, such as the *bank prime rate* (the interest rate banks charge their best customers) or the Federal Reserve *discount rate* (the rate at which banks can borrow from the Federal Reserve) are set by some group, and are called *administered rates*. However, these administered rates would not prevail for long if they did not reflect underlying market forces—ultimately they will reflect market rates.

These comments will initially focus on forces that affect the movement of interest rates generally rather than on rates of particular kinds of investments or their relationships with one another.

FACTORS AFFECTING INTEREST RATES

What are the major forces to watch in evaluating the future movement of interest rates? They include the economy, inflationary pressures, the federal government, international, the dollar, and U.S. financial institutions.

The Economy

Interest rates are strongly influenced by the expansion or contraction of the economy. When the economy is expanding, consumers have jobs and savings to lend, but also need to borrow for large purchases, such as a home or a car, or to finance other purchases by using credit cards. Business people need to borrow to build inventories or plants or to run their businesses generally as economic activity rises. As the demand for funds increases faster than the supply of savings grows, interest rates rise and act to ration the funds available. Of course, the opposite is also true; when the demand for funds is slack, interest rates fall.

Inflationary Pressures

Inflationary pressures also have an effect on interest rates, because the rates paid on most loans are fixed in the contract. A lender will be reluctant to lend funds for any period of time if the purchasing power of these funds will be less when they are returned. Consequently, the lender will demand a higher rate, a so-called *inflationary premium*, to lend money. Inflation pushes interest rates higher; deflation sends rates down.

Inflation pressures arise for a number of reasons, including the expansion of money and credit in excess of savings to support it, the purchase of federal debt by the banking system, or an increase in import prices (and indirectly domestic prices) because of a falling dollar.

The Federal Government

Another factor influencing interest rates is the actions of the nation's largest borrower, the federal government. Vast taxing powers of the federal government accords its debt the highest credit rating and therefore it is a preferred investment. Its operation is vital to the country; the federal government has first claim on the funds available in the marketplace. As discussed in Chapter 6, the fiscal posture of the federal government has shifted in fiscal year 1998 from a string of years of budget deficits to surplus, which is expected to continue into the immediate future. Consequently, the amount the Treasury has to borrow has been reduced significantly. Whether this happy condition will continue depends on Congressional action on spending, tax reduction, and adjustments to spending for social security and Medicare as well as the state of the economy. As it has in the past, the federal government could again become a significant borrower in the financial markets.

International

International forces have exercised an increasingly important influence on U.S. interest rates. Several years ago, when U.S. interest rates were high relative to those of other major industrial countries, foreigners were eager to invest in the United States, which increased the supply of funds and exerted downward pressures on interest rates. To the extent that foreign investors are willing to lend funds to the United States, they supplement domestic sources of funds and push rates down. Should they decide to reduce their lending or, worse, sell their holdings to reinvest elsewhere in the world, funds needed in the United States would have to come from domestic sources, pushing rates up. Consequently, an important consideration for the Federal Reserve in setting monetary policy is whether U.S. rates are sufficiently high to maintain foreign interest in U.S. securities.

From time to time, overseas funds flow into the United States as a safe haven because of some international political or economic event. Such a development occurred in December 1997 and again in June 1998, when overseas funds from Asia poured into long-term U.S. Treasuries, seeking both a safe haven and the higher yields available on U.S. Treasury securities. This inflow pressed U.S. long-term interest rates down. At the same time, in an effort to bolster the value of the Japanese yen in foreign exchange, the Bank of Japan and the Federal Reserve were reported to have engaged in a carefully controlled selling of Japanese holdings of U.S. short-term Treasury securities, which drove short-term interest rates up. (The proceeds were used to buy yen in the foreign exchange markets to curtail its depreciation, which was caused by the turmoil in Asia and which would drive the yen and therefore the price of Japanese exports to the United States to unacceptable levels.) As a result of these international developments rather than any domestic U.S. events, the yields on U.S. Treasury securities shifted into a pattern that was not typical for the economic conditions then prevailing in the United States.

The Dollar

The dollar is the main currency in international trade and is used extensively in world markets. Orderly fluctuations of the dollar in foreign exchange markets are essential for domestic and international stability. Major or very volatile exchange rate movements in the dollar may force the Federal Reserve to intervene and may also affect U.S. monetary policy and interest rates.

U.S. Financial Institutions

At times, some of the major banks or thrift institutions may face difficulties due to poor lending policies or a business contraction that affects the ability of many borrowers to repay their bank loans. If any large institution is threatened with failure, it would not default on the funds owed to its depositors, as happened in the

1930s. Federal government actions would be taken to ensure the integrity of the deposits, regardless of the impact on the federal budget deficit. The Federal Reserve would make bank reserves available as necessary. This action would increase the supply of funds in the market. Initially interest rates would move down, but ultimately the increase in inflationary pressures would send rates higher. Changes in the health of the U.S. financial system have a significant effect on U.S. interest rates.

THE FEDERAL RESERVE SYSTEM

Probably the most important force to watch in evaluating future interest rate trends is the Federal Reserve. The Federal Reserve controls credit availability, for example, the *amount* of funds available to lend, and the *level of interest rates* at which this credit is made available. Its importance in the functioning of the financial system requires a longer discussion of the purpose, organization, and some of the responsibilities of the Federal Reserve.

Purpose

The Federal Reserve System was created by Congress in 1913 to provide for a safer, more flexible banking and monetary system. Over time, this original purpose has shifted to broader national economic and financial objectives:

Stability and growth of the economy;

A high level of employment;

Stability in the purchasing power of the dollar; and

Reasonable balance in transactions with foreign countries.

As the nation's central bank, the Federal Reserve contributes to the achievement of these broad objectives by its ability to influence money and credit in the economy.

The Federal Reserve is but one of the many forces that affect the economy. Other forces include federal government policies on taxes and spending (fiscal policy), wage and price policies of business, price shocks, economic and political developments overseas, and changing expectations of businesses and consumers that affect their spending patterns. Nevertheless, the Federal Reserve exerts significant influence on the path of the economy.

Organization

The governing body of the Federal Reserve System is the Board of Governors, located in Washington, DC. The seven members of the Board are appointed for a 14-year term by the President, with confirmation by the Senate. The Chairman and Vice-Chairman are selected from Board members for four-year terms, also by the President with the confirmation of the Senate. The Board is not a part of the Administration. It is an independent agency of the federal government, although Congress can change its powers and duties by legislation.

The United States is divided into 12 Federal Reserve Districts, each with a district Federal Reserve Bank and its own president and directors. These banks have the duty of making recommendations to the Federal Reserve Board for changes in the *discount rate,* the interest rate that financial institutions must pay to borrow from the Federal Reserve. In addition, these banks hold the reserve balances for and make loans to depository institutions, furnish currency, collect and clear checks, and handle U.S. government debt and cash balances.

In addition to its responsibilities in regulating the supply of reserves in its efforts to influence economic activity, the Federal Reserve has other functions that should be mentioned briefly. The Federal Reserve acts for the government in foreign exchange markets, in close cooperation with the U.S. Treasury. In a world of flexible exchange rates, one of the objectives is to prevent disorderly conditions on exchange markets. The Federal Reserve watches international developments, such as changes in interest rates overseas, in order to temper their effects on the U.S. economy.

The Federal Reserve also has supervisory and regulatory functions, which it shares with other federal banking agencies. The Federal Reserve supervises state-chartered banks that are members of the Federal Reserve System and all bank holding companies. (The Office of the Comptroller of the Currency supervises national banks, and the Federal Deposit Insurance Corporation [FDIC] supervises insured nonmember commercial banks and insured state-chartered savings banks.) The Federal Reserve also acts as the banker for the federal government, sets margin requirements for the purchase or carrying equity securities, and establishes and enforces rules that offer protection to consumers in financial operations. However, the most important function of the Federal Reserve is its control over banking reserves.

The members of the Federal Reserve Board are a part of the Federal Open Market Committee (FOMC). Other members of the FOMC are the President of the Federal Reserve Bank of New York and four other Reserve Bank presidents, who serve on a rotating basis. The FOMC directs the Federal Reserve's open market operations, the chief instrument of monetary policy, described in more detail later in this chapter. The FOMC meets formally eight times a year and more often if necessary.

About 39 percent of the roughly 11,200 commercial banks in the United States belong to the Federal Reserve System. National banks chartered by the federal government must belong to the system, and state banks may also be members. Since 1980, all depository institutions (commercial banks, foreign-related banking institutions, savings banks, savings and loan associations, and credit unions) are required to maintain reserves with the Federal Reserve System; they may also borrow from the Federal Reserve as necessary.

Member banks must subscribe to stock in the Reserve Bank of its district equal to 6 percent of its capital and surplus, 3 percent of which is paid in and the remainder subject to call by the Board of Governors. Owning this stock does not give member banks control of the policies of the Reserve Banks; however, member banks do receive a statutory dividend each year of 6 percent on the value of their paid-in stock. After paying expenses and the 6 percent dividend, the remaining earnings of the Federal Reserve, about 95 percent of the total, are turned over to the U.S. Treasury.

Reserves of Depository Institutions

The Federal Reserve influences overall monetary and credit conditions, and thus movements in the economy, through actions that affect both the *amount and cost of reserves* of depository institutions.

Reserves are defined by law as cash (currency and coin) held by depository institutions in their vaults plus the accounts of these institutions with their district reserve banks. Total reserves have two components. The first is *required reserves,* defined as the minimum percent of deposits the Federal Reserve requires a depository institution to hold (for most accounts, now 10 percent). Total reserves less required reserves are called *excess reserves.*

Reserves are provided in two forms. *Nonborrowed reserves* are obtained by depository institutions primarily from the Federal Reserve through Federal Reserve open market operations. *Borrowed reserves* are accomplished by a loan to the depository institution by the Federal Reserve. When borrowed reserves are subtracted from excess reserves, the balance is called *free reserves.* These reserve balances are reported weekly in financial newspapers as part of the consolidated balance sheet of the Federal Reserve Banks.

Another measure that is published together with the reserve information is called the *monetary base,* which includes currency held by the public and in the vaults of depository institutions plus reserves of depository institutions. Of the two components, currency comprises the larger, more than 80 percent. The monetary base, in effect, comprises the Federal Reserve's liability for currency in circulation and for reserve balances; it also represents monetary instruments that can function as reserves in the banking system. Some economists argue that the monetary base should be used as an operating target for monetary policy, but it is more generally used as an analytical device.

The fractional reserve system provides the Federal Reserve with a powerful tool to influence the amount of money and credit in the economy and thus the level of economic activity. If, for example, a reserve of 10 percent against deposits were required, every dollar of bank reserves held by the Federal Reserve would support ten times that amount in deposits in the banking system. For every dollar of excess reserves (reserves above those necessary to support the current level of deposits), the banking system can create new deposits and make loans to ten times the amount of excess reserves. (For example, on December 17, 1997, the Federal Reserve reported that total reserves equaled $46,246 million and excess reserves $1,482 million. Subtracting $240 million of bank borrowings from the Federal Reserve, free reserves equaled $1,242 million, which could support additional bank lending of ten times that amount.) The Federal Reserve can significantly affect the ability of the banking system to expand or contract loans and deposits by taking action to increase or shrink reserves.

Influencing Reserve Positions

The Federal Reserve can affect the supply of reserves in three ways:

1. *Setting bank reserve requirements,* which is done by the Federal Reserve Board. Changing reserve requirements is considered a major step not often used. It affects all depository institutions and can have a significant impact on reducing or increasing funds available for lending.

2. *Discount lending.* Financial institutions may borrow from the Federal Reserve by pledging securities or loans they own, paying an interest rate called the *discount rate.* This rate is approved by the Board on the recommendation of the district Reserve Banks. Raising or lowering this rate can hinder or encourage borrowing and hence the supply of bank reserves. However, banks usually borrow from the Federal Reserve only for temporary or unusual reasons. Changes in the discount rate are more symbolic of the central bank's intentions than a major tool of monetary policy.

3. *Open market operations.* The most frequently used and most flexible tool of monetary policy is open market operations, which are directed by the FOMC. When the Federal Reserve sells U.S. Treasury securities out of its portfolio to securities dealers, these dealers pay for the securities with checks drawn on financial institutions; the Federal Reserve collects from these financial institutions by reducing their reserve accounts at the Federal Reserve. This step reduces the lending ability of financial institutions substantially more than the amount of the payment because of the operations of fractional reserves. When the Federal Reserve buys securities and pays for them by crediting bank reserve accounts, the opposite effect occurs. These actions work indirectly on the economy through the supply and the cost of funds, with a response lag that may vary depending on the reserve position of the banking system and the many other forces that influence the economy.

Actions of the Federal Reserve are not the only factors that cause changes in nonborrowed reserves. Currency in circulation reflects public demand for money and has a significant seasonal pattern, for example, a big increase around holidays. The Federal Reserve float—the difference between checks credited to bank reserve accounts but not yet collected from issuing banks—is affected by random factors, such as storms or transportation strikes. Thus, Treasury and foreign official balances at Federal Reserve Banks are very difficult to predict.

What the Federal Reserve Watches

What guides does the Federal Reserve use in determining monetary policy? Prior to October 1979, the Federal Reserve operated monetary policy by managing reserve positions to achieve a certain level of the federal funds' rate. (*Federal funds* are excess reserves that banks lend to each other for brief periods, mostly overnight; the lending bank has excess reserves and the borrowing bank needs to cover a temporary reserve deficiency. The Federal Reserve actions impact reserve positions; therefore the federal funds' interest rate is the easiest to influence through open market operations.)

In October 1979, this procedure was altered to focus on achievement of a certain growth rate in the money supply. Since late 1982, a more judgmental approach has been used, with the economic outlook, commodity prices, the monetary aggregates, interest rates, credit conditions, the foreign exchange position of the dollar, and other factors being considered.

Overall economic conditions are a primary focus of Federal Reserve analysis. In Chapters 2 through 8 a framework for such an analysis was provided. The Board has an exceptionally talented staff that analyzes available business and financial statistics to determine the current position and likely future path of the economy. In addition, the Board has an excellent intelligence network in the district banks, which submit regular reports on district conditions. These reports, contained in the so-called beige book, are usually summarized in the financial press, and the complete report is available on the Federal Reserve Board's web site—http://www.bog.frb.fed.us

The Money Supply

Another important monitoring tool is changes in the money supply. It is useful because it provides a clue to changes in the *amount* of money available to the public rather than the *cost* of this money. Several problems arise when the focus of monetary policy is on controlling changes in the money supply.

Before banking deregulation, a clear distinction could be made between funds held for transactions purposes and funds held as a store of wealth, or savings. Transactions accounts did not pay interest and were comprised of currency and demand deposit or checking accounts at banks. Savings accounts were interest-bearing deposits at banks and other savings institutions.

With deregulation, however, the picture has changed. Demand deposits may now pay interest. Checks can now be drawn against savings accounts; and the kinds of accounts have proliferated, including money-market mutual funds with checking privileges. Whether a deposit is for transactions or for savings is really in the mind of the owner of the account, which may change from time to time. The name or nature of the account is of little help.

As a result, measures of the money supply have had to be expanded, and long-time historical relationships reconsidered. The definitions of the money supply now include the following:

1. *M1* includes balances (currency, travelers checks, demand deposits, and interest-bearing accounts with unlimited checking authority) that are commonly used for transactions purposes to purchase goods and services;

2. *M2* includes Ml plus liquid assets whose nominal values are fixed and can be converted into transactions balances with relative ease, for example, money-market accounts, time and savings deposits, and money-market mutual funds;

3. *M3* includes both Ml and M2 as well as liquid assets held by large asset holders, for example, $100,000 or more.

Statistical analysis indicates that, in the long run, prices in the economy will rise in proportion to the rise in the money supply. M2, among the aggregates, is the measure that most closely conforms to movements in GDP in current dollars. This relationship implies that the Federal Reserve can control the trend in nominal GDP by controlling M2, which is why many economists emphasize the use of this measure to establish and monitor monetary policy.

However, several difficulties are encountered in using the money supply for this purpose. The first is the blurring of the distinction between money used for *transaction balances* and for a *store of wealth*. The transaction balances are those involved in attempting to control economic activity. The second is the difficulty in identifying changes in the trend of money supply movements, determining the lead time between these turning points and then the subsequent impact on business. It is one thing to look at a chart of historical movements in the money supply and business activity; it is another to pick turning points contemporaneously as these lines jiggle up and down. The final problem is that money has not only quantity but also velocity, that is, the rapidity with which it changes hands varies.

For all these reasons, many economists question the utility of using the money supply as the principal tool in setting monetary policy, regardless of the theoretical basis for its use. However, it is a useful measure to watch in anticipating changes in Federal Reserve policy.

Watching the Federal Reserve

Officials at the Federal Reserve tend not to indicate plainly what their intentions are with respect to monetary policy; these must be determined by watching what they watch and watching what they do. As indicated earlier, they watch business conditions; an average individual can do this as well. Granted the economists at the Federal Reserve have many and more sophisticated tools at their disposal, but understanding the strength or weakness of the economy and anticipating major turning points are well within the abilities of the average individual willing to take a little time to develop a perspective of what is going on.

Clues as to what the Federal Reserve is going to do can be obtained by watching movements in the money supply, changes in bank reserve positions, and changes in the federal funds rate. Another important clue is to watch the speeches and statements of Federal Reserve officials. The Chairman is required to testify before Congress twice a year (February and July) on the Federal

Reserve's assessment of the economy, credit conditions, and their projected growth rates of the money supply for the year ahead. In addition, the minutes of the FOMC are reported in the press. Unfortunately the release is made about 45 days after each meeting, considerably reducing their usefulness. In addition, members of the Board often make speeches that touch on their views of monetary policy, and these speeches are reported in the financial press and are available on the Board's web site.

One way of watching the Federal Reserve's actions is to monitor changes in the federal funds' rate and the discount rate. Figure 8.1 plots the monthly movements of these rates from January 1987 into 1998. The upward movement in the funds' rate through early 1989 raised the cost of borrowed funds, clearly indicating the concern of the FOMC with inflationary conditions. This concern gradually abated through the fall of 1990. The worry became the weakness of the economy, which was very evident in late 1990. Policy was eased quickly, as indicated by the sharp fall in both the funds' rate and quick cuts in the discount rate. Interest rates generally, especially short-term rates, fell rapidly. Monetary policy was relatively steady into 1998; the only move was a slight increase in the funds' rate in March 1997.

Figure 8.1   Federal Funds and the Discount Rates, 1987–1998

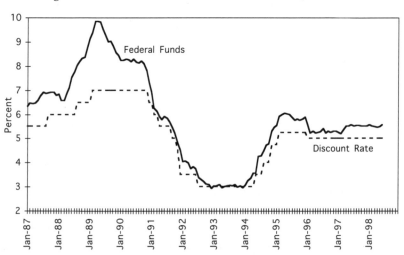

Source: FRB, Historical data bank

Another method of watching the Federal Reserve's actions is to plot the dollar value of the M2 money supply and match its movements against growth targets the Federal Reserve has made public in the Chairman's Congressional testimony each February (reviewed again in July). Figure 8.2 presents this information from the fall of 1995 through mid-1998. As the chart indicates, the Federal Reserve has kept the money supply close to the upper limit of its target range during this period; the range was set at 1 to 5 percent.

Figure 8.2   M2 Money Supply, October 1995–June 1998

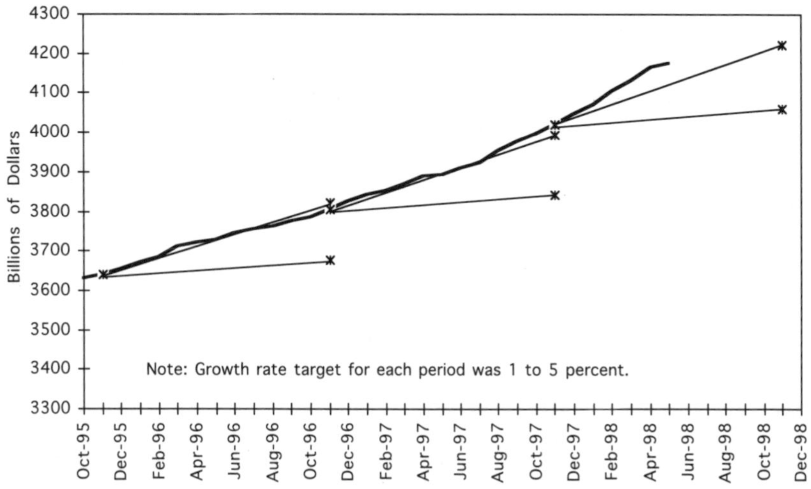

Source: FRB H.6

INTEREST RATES

In Chapter 1, interest rates were briefly mentioned, indicating that short-term interest rates (i.e., the rates on money lent for short periods of time) are more volatile than long-term interest rates. The pattern of interest rates during most of the postwar period was also reviewed, finding that these rates were responsive to cyclical movements in the economy and also had long trends that were related to movements in the inflation rate. Some additional characteristics of interest rate movements need to be added.[1]

In addition to the level of interest rates (covered in Chapter 1), two other characteristics of interest rates are worth understanding. The first is changes in the so-called *yield curve,* which refers to the relationship among yields of securities with different maturities. The second characteristic is *yield spreads,* which refers to the relationships among bonds of different maturity or quality.

The Yield Curve

The interest payment on a fixed-income security relative to its current market price provides a measure of the security's yield. The yield curve reflects the structure at a point in time of the yields of various fixed-income securities of the same quality (usually U.S. Treasury securities) as the maturity lengthens from short- to intermediate- to long-time periods to maturity.

The shape of the curve will change each day, reflecting both changes in the level of interest rates generally and changes in the shape or the slope of the curve as the yields for securities of particular maturities reflect price movements at different rates.

How Does the Yield Curve Change?   Financial economists generally identify three broadly defined shapes of the yield curve, with the shape moving from one kind to another over time:

Upward sloping, a shape that has prevailed most of the time in recent years, when the yield on short-term maturity securities has been lower than that of long-term securities, so that the slope of the curve is upward. Such a pattern of yields prevails most of the time, as investors demand a higher interest payment for waiting longer for the return of the principal they have lent;

Downward sloping, a pattern that occurs less frequently and often lasts for short periods. In this case, short-term securities have a higher yield than securities with a longer maturity and the curve slopes downward;

---

[1] This discussion will be confined to interest rates. Information about the bond market and bond portfolio management will be found in a companion volume written by the staff of the New York Institute of Finance, *How the Bond Market Works* (New York Institute of Finance, 1996).

Relatively flat, indicating that yields are roughly the same at all maturities, as investors appear indifferent to the length of the time they wait for repayment of the principal of their investment. Such a curve also may reflect different forces influencing different sections of the curve.

Why Does the Slope Change?   The level of yields basically reflects the supply and demand for funds. The shape of the yield curve is influenced by two factors: expectations of borrowers and lenders about the future path of interest rates, and the monetary policy of the Federal Reserve.

Reflect for a moment on the attitudes of both lenders and borrowers if they expect interest rates to rise considerably in the future. Lenders will prefer shorter maturity investments, which will fall less in price as rates rise, and anticipate better buying opportunities later. Borrowers, however, will prefer longer maturity investments so that they can lock up current low rates in order not to have to pay higher interest later. With the downward pressure on short rates as lenders provide short-term funds and upward pressure on long rates as borrowers try to lock in prevailing rates, the yield curve slopes upward. The reverse is also true; the yield curve has a downward slope when interest rates are expected to fall significantly, as lenders seek to lock in higher long rates and borrowers seek short maturities that can be extended at a later date.

The Federal Reserve can also affect the yield curve as it alters monetary policy. The Federal Reserve usually confines its open market operations to shorter maturity securities; the economic effects and the reflection of monetary policy in long rates takes a little longer. Longer rates reflect supply and demand for funds and inflation expectations of investors rather than Federal Reserve policy.

The Yield Curve and Business Cycles.   As a generalization, an upward sloping yield curve is steepest at the trough of a business cycle. At the trough, interest rates are expected to rise in the future and borrowers are beginning to increase their activity, thus demanding long-term funds and trying to get rates as low as possible. Lenders, however, prefer to supply funds for short periods of time because they expect to get higher rates later.

As the economy expands, interest rates move up; either because of increasing demand for funds or, as the economy nears full employment, the Federal Reserve tightens monetary policy, pushing interest rates up in order to slow the economy and control inflation. As rates move up, investors' and borrowers' expectations of the future level of interest rates change; they become less concerned about the time to maturity of a loan and the yield curve flattens.

Toward the peak of a cycle, when lower rates can be anticipated at some future time when the economy contracts, the upward pressures on the short end of the market intensify; lenders are more willing to supply long-term funds while borrowers have a greater interest in short-term borrowing. Moreover, monetary policy is at its tightest toward the end of the cycle. Consequently, short rates go up more than long rates, and the yield curve often becomes "inverted," with short rates becoming higher than long rates.

In past business cycles, an inverted yield curve has preceded a contraction in business activity, with the lead time from the inversion to the business cycle peak varying from five to seven quarters. The level of all interest rates, however, usually does not turn down until the cycle itself has peaked.

Figure 8.3 shows the three types of yield curves at varying times in recent years. An upward sloping yield curve in October 1992 occurred during a period of very sluggish economic activity when the Federal Reserve was pursuing an easy monetary policy. An inverted yield curve occurred in June 1989, when inflation was a serious concern and the Federal Reserve was pursuing a tight monetary policy. The flat yield curve in December 1997 was not the result of any action by the Federal Reserve, which had been pursuing a neutral policy since March of that year. It rather reflected the impact on the U.S. Treasury market (discussed in Chapter 6) of the turmoil in Asia toward the end of 1997. The short end of the Treasury yield curve was pushed up because the Bank of Japan, with the cooperation of the Federal Reserve, was very carefully selling U.S. Treasury bills to get dollars to buy yen, because a cheapening yen was threatening to exacerbate the U.S. trade deficit by a surge in Japanese imports. By contrast, yields in the long end of the Treasury market were being pushed down by a flood of funds from overseas and within the United States seeking safety and a high return.

Figure 8.3   *Examples of U.S. Treasury Yield Curves*

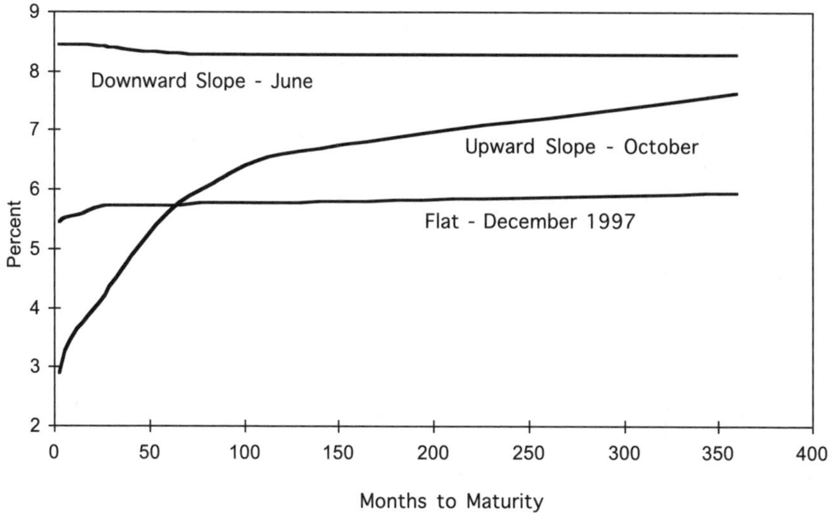

Source: FRB, H.15 Historical data

Depending on the investor's objectives, time horizon, and risk tolerance, watching the yield curve can help in anticipating future moves in interest rates and open up investment opportunities.

Bond Maturity Spreads

Another way of examining differences in bonds is to measure the spread or *yield difference between bonds of the same quality but of different maturities*. Figure 8.4 shows the monthly yields of three-month Treasury bills compared with the yields of ten-year Treasury notes (the two lines at the top of the figure) and then the difference in percentage points between the two (the dash line at the bottom of the chart). U.S. Treasury securities are used because they are of the highest quality, and price movements therefore reflect only maturity differences.

The movement of the bottom line indicates that the shape of the yield curve changes over time. For example, from early 1988 to the spring of 1989 the Federal Reserve maintained a tight monetary policy in an effort to slow a rising economy and contain inflation. This policy was effective, and a sluggish economy became a more important concern of the Federal Reserve; the federal funds' rate peaked in March, as shown in Figure 8.1.

As short rates moved up in 1988 to 1989, the yield on the longer maturity issue remained relatively flat, so that the yield curve flattened, as typically happens as the peak of a business cycle approaches. (See Figure 8.4.) Yield spreads continued to fall, and an inversion of the yield curve almost occurred in June 1989. Thereafter, short rates fell more than long rates, and the yield curve became more upward sloping. An investor who understands these yield shifts between short- and long-maturity securities, and correctly anticipates major turning points in interest rates can improve investment performance by shifts between securities with different maturities.

Bond Quality Spreads

Another interesting shift in interest rates occurs in the *yield differentials between bonds of different quality.* Figure 8.5 plots the monthly yield difference between corporate bonds of the highest quality (Aaa rating) and those of the lowest investment quality (Baa).[2] Just as investors shift their preferences in maturities, they also shift their interest in issues of different quality.

As the economy expands, investors are more confident of the ability of corporations to maintain payments on their bonds, and bonds of lower quality but higher yield are in greater demand. Thus, the spread between high- and low-quality issues narrows. Of course, the opposite is true as investors anticipate a business contraction. Figure 8.5 indicates the narrowing of the yields from mid-1996 through mid-1998 as investors seeking higher returns increased their demand for lower-quality issues.[3]

---

[2] Bond ratings range from Aaa, the highest quality, through Aa, A, and Baa. Bonds rated Ba and below are not considered of investment grade, and are often referred to as either *high yield* or *junk* bonds.

[3] Other differences among bonds are routinely considered by investors in managing bond portfolios, such as the tax status of the bond, the coupon rate, and the ability of the issuer to call the bond for refunding before maturity. These factors are beyond the scope of this book; explanations can be found in books on bond portfolio management (e.g., H. Gifford Fong, "Portfolio Construction: Fixed Income," in *Managing Investment Portfolios*, 2nd ed., John L. Maginn and Donald L. Tuttle, eds., Warren, Gorham & Lamont, 1990).

Figure 8.4   U.S. Treasuries, Yields, and Yield Spread, 1985–1998

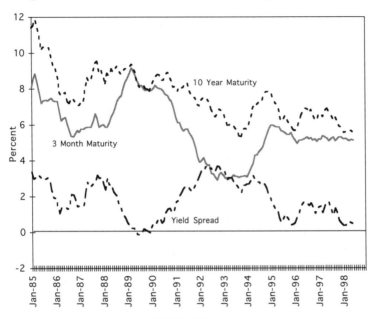

Source: FRB, H.15 Historical data

Figure 8.5   Corporate Bond Quality Yield Spreads, Aaa vs. Baa, 1987–1998

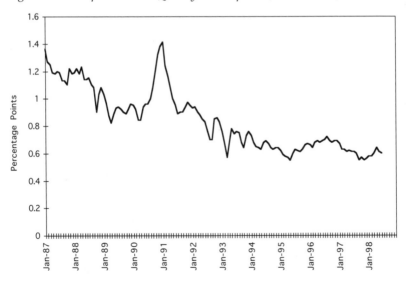

Source: FRB, H.15 Historical data

USING FEDERAL FUNDS FUTURES TO ANTICIPATE FEDERAL RESERVE ACTION[4]

Futures markets primarily are a trading area, but they also provide a lot of helpful information. For example, the federal funds futures markets make available the expectations that thousands of investors have about future Federal Reserve activity, which may be a lot more useful than relying on the views of one or two "experts." This information is available daily and can easily be found in the *Wall Street Journal*, usually in the third section on the page labeled "Futures Prices." Under the heading "Interest Rates," you will find quotes for 30-day federal funds from the Chicago Board of Trade as of the close of the previous business day. You can read the market consensus by a simple exercise:

1. Note the price for every active contract.

2. Calculate the interest rate implied by each price by subtracting it from 100 (e.g., 100–94.49 implies a rate of 5.51 percent).

3. Determine the spread from one month to the next.

For example, on April 3, 1997, the following information was shown:

	Futures Prices	Implied Rate	Spread Over Previous Month
April	94.49	5.51	—
May	94.45	5.55	+ .04
June	94.35	5.65	+ .10
July	94.24	5.76	+ .11
August	94.18	5.82	+ .06

At that time, the Fed funds market seemed to be anticipating another 25 basis points increase in the Fed funds target rate. (The

---

[4] I am grateful to Keith Schap of the Chicago Board of Trade for calling my attention to this useful tool and for helping me learn how to interpret it.

last increase had been at the March 25 meeting.) But the futures market was saying that the move would come after the July FOMC meeting. The 10 basis points spread from May to June left open the possibility of a move at the May meeting, but the 25 basis point April-to-June spread argued for any action coming after July.

Moving on to June 6, 1997, the funds configuration was as follows:

	Futures Prices	Implied Rate	Spread Over Previous Month
June	94.49	5.51	—
July	94.47	5.53	+ .02
August	94.34	5.66	+ .13
September	94.31	5.69	+ .03
October	94.23	5.77	+ .08

While the July–August skip from 2 to 13 basis points might indicate a belief by some market participants that the Fed would tighten in July, the spread configuration in general argued against any move in the near future. And the Fed went through 1997 with no further tightening.

It takes less than five minutes a day to plot and record these changes, but following them on a daily basis over a period of time develops a sense of what the markets are saying. These markets can change very swiftly, but they can be a most useful indicator of what the markets think the Fed will do.

SUMMARY

This chapter provided an overview of interest rates and the factors that influence their movements. Particular attention was paid to the operations of the Federal Reserve System and the relationship of fixed-income securities with various characteristics. Following actions of the Federal Reserve can be accomplished by careful reading of the financial section of leading newspapers. However, a good rule of thumb is that shifts in Federal Reserve policy are predicted about ten times more often than actually occur.

Interest rate movements are often charted in the financial media, especially the *Wall Street Journal*. Financial publications are available from the Federal Reserve Board and the district banks that provide data on interest rates. Moreover, as even a casual glance at the financial press will indicate, commentaries on Federal Reserve policy are legion.

It is not the purpose of this chapter to assist an investor in managing a bond portfolio. This is a highly skilled task best left to experts. However, we have tried to provide some guidance for the many decisions an individual must make that require some knowledge of interest rate movements. Trying to call short-term fluctuations in interest rates, however, is nearly as difficult as calling short-term movements in stock prices. The financial press often publishes surveys of economists' predictions of interest rates in detail by calendar quarters a year or more ahead. Some forecasts are, at best, a triumph of optimism over reality. Nevertheless, one who follows the economy and financial markets reasonably closely should be able to determine the following factors about interest rates, with increasing degrees of difficulty and uncertainty:

1. The current *trend* of interest rates, either up or down;

2. Whether a significant *turning point* in rates has occurred, preferably within a short time after the turning point; and

3. The *extent of the expected movement* in rates, or at least identifying the factors that will determine the extent of the change.

Given the many forces acting on rates, however, it is almost impossible to predict other factors.

CHAPTER 9

Economic Trends and Cycles

Understanding the monthly movements in the economy is easier if they are examined in a broader perspective of the past and potential real growth of the economy, the prospects for inflation, and the present phase of the business cycle. This chapter provides the following background information to provide this perspective:

Judgments about long-term economic growth rates are made by estimating the future size of the *labor input* and the *productivity* of that input. The Congressional Budget Office (CBO), a nonpartisan body created by Congress in 1974 to provide objective and impartial analysis, has studied this issue and concluded that economic growth between 2 and 2½ percent per year in real GDP is a reasonable range to use for the next ten years;

A review of the pattern of prices in the United States since the Civil War reveals an upward sweep of prices after World War II, suggesting that an *inflationary bias* may exist in the U.S. economy. A review of forces that will push prices up as well as down suggests that inflation rates between 3 and 5 percent are likely in the years ahead;

Business cycles are periods of expansion and contraction characteristic of nations that organize their work through private business enterprises. They vary in their length and severity, and no two cycles are alike. Certain repetitive characteristics have been identified, but no single explanation for cycles has been determined. One method of tracking cycles is by following groups of time series called *economic indicators* that have historically led, coincided with, or lagged cycle turning points.

ESTIMATING FUTURE ECONOMIC GROWTH [1]

A carefully watched statistical measure of the health of the economy is the annualized growth rate of inflation-adjusted or "real" GDP. Each month the Department of Commerce estimates the annualized growth rate for the most recent calendar quarter. Each July data are revised for the previous three years, and periodically revisions are made for longer time periods. Economists for both public and private organizations make estimates of growth rates for future years. Yet little is said about how fast this growth should or could be.

Potential Output

How fast the economy *should* grow is important for government decisions about fiscal and monetary policy. An especially fast growth rate can cause increased demand that cannot be satisfied by the current supply of labor and industrial capacity, leading to higher inflation. A sluggish growth rate causes lost output of goods and services and higher unemployment. Economic policy

---

[1] The comments in this section are based on two studies of the Congressional Budget Office: *The Economic and Budget Outlook: Fiscal Years 1998-2007*, January 1997, and *The Economic and Budget Outlook Update*, September 1997.

attempts to modify growth rates in order to achieve balanced output and price stability.

Knowing how fast the economy *could* grow, that is, its *potential output*, permits a more intelligent interpretation of past or projected growth rates. Potential output may vary from actual output for many months because of cyclical variations in the economy.

The concept of potential output is important because it provides a benchmark against which policymakers can evaluate the economy's actual performance and determine what actions, if any, are necessary to modify the pace of activity. Understanding where the economy is with respect to potential enables the observer of the economy to anticipate and evaluate policy changes.

In estimating potential output, a somewhat different approach is used in contrast with the estimates of GDP that reflect the demand for goods and services and how they are taken off the market by consumers, business, government, and net exports. Instead, the potential is measured by *labor input* (the employed civilian labor force multiplied by the number of hours worked per year) and the *productivity* (or real output per hour) of that input. Growth above potential means that either or both of these factors are utilized at above historic levels.

Trends in Potential Output

The long-term trend of potential real output in the United States has been upward because of the growth in labor input and improvements in labor productivity; however, this rate of growth has slowed. The Congressional Budget Office has estimated that potential real output fell from an annual growth rate of 3.7 percent in 1960 to 1969 to 3.0 percent in 1970 to 1979 and 2.4 percent in 1980 to 1990. Diminishing productivity growth and more recently the slower growth of the labor force have been the primary causes of this slowing.

Figure 9.1 presents these estimates of potential prepared by the Congressional Budget Office and compares them with actual output. In this instance, the output measure is GDP, which measures output by factors of production in the United States only and excludes income from abroad. The movement of the solid line, actual output, above and below the dashed line, potential output, reflects the variations mentioned earlier.

Figure 9.1   Potential and Real Output, 1950–2010

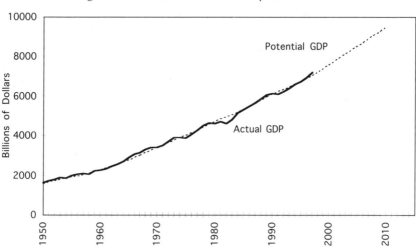

Source: Actual: SCB August 1997, Table 2A, p. 152; June 1998,
Table 1.2, p. D-2; Potential: CBO

What about future potential growth? Estimating future economic growth requires estimating changes in the labor input and
changes in labor productivity. Labor input depends on growth of
the labor force and to a lesser extent the number of hours worked
per worker each year. Changes in productivity depend on improvements in the quality of labor as well as increases in the quantity and
quality of capital (the tools and equipment that labor uses).

The CBO regularly does a careful estimate of near-term and
long-term growth of the U.S. economy. A full-scale analysis is published each January, with a follow-up in the summer or fall. The
focus is on the near-term (two-year) outlook, but a longer-term
estimate is made for the next ten years. These publications are
available from the Superintendent of Documents, Washington, DC
20402.

In September 1997, the CBO revised its projections of the previous January because of the availability of new economic data,
including the comprehensive revision of the national income and
product accounts in mid-1997, and the effects of the budget agreement, which is designed to bring the budget into balance by 2002.
The new projections indicate growth in real GDP of 2.3 percent

from 1999 to 2007, just slightly below the potential output for that period. These projections were relatively unchanged in the January 1998 projections.

In preparing these projections, the CBO does not attempt to estimate cyclical movements of the economy but rather to reflect the approximate level of economic activity on average. The CBO uses historical relationships to identify trends in factors underlying the economy, including the growth of the labor force, the rate of national saving, and the growth of productivity. The projections of real GDP, inflation, and real interest rates are then based on the trends of those fundamental factors.

The slower rate of growth of the labor force accounts for almost all of the reduction in the rate of growth compared with the 1980s. This slower growth reflects both the slowing population growth as the "baby boomers" after World War II get older and also a peaking of the percent of women in the labor force. The civilian labor force is assumed to grow at an annual rate of 1 percent from 1996 through 2007, compared with 1.6 percent from 1981 to 1990. The projection of labor productivity is an average of 1.2 percent or slightly higher, which is close to the advance posted in the 1980s.

The importance of these projections is to make clear that economic growth is primarily a function of demographic forces, that is, labor force growth, and the efficiency with which this labor is used, that is, the plant and equipment at their disposal. Capital also must be made available to procure this plant and equipment, but that has not been a retarding factor in the United States. Economic policies that attempt to stimulate growth beyond these broad limits are unlikely to achieve their purpose. Comparing economic growth of a mature economy, such as the United States, with growth rates of emerging economies is not realistic.

INFLATION

Chapter 3 touched briefly on inflation, the inequities it causes, and the various ways price changes are measured. In this section the outlook for inflation in the next several years is examined. Such an outlook is important in evaluating economic policies and the economic outlook, and is critical in making investment decisions.

Figure 9.2 provides a very long perspective on the level of prices in the United States, showing an annual consumer price index (CPI) from the Civil War to 1990. The figure indicates the very moderate increases in prices prior to the end of World War II. Two periods of rising prices are evident—just after the Civil War and during the 1920s—but they were followed by periods of price declines. However, prices increased significantly after World War II.

Another way to look at the price changes is as follows: Prices doubled from 1860 to 1945, a period of 85 years; they doubled again in the next 24 years, 1946 to 1969; they doubled again in the next 10 years from 1970 to 1979. True, during this period of price increases, less rapid price gains occurred. For example, from 1952 to 1969, the average annual price increase was 1.5 percent and in only one year did the increase exceed 3 percent. More recently, from 1992 to 1998, price increases averaged 2.8 percent. A focus on the post-World War II experience may be useful.

Figure 3.3 showed the December-to-December changes in the CPI from 1950 to 1997, and Figure 3.1 plotted the CPI less food and energy prices, *the core inflation rate*. Figure 9.3 plots these two price indexes on the same chart for the 1958 to 1997 period. (Data for 1950 to 1957 are not available for the CPI less the food and energy components.)

Figure 9.2   Consumer Price Index, 1860–1997

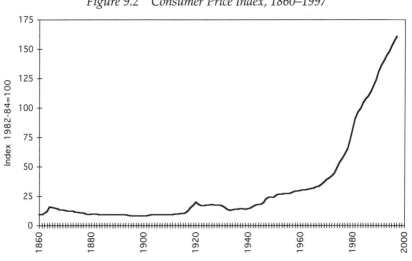

Source: Historical Statistics of the U.S., Series E135, pp. 210–211;
ERP, 1998, Table B-59, p. 348

Figure 9.3   CPI With and Without Food and Energy Prices, 1958–1997

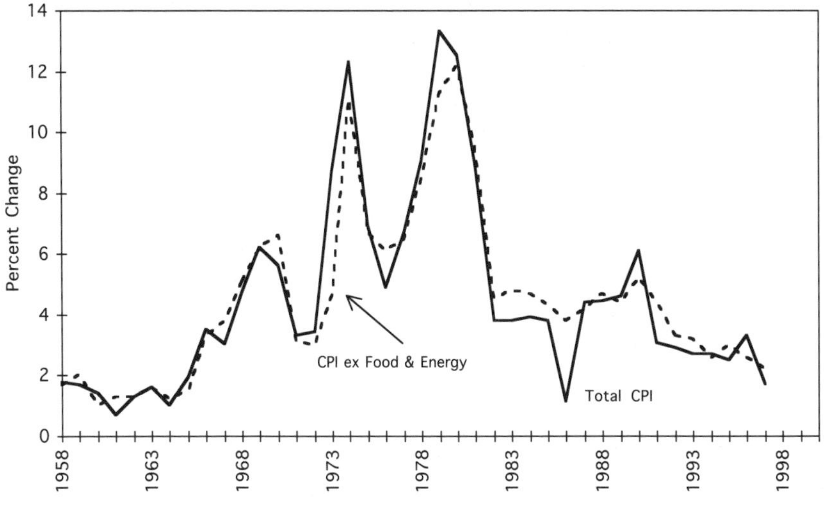

Source: ERP, 1998, Table B-63, p. 353

The two price series track each other reasonably well, with the CPI more volatile because of greater fluctuations in food and energy prices. Food price fluctuations can be blamed on the weather and are random events that ordinarily correct themselves. Energy prices are a different matter. While energy prices can be removed from price indexes, it does not eliminate the secondary effects as higher energy costs get embedded in the prices of products that use energy in production. Such effects can be seen in the price changes in 1974 and again in 1980 to 1981 and 1990.

The average price increase for both series is about the same; 4.48 percent for the total CPI and 4.53 percent for the core rate for the 1958 to 1997 period. However, if the two series are averaged for subperiods, the results are different (see Table 9.1).

In Table 9.1, the first period, 1958 to 1972, the average change in the two series was about the same although inflation was higher in 1966–1972. However, in the 1973 to 1981 period, the inclusion of energy prices caused the CPI to increase faster than did the index without food and energy. In the 1982–1997 period, when oil price changes were more subdued, the CPI moved up less. In the four years 1994–97, the core rate has been 3 percent or less, similar to the 1958–65 period.

Table 9.1
Average Annual Percentage Changes, CPI and
CPI Excluding Food and Energy

	CPI	CPI Excluding Food and Energy
1958 to 1965	1.43	1.45
1966 to 1981	7.06	6.73
1982 to 1990	4.00	4.51
1991 to 1997	2.71	3.04

Future Price Expectations

With this background, what is the inflation rate, as measured by the CPI, likely to be over the next five years or so? Are we in for a period of deflation, as some economists predict? Or are forces building that may lead to a period of renewed inflation?

Oil Prices.   When examining the forces that may push prices up, oil prices are a good place to start. Prior to the summer of 1990, oil prices tumbled. Overproduction and price cutting by OPEC (Organization of Petroleum Exporting Countries) increased production from new sources, lower world demand due to sluggish economic growth, and more efficient energy use pulled prices down to between $15 and $18 a barrel. Prices jumped quickly when Iraq invaded Kuwait, and the threat of losing a substantial portion of Middle East supply drove prices up to $40 a barrel, with higher prices predicted. With the successful military action of the Coalition forces, the threat of Iraqi domination of oil supplies was significantly reduced. Meanwhile other oil producers stepped up production, so that supplies quickly regained their prewar level and prices fell back to under $20 a barrel again.

This recital of events indicates one thing: Supply is ample but very unstable. OPEC supplies somewhat less than 40 percent of the world demand for oil, and the political turmoil of that area was demonstrated clearly by the invasion of Kuwait and its aftermath. The political instability in the Middle East as the century draws to a close is as great as ever. Should some unpredictable event cut off OPEC oil or severely restrict its availability, alternative sources could not make up the loss and higher oil prices would be inevitable.

The Dollar.   Chapter 6 discussed the decline in the dollar relative to other major currencies. The dollar's decline causes increases in import prices as foreign producers charge more dollars for their products to avoid losses when they convert dollars into their own currencies. Initially they may accept lower profit margins to maintain market share, but this policy has limits. When foreign producers raise their prices, experience indicates that U.S. producers raise their prices also instead of trying to increase their market share.

A lower dollar also makes investment in the United States less attractive to overseas investors—they have been major purchasers of U.S. Treasury bonds issued to finance the federal deficit. A change in attitudes about the attractiveness of U.S. investment would force these funds to be raised in the United States, forcing U.S. interest rates up. Higher U.S. interest rates either curtail U.S. demands for funds or lead to higher prices to offset higher costs.

During 1997 and in the first half of 1998, the dollar was stronger rather than weaker. In the first half of 1997, the sluggish recoveries in Europe and Japan and the higher returns on investments in the United States caused funds to flow to this country. Then in the closing months of 1997 the turmoil in Asia, which started in Thailand, Indonesia, and Hong Kong but soon spread to South Korea and Japan, caused a flight to the safe haven of U.S. investments, mostly U.S. Treasury securities. While an immediate reversal of this flow is not likely, should stability return to Asia that area might become again a place for both direct and security investment. The dollar outflow would resume and the dollar would decline again. In addition, the start of the European Currency Union on January 1, 1999, may also cause a flow of funds out of the United States to Europe. In any event, the favorable conditions for the dollar that prevailed at the end of 1997 are by no means assured to last for an indefinite length of time, and the unfavorable results of a declining dollar discussed above could come into being again.

Compensation.   Another potential inflationary force is the erosion of real employee compensation in the United States; in almost half the years since 1975, the increase in compensation was less than the inflation rate. Figure 9.4 plots the annual increase or decrease in real hourly compensation (hourly compensation less the CPI in each year) from 1960 through 1997. The deterioration in real earnings from 1975 to 1995 is evident. Whether this deterioration is reversing is an open question, but it is unlikely that workers will accept lower living standards indefinitely. In 1997, hourly compensation was creeping up, and reports of labor shortages in many areas of the country were increasing. Higher real wages inevitably will lead to higher prices.

Figure 9.4   Change in Real Nonfarm Compensation per Hour, 1960–1997

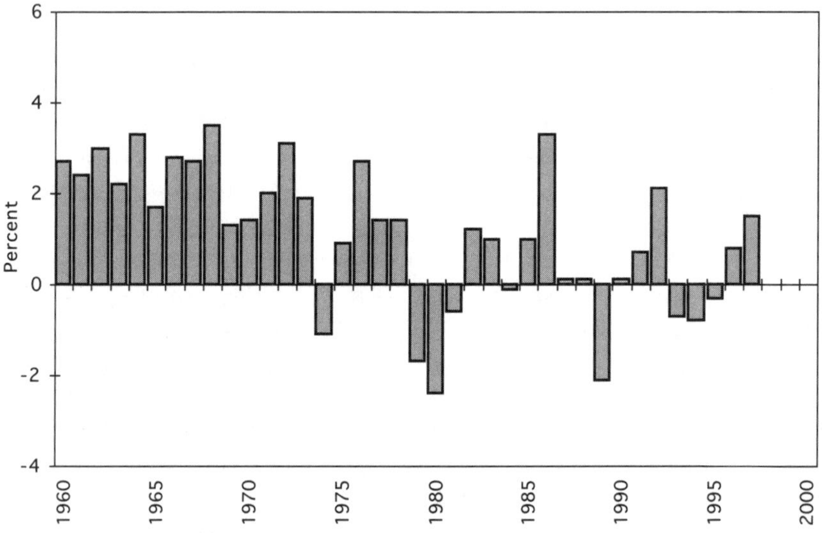

Source: ERP, 1998, Table B-50, p. 339; BLS Release Productivity and Costs, First Quarter 1998, June 4, 1998, Table 2

The Federal Deficit.   Chapter 7 discussed the federal deficit, the fragility of the 1997 budget agreement, and the inflationary implications of how a deficit is financed. Deficits that have to be financed through the banking system are inflationary. While this does not seem a near-term threat, the potential for renewed deficits will require positive action by Congress and the executive branch to avoid bigger deficits in the future.

A "New Era"?   Toward the end of 1997, the argument was advanced both in the press and in academic circles that the United States had entered a new era of higher productivity, low interest rates, and low inflation. Two features distinguish the current business cycle:

- In its eighth year, this cycle is one of the longest on record.
- The good news continues—healthy rates of economic growth, low and stable unemployment, rapidly growing corporate profits, high stock prices, growing tax revenues, and shrinking government deficits.

The key to whether this good news will persist depends on whether the economy will continue to experience a prolonged period of modest price increases or whether a resurgence in prices has just been deferred. The answer to this question depends on whether productivity, or output per hour, has picked up relative to past performance, so that wages and profits can accelerate while inflation holds steady.

Economists who believe that productivity has picked up but has not been detected in the usual measures argue that the error is in the data. The improvement in productivity has been concealed because of the method in which economic growth is measured, that is, using expenditure measures rather than income growth. In addition, areas of the economy where productivity growth is hard to measure, for example, the service sector, are increasing in their proportion of total output.

The other side of the argument states that, to explain accelerating wages and profits along with stable prices, the degree of understatement should have increased, and it has not. This view holds that temporary factors have held prices down in the past few years:

- Dollar appreciation has held down the prices of imports.
- The cost of medical care has had a one-time drop because of the shift to managed care.

- Lower energy prices held inflation down in 1997 and early 1998.

- Technical adjustments in the way prices are measured by the Bureau of Labor Statistics may lower the inflation rate; these adjustments affect the way prices are measured, not the underlying inflation rate.

These temporary factors may be reversed in 1998 and following years. If the economy continues to expand at a rate faster than its potential growth rate of 2.2 to 2.3 percent a year, the unemployment rate will fall further, labor shortages will intensify, and the inflation rate will go up.

In January 1998 projections of the U.S. economy by the CBO, real economic growth was forecast at about 2.7 percent rate for 1998, 2.0 percent for 1999, rising to 2.3 percent by 2003–04 and falling back to 2.2 percent from 2005 to 2007. As a result, the CPI is forecast to remain under a 3.0 percent rate, and interest rates to rise moderately through 1998 but decline slightly thereafter.

The CBO hastens to add that there are risks to these forecasts. Near-term economic growth could accelerate, putting upward pressure on inflation and causing a tightening of interest rates by the Federal Reserve. The Asian crisis is another potential negative. Another risk to the forecast on the positive side is that productivity may have surged more than the statistics reveal, and a higher growth rate could be sustained without creating unacceptable inflation rates.

Outlook.   What conclusions seem reasonable as this is written in mid-1998? Assessing the evidence, a reasonable conclusion is that the long post-World War II history suggests that an inflationary bias still exists in the American economy, and that the slow pace of price increases in the past few years is more likely to be temporary than permanent. A likely range of inflation for the next five years is 2½ to 4½ percent, with occasional bursts outside that range. In any event, some inflation protection should be a part of all business and investment plans; the inflation dragon may not be dead but only sleeping.

BUSINESS CYCLES

Business cycles are periods of *expansion* and *contraction* in aggregate economic activity found in nations that organize their work mainly in private business enterprises.[2]

Business cycles vary in how long they last, how high or low the economy moves during the cycle, and how broadly the economy is affected. In the United States, peacetime expansions have averaged about 1.5 to 3 years, contractions have averaged about 1 to 2 years, and the total cycle about 2.5 to 5 years. Considerable deviations around these averages have occurred, and each cycle has its own particular characteristics. However, business-cycle expansions generally have been longer and contractions much shorter after World War II than before, and the contractions have been less severe. Table 9.2 shows the peaks, troughs, and duration of cycles since World War II.

Several explanations have been offered for this change in cycles after World War II. Spending for services has increased, and such spending does not vary much during a cycle. (Examples are housing costs, household maintenance, and medical care, which account for almost two-thirds of consumer spending for services.) The size of the government sector is larger, and government employment is relatively stable during the cycle. Better methods of inventory control also have contributed to this reduced severity.

A variant of the typical business cycle in the postwar period has been labeled by some economists a *growth recession*, a period of sluggish growth not marked by a downturn in overall economic activity. Such periods occurred in 1965 to 1967 and again in 1984 to 1985. If in 1989 to 1990 the so-called soft landing that was the objective of the Federal Reserve in tightening monetary policy had been successful, there would have been a growth recession.

Cyclical movements should be distinguished from three other types of movements, which can be segregated in the reports of economic data by statistical techniques:

---

[2] *Contraction* is a better word to describe the downside part of a business cycle than *recession*. Recession was a political euphemism invented in 1938 to avoid calling the contraction at that time a *depression*, a word that recalled the deep contraction of 1929 to 1932. Neither recession nor depression is a word with a precise meaning in an economic sense, in spite of their widespread usage.

Long-term growth trends;

Seasonal fluctuations, or variations within a year due to weather or other seasonal factors, for example, Easter may fall at different times in different months, making the usual seasonal adjustments inadequate for the surge in spending that occurs before Easter;

Irregular or *random movements,* such as strikes or natural disasters (e.g., hurricanes or earthquakes).

Table 9.2   Business Cycles Since World War II

Business Cycle Dates		Expansion Duration	Subsequent Contraction Duration
Trough	Peak		
Oct 1945	Nov 1948	37	11
Oct 1949	July 1953	45	10
May 1954	Aug 1957	39	8
Apr 1958	Apr 1960	24	10
Feb 1961	Dec 1969	106	11
Nov 1970	Nov 1973	36	16
Mar 1975	Jan 1980	58	6
July 1980	July 1981	12	16
Nov 1982	July 1990	92	8
Mar 1991	?	>81	—
Average 1945–1991		50	11

Source: National Bureau of Economic Research, Cambridge, MA

Features of Cyclical Behavior

The most extensive studies of U.S. cyclical history have been conducted under the auspices of the National Bureau of Economic Research, a respected private research organization in Cambridge,

MA. These studies have indicated certain repetitive characteristics of business cycles:

1. Most industries and sectors of the economy are affected by business cycles (agriculture and the extraction of natural resources are exceptions);

2. Durable producer and consumer goods are affected more than nondurables and services;

3. Private investment expenditures have greater percentage fluctuations in a cycle than consumer spending;

4. Production fluctuates more than sales, causing still greater movement in inventories;

5. Profits have cyclical movements that conform to business cycles, but profit fluctuations are much greater than those of wages and salaries, dividends, interest payments, and rental income;

6. Industrial prices fluctuate more than retail prices (before World War II, business contractions were periods of price *declines;* in postwar contractions, the rate of price increases has slowed);

7. Short-term interest rates have relatively large movements that conform to cyclical changes. Turning points in long-term interest rates lag behind short-rate turns and have smaller amplitudes; as a result, near cyclical peaks, short rates tend to exceed long rates, resulting in an inverted yield curve.

In addition to economic movements that conform to cycles, certain *timing sequences* with respect to cyclical peaks and troughs have been observed:

1. Months before a cyclical peak, certain activities start to decline, for example, new business formations, commercial and industrial construction contracts, new orders for machinery and equipment;

2. Profit margins decline before profits, which, together with stock prices, tend to lead cyclical downturns;

3. Business inventory changes conform positively to cycles and are highly sensitive and volatile, although better methods of inventory control have diminished the volatility of the inventory cycle. Inventory investment is an important part of short and mild cycles, while fluctuations in fixed investment cause longer and larger cycles;

4. Monetary aggregates show low cyclical conformity and more random fluctuations, limiting their usefulness as a forecasting and possibly as a policy tool.

Causes of Business Cycles

Prior to the 1929 to 1932 severe contraction, little attention was paid to business cycles, which were believed to be short, mild, and essentially self-correcting. The severity of that contraction initiated many studies of the cycle. Although no one theory of the causes of business cycles has as yet been generally accepted, several explanations have been offered by economists.

The explanation usually advanced as to the causes of a cyclical downturn can be summarized briefly. A long and complex chain of production exists for both long- and short-lived goods. This chain also produces a stream of income that supports the demand for the output produced. However, an interruption in final demand for whatever reason will reduce income, reduce demand further, and lead to curtailed production and an economic contraction. (Some reasons for a temporary reduction in demand might be consumers having a plentiful stock of durable goods such as automobiles, or business having excessive inventories or plant capacity.) Moreover, wages and prices are sticky. They do not respond quickly to changes in the supply or demand for goods and services, and may not adjust enough to avoid excessive unemployment. A down cycle results, which will correct after the excesses in the system are worked off.

The cycle, although temporary, can be harmful to the country's welfare, so that government action is desirable to temper these adverse effects. Monetary action by the Federal Reserve can influence the supply of money and credit and the level of interest rates. Fiscal policy includes the influence on the private sector of federal spending, receipts, and the budget surplus or deficit. Either or both of these policy tools have been used to offset the effects of either a contraction or an overheated expansion.[3]

Other explanations of the cycle disagree with the desirability of government action to offset cyclical changes. The monetarists argue that changes in the money supply are the causes of cyclical fluctuations; thus, a steady rate of growth in the money supply and no monetary policy shifts are the way to dampen cyclical fluctuations considerably.

In the 1970s, another view of the cycle argued that changes in the money supply could affect real variables such as employment. However, public expectations about changes in the money supply are formed rationally and the changes would always be anticipated. Therefore, controlling the money supply does not affect real variables such as employment and output and is therefore undesirable.

In the 1980s, another school of thought argued that changes in the economy are more permanent than temporary and are due to things such as technological change or shocks (e.g., wars or changes in the price of oil). This group doesn't believe in temporary cycles— it questions the desirability of any government intervention to affect employment and output.

These very brief summaries hardly do justice to the vast literature on the causes and control of business cycles. They are presented to illustrate the differences in current thinking on the causes of cycles and the appropriate government response to cyclical fluctuations. In spite of these alternative views, government action, through fiscal and monetary policy changes, to offset cyclical fluctuations are still a cherished belief of most economists, politicians, and private citizens.

At this time, use of fiscal policy to counter a cyclical downturn is limited because of the enormous size of the federal deficit and the efforts to reduce it. Therefore, Federal Reserve monetary policy is the primary countercyclical force available. Yet monetary

---

[3] Note that this explanation of the down cycle depends on demand shifts due to excessive stocks of goods, plant, and inventories that must be worked off. Some economists have suggested that contractions in demand can be intensified by vulnerability in financial positions, that is, debt-burdened consumers and highly leveraged businesses. Fiscal policy stimulation can be immobilized by efforts to reduce the federal deficit, and changes in the financial structure may limit the effectiveness of monetary policy; thus, these changes could intensify the severity of contractions.

policy is also constrained by concern over inflation, the position of the dollar in foreign exchange, and by the limited tools (mostly working on short-term interest rates) at the Federal Reserve's disposal.

Tracking the Cycle

Considerable research has been devoted to developing tools to analyze business cycles. The National Bureau of Economic Research (NBER) has tracked economic time series for many years, that is, monthly or quarterly data on particular economic activities such as production, inventories, stock prices, and so on. These series often have turning points followed by irregular but extended periods of advances and declines. When turning points of many of these series cluster together at a particular month or quarter, these months or quarters have been labeled reference dates, that is, the date in which general business activity peaked or bottomed out.

The NBER has formed a committee of economists that establish these reference dates, and these dates are generally accepted. Unfortunately, the committee's decisions are made well after turning points have occurred.

After the reference dates for peaks and troughs of economic activity were established, further research revealed that some of the economic time series have peaks and troughs of their own that occurred consistently before, coincident with, or after the peak or trough reference dates; other series could not be so classified. Those with the most consistent patterns were combined into indexes of leading, coincident, and lagging indicators; these indicators have been revised several times as the economy has changed. The indicators formerly were released monthly by the Department of Commerce, but that responsibility has now been assumed by The Conference Board, a private, nonprofit research organization in New York City. The indicators include measures of employment; production and income; consumption; trade orders and inventories; capital investment; prices, costs, and profits; and money and credit. A weighting system has been adopted to prevent the more volatile series from dominating the indexes. The system is also designed to give the better performing series a heavier weight.

Most of the components of the cyclical indicators, or broader indicators of which these are a part, have been discussed earlier in this book. The components of the leading index are as follows:

1. Average weekly hours in manufacturing
2. Initial claims for unemployment insurance, in thousands
3. Manufacturers' new orders, consumer goods, and materials
4. Vendor performance, slower deliveries diffusion index
5. Manufacturers' new orders, nondefense capital goods
6. Building permits, new private housing units
7. Stock prices, 500 common stocks
8. Money supply, M2
9. Interest rate spread, ten-year Treasury bonds less federal funds
10. Index of consumer expectations

The components of the coincident index are as follows:

1. Employees on nonagricultural payrolls
2. Personal income less transfer payments
3. Industrial production
4. Manufacturing and trade sales

The components of the lagging index are as follows:

1. Average duration of unemployment, in weeks
2. Ratio of manufacturing and trade inventories to sales
3. Change in labor cost per unit of output
4. Average prime rate charged by banks
5. Commercial and industrial loans outstanding
6. Ratio, consumer installment credit outstanding
7. Change in consumer price index for services

These indicators have provided a useful method of tracking the cyclical path of the economy. However, some myths have crept into the analysis of the indicators; for example, it is popular to say that three months of a decline in the leading indicators forecast a "recession" in the near future. But because some of the data in the time series used are often revised, it takes a number of months to be sure that three months of actual decline have occurred. Moreover, three months of decline historically have predicted more erroneous turns at peaks and troughs than they have true turns. Using a greater number of months of declines and increases improves the accuracy, but by then the economy is either *in* a downturn or upturn! Remember also that all of the components of the indexes have been released prior to the release of the indexes; following them on an individual basis can provide a good clue to future indicator movements that will be reported.

The measures have also been criticized because they do not actually reflect the complex economy we have. For example, the majority of employment in recent years has been in the services sector, which has been growing in importance, but services activity is not well represented in the indexes. In addition, the United States is becoming more and more a part of a global economy, while the indexes reflect primarily domestic activity. Future revisions of the indexes may address these weaknesses.

Although cycles share some common characteristics, each cycle is individual in nature. Its causes may differ, its duration will differ from the average, its severity will vary, and its turning points will not be recognized until after the fact. Relying on averages of historical relationships may not always be helpful for forecasting the future; it was of little help in assessing the length of the 1982 to 1990 expansion, which was the second longest in history, or the expansion that started in March 1991. The indicators can be more useful for tracking the economy than for predictive purposes.

One method of following the indicators is to subscribe to *Business Cycle Indicators*, a monthly report issued by The Conference Board, 845 Third Avenue, New York, NY 10022-6679. The cost is $120 a year for first-class mail service and $95 for second-class mail service. The report contains information in charts for the indicators and many other business cycle series, with the dates of the past five cycles clearly marked. In addition, data are provided in tabular form for the past two years and for the past thirteen months. Each month also has a commentary on research in business cycles. The monthly press release of the Conference Board reporting on the latest performance of the indicators also is available on the government's statistical page on the Internet through STAT-USA.

Figure 9.5 is a copy of the first page of charts showing the movement of the three composite indexes since 1958. The peaks and troughs of the business cycles are indicated, so that the indicators can be seen relative to business-cycle turning points. In addition, at the bottom of the figure, a separate computation of the ratio of coincident to lagging indexes is plotted; this ratio, at times, had a better predictive record than the leading index.

SUMMARY

This chapter covered three major characteristics of the economy: long-term trends, price movements and prospects, and cyclical fluctuations. Trends estimated by the CBO place the growth of real GDP between 2 and 3 percent for the next 10 years; price inflation is expected to be about 3 percent. Our own inclination would be to expect inflation to range between 2½ and 4½ percent during the next decade. Cyclical fluctuations have some common characteristics but each cycle is different. The causes are still debated, but a good way to follow cyclical trends is to watch the economic indicators and their components. The peak of the most recent cycle was probably in July 1990, with the trough not yet determinable at this writing.

Figure 9.5   Cyclical Indicators and Composite Indexes

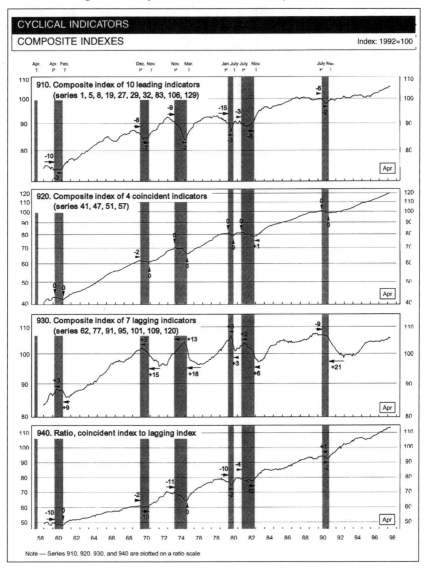

Source: Business Cycle Indicators, used with permission

CHAPTER 10

Understanding Corporate Profits

In a profit-oriented economy like that of the United States, tracking profits helps answer the question of how well the economy is doing. As discussed in Chapter 1, the economy affects corporate profits, which in turn affect stock prices. Profits are a good indicator of future business investment (as discussed in Chapter 5) because profits are a volatile part of corporate cash flow. Investors track the movements of profits to evaluate stock market changes. Investors also follow the past and expected changes in individual company earnings and dividends to compare them against movements in profits and dividends as a whole. Understanding how profits are measured and examining the factors that influence profit changes can be very useful in appraising the economy and the shifts in the stock market.

This chapter will discuss:

Different measures of corporate profits defined as:

Shareholder reported profits

NIPA profits

Profits reported for tax purposes

Uses of shareholder profits measures

Uses of NIPA profits measures:

NIPA operating profits, profits before tax, profits after tax

Rest of world profits

Financial corporate profits

Nonfinancial profit details

Corporate profits can be measured in three ways: profits reported to shareholders, profits as reported in the National Income and Product Accounts (NIPA), and profits reported for income-tax purposes.

Compilations of *reported profits to shareholder* as well as profits for individual companies and groups of companies are useful for investment purposes. As discussed in Chapter 1, future profits and dividends are one of the causes of changes in stock prices. Profit compilations can be related to appropriate stock market price indexes for an evaluation of the current level and future prospects for stock prices generally or for specific groups of stocks.

NIPA profit measures reflect profits from current production, defined as profits:

Before taxes;

After adjustment to place inventories on a current cost basis rather than the many ways corporations treat inventories on their books; and

After adjustment to place depreciation on a current replacement cost basis and estimates of the useful service lives of plant and equipment.

The resulting profits, called *operating* or *economic profits,* permit uniform comparisons of profits over time.

Major divisions of profits are for *domestic nonfinancial corporations, domestic financial corporations,* and *rest of the world* profits; this latter category includes the contribution to profits of overseas earnings after deducting U.S. earnings sent overseas.

For those interested in a detailed analysis of nonfinancial profits, the labor costs, capital consumption, net interest, indirect business taxes, and profits are reported per unit of real nonfinancial output. This information provides valuable insights into costs and profit margins that are not available in corporate shareholder reports.

Compilations of profits reported for tax purposes are of limited use for current business analysis because of the long delay before they are available. Individual tax returns are, of course, confidential.

DIFFERENT MEASURES OF CORPORATE PROFITS

Profits are measured in several ways, and it is important to understand the differences among them for economic and investment analysis.

Shareholder Profits

A profits measure most familiar to most people is *profits reported to shareholders,* which reflect how the management of a particular corporation evaluates the company's operations, ordinarily checked by an independent audit as performed by a recognized accounting firm. Generally accepted accounting principles, as defined by the Financial Accounting Standards Board, do bring a certain uniformity to shareholder-reported profits. However, corporations have some degree of flexibility in the degree of consolidation of subsidiaries and the treatment of depreciation.

Shareholder reports are often based on worldwide consolidation of earnings, while tax returns submitted to the IRS are not. In addition, shareholder reports usually reflect straight-line depreciation, that is, depreciation of an asset in equal amounts each year over its estimated useful life. However, tax returns may use any of several depreciation methods to permit accelerated write-offs. (Depreciation is a before-tax charge to earnings that of itself does not represent a cash outlay; therefore, higher depreciation charges reduce taxable earnings but increase the cash flow a company may retain.) Accelerated write-offs may result in lower depreciation for shareholder reports than is reported on tax returns. As a result, higher earnings are reported to shareholders than to the Internal Revenue Service; both procedures are permitted and are perfectly legal.

National Income Account Profits

A second and less well-known measure of profits is reported by the Department of Commerce and included in the information on the quarterly GDP.

Chapter 2 mentioned one way of viewing GDP—to consider it the sum of incomes generated in producing the nation's output; this income equals the costs of production plus profits. Profits include corporate profits, incomes of proprietorships and partnerships, and rental income received by persons. The corporate profits figure is *not* the sum of all of the profits reported by all the corporations in the country. The figure is rather an attempt to measure the *earnings of corporations arising from current production that is distributed to the residents of the United States.*

The basic source of the information about corporate profits is corporate income-tax returns. However, because of the delay in obtaining this information, the most recent year's estimates are an approximation of what these returns will be when they are finally compiled.[1]

In order to reflect profits from current production, two major adjustments are made to the profits figures:

Inventories used in production are not valued by the various methods corporations use to carry inventories on their books (that is, first-in, first-out [FIFO] or last-in, first-out [LIFO]). Instead, inventories are valued at an estimate of the physical

---

[1] Certain adjustments are made to the tax-based profits in order to conform to national income account concepts. The basic profits figure to which these adjustments are made includes the income of corporations organized for profit as well as those of mutual financial institutions (e.g., mutual insurance companies). Intercorporate dividends are excluded to avoid double counting. Net inflows of dividends from abroad (to corporations as well as individuals) and reinvested earnings of foreign affiliates of U.S. corporations are both included.

volume of inventories adjusted to prices in the calendar year or quarter being reported, referred to as the "current period." The purpose of this adjustment is to eliminate from profit compilations any profits (or losses) due to using inventories in current production that are valued at costs different from current costs.

Depreciation charges are adjusted to place them on a current replacement cost basis. This adjustment is called the *capital consumption adjustment*. The purpose of this adjustment is to prevent overstatement (or understatement) of profits because of insufficient (or excessive) depreciation of plant and equipment. Insufficient depreciation results if the replacement cost of plant and equipment is greater than the original cost. Excessive depreciation may result if accelerated depreciation is permitted for income-tax purposes, so that plant and equipment may be written off before the end of its useful life. Congress has authorized this process from time to time as an incentive for increased capital spending.

It should not be surprising that compilations of shareholder and tax-based reports differ considerably. *Nevertheless, shareholder-reported profits are the basis of earnings per share numbers reported by companies and estimated by financial analysts, and are the profits reflected in stock prices.*[2] Shareholder profits are also the basis of profit compilations made by investment organizations and the business press, such as *The Wall Street Journal* or *Business Week*.

Profits Reported for Tax Purposes

The most comprehensive compilation of profits available is that based on corporate income-tax returns. These reports have a considerable degree of uniformity because they are prepared in accordance with the provisions of the Internal Revenue Code.[3]

---

[2] However, financial analysts and other investors often make their own adjustments to earnings to increase comparability over time and among companies.

[3] The Internal Revenue Code (the codè) does permit varying treatment for such items as depreciation, depletion, installment sales, and gains and losses on property sales. Treatment of foreign profits and the degree of consolidation used in reporting for related corporations also affect the comparability of the data. As a generalization, intercorporate dividends and capital gains and losses are included, special revenues are excluded, and foreign subsidiary earnings are included only to the extent that dividends are remitted to the parent company.

The information about corporate tax returns is released by the IRS in an annual report called *Statistics of Income—Corporate Income Tax Returns*. Unfortunately, this report is not available until several years after the end of the tax year. For example, data for taxable years that end between July 1996 to June 1997 will not be published until mid-1999. Consequently, the information is of historical interest but of limited use for current business analysis.

USES FOR SHAREHOLDER EARNINGS

With this selection of reports available, which is the best one to look at when evaluating profits trends? For the investor, probably the most useful compilation of profits is the estimate of earnings on the well-known stock market averages, such as the Standard & Poor's and the Dow-Jones Industrial Average. The historical data are available from either of the two organizations that compile the averages or can be found in the reference section of many public libraries and brokerage firms.

Many brokerage firms also report their own estimates of current as well as next year's earnings for individual companies and for composites of earnings. Consequently, the trends of both earnings and price to earnings (P/E) ratios can be reviewed and current earnings and P/E multiples may be compared with the historical record. These aggregates also provide a base against which to compare earnings reports for individual companies.

One caution is necessary when using these estimates of current earnings. Experience over many years indicates that estimates for a particular year, either for an individual company or for an aggregate of companies, are almost invariably optimistic. Rarely is a forecast made for a contraction in business activity or profits, and early estimates (the estimating season usually starts about August for the following year) also do not anticipate unforeseen events. Consequently, these earnings estimates should be taken with a grain of salt until at least one or two quarters of earnings in a forecast year have actually been published and analyzed.

One further caution should be observed. Traditionally, earnings are reported compared with earnings of the previous year or the same quarter of the previous year; by now readers should be aware of the need for comparisons for a period longer than one year. Moreover, quarterly comparisons can be misleading; earnings may have declined for two quarters but still be above those of the same quarter of the prior year. Unfortunately, quarterly earnings at seasonally adjusted annual rates are found only in the aggregate profits reports in the NIPA.

USES FOR NIPA PROFITS

The monthly estimates of quarterly profits in the NIPA of the Department of Commerce are probably the most useful to gain greater insights into the factors influencing total earnings. The quarterly profits are estimated on a seasonally adjusted annual rate basis, thus avoiding the year-over-year comparison. Total corporate profits are estimated; they are also reported for financial and nonfinancial corporations as well as for major industry groupings.

These profits are before income taxes and are adjusted for inventory valuation and depreciation, as discussed earlier. The resulting profits are often called *operating profits* or *economic profits* or *profits from current production.* Over time, operating profits have had the closest relationship to broad stock price movements, because they reflect underlying economic factors that affect profits and eliminate the distortions due to inventory profits, different depreciation methods, and varying tax rates.

In addition, the Commerce Department also reports profits without adjustments for various inventory valuation and depreciation methods. The result, called *profits before taxes,* indicates what profits would be before taxes if tax-allowed depreciation were used and inventories were valued as companies value them on their income-tax returns. When the estimated sum of all federal, state, and local income taxes on corporate earnings is subtracted from profits before taxes, the remainder is an estimate of *profits after taxes* in the economy. Commerce also reports total *corporate dividends,* which reflect dividend payments by corporations located in the United States and abroad to stockholders who are U.S. residents. The payments are net of dividends received by U.S. corporations.

Figure 10.1 shows these three profit measures annually from 1950 to 1997. The differences between operating profits and pretax profits were minor before 1972, but thereafter the differences were significant. The effects of inflation as well as changes in the tax laws accounted for these differences. The changing differences between pretax and after-tax profits is caused by changing tax rates.

Figure 10.2 provides a better understanding of the causes of the major adjustments between operating profits and pretax profits. The solid line indicates the capital consumption adjustment from 1950 through 1997; the dotted line reflects the inventory valuation adjustment. Although neither adjustment was very significant before 1962, the rising inflation thereafter, especially that caused by the surges in oil prices in the 1970s, created significant inventory profits that overstated pretax profits. The deflation associated with the 1980 to 1982 business contractions gradually reversed inventory profits, but more recently such profits have increased again. However, as dollar profits have increased and inflation has been moderate, inventory profits have become a relatively small percent of total profits.

From 1950 to 1974, depreciation allowances were roughly equal to replacement costs, and the capital consumption adjustment was minor. However, a combination of high inflation in the 1970s and restrictions on allowable depreciation resulted in tax-permitted depreciation less than replacement costs. Inadequate depreciation inflated earnings, and operating profits fell below pretax profits. In the early 1980s slowing inflation and a new depreciation law caused tax depreciation allowances to increase sharply, and the capital consumption adjustment turned positive; operating profits were again greater than pretax profits. In 1986 the depreciation law was changed once again, permitting faster depreciation, but as the effect of this law diminished, the adjustment fell until 1992 and then rose again.

The combination of these two adjustments explains the differences between operating and pretax profits after 1971. In effect, pretax profits were overstated from 1973 to 1983, understated from 1984 to 1988, and have been roughly the same in 1989 to 1990. Because of the frequent distortions introduced by inflation and changing depreciation laws, operating profits are a better measure of underlying corporate profitability.

Figure 10.1   NIPA Corporate Profits, 1950–1997

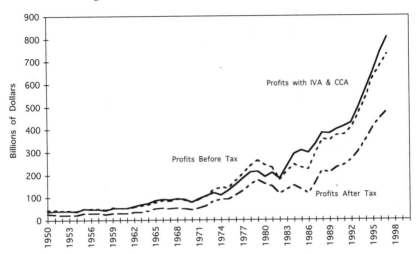

Source: SCB, August 1997, Table 1, p. 164; BEA, GDP press release, June 15, 1998

Figure 10.2   *Inventory and Capital Consumption Adjustments, 1950–1997*

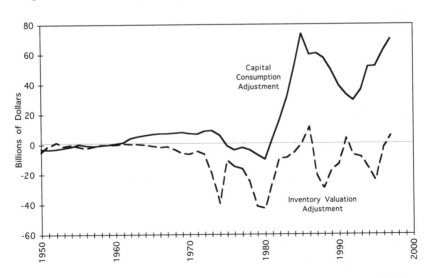

Source: SCB, August 1997, Table 4, p. 164; BEA, GDP press release, June 25, 1998

SOURCES OF NIPA PROFITS

Profits as reported in the NIPA come from three sources: non-financial corporations, financial corporations, and the rest of the world component. Table 10.1 illustrates how these various profit components relate to total corporate profits—domestic operating profits, inventory and capital consumption adjustments, domestic pretax profits, and total corporate profits after tax.

The rest of the world profits and financial corporate profits are the smaller components of total profits. More extended discussion is required of nonfinancial corporate profits because considerable detail is available to permit a more thorough analysis of the cost factors that influence movements of this profit series.

Table 10.1   Corporate Profit Components—1997 (Billions of Dollars)

Nonfinancial operating profits	596.9
Financial operating profits	109.5
Total domestic operating profits	706.4
Nonfinancial inventory valuation adjustment	5.5
Nonfinancial capital consumption adjustment	69.7
Financial capital consumption adjustment	-10.0
Total financial and nonfinancial adjustments	65.2
Nonfinancial pretax profits	511.7
Financial pretax profits	119.5
Total domestic pretax profits	631.2
Nonfinancial after-tax domestic profits	346.3
Financial after-tax domestic profits	35.4
Rest of world profits	98.6
Total corporate profits after tax	480.3

Source: BEA, GDP press release, June 25, 1998

Rest of World Profits

Rest of world profits reflect receipts by all U.S. residents (corporations and individuals) of:

Earnings (both distributed and reinvested) of foreign affiliates of U.S. direct investors;

Plus the dividend portion of other private receipts;

Less corresponding outflows;

Less income taxes and capital gains and losses.

In short, this component can be viewed like a net import of profits from abroad. It has been growing in importance, as Figure 10.3 indicates. In 1997, it equalled about $99 billion, about 21 percent of profits after taxes.

Figure 10.3   Rest of World Corporate Profits, 1953–1997

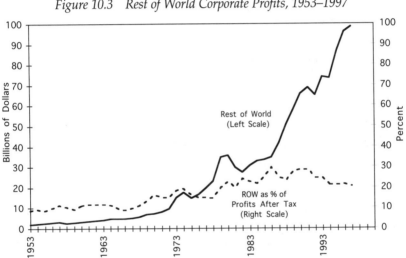

Source: NIPA, Historical data, Table 4, Series 1.15;
BEA, GDP press release, June 25, 1998

Financial Corporate Profits

Financial profits deserve special consideration because, in the NIPA, they are not just a summary of the profits of financial corporations in the United States. Financial pretax profits include two unusual items: profits of the Federal Reserve System and the contributions less the payouts of corporate pension plans not insured by insurance companies. Payouts of corporate pension plans are considered like dividend payments; they are included in financial pretax profits because they are corporate income that is not taxed. However, because contributions to these plans now exceed payouts, the net contributions are included in financial pretax profits as a negative number.

Financial profits after taxes have another unusual feature. As we have mentioned earlier, the Federal Reserve pays about 95 percent of its pretax income to the U.S. Treasury. The effective corporate tax rate of the Federal Reserve thus has no relation to the general corporate tax rate. The total financial component of NIPA profits is therefore not especially helpful for tracking movements of either pretax or after-tax financial corporate profits.

ANALYZING NONFINANCIAL PROFITS

The information discussed thus far is sufficient to understand the various profits reports in the press and in financial publications. For those persons interested in major factors impacting profits, the large component of nonfinancial profits can be analyzed in considerable detail. Such detail is not available in company shareholder reports nor in compilations of shareholder profits. However, it is invaluable in understanding cyclical and longer trends in profit performance.

Some of this additional information is available in a quarterly report of the Bureau of Labor Statistics (BLS), *Productivity and Costs,* available from BLS, Washington, DC 20212. Each quarter, approximately two months after the end of the quarter, a report is published on nonfinancial output, productivity, labor costs, nonlabor costs, and prices, thus facilitating analysis of unit labor and nonlabor costs, prices, and unit profits. Thus, information on costs as well as profits per unit of real output is available. An analysis of this information follows.

Figure 10.4 indicates for each quarter from 1988 through 1997 the change in *nonfinancial corporate physical output* (thin solid line) and the *hours required to produce that output* (dashed line). The ratio of the two is *output per hour,* or, as it is often called, *productivity* (thick solid line). The data plotted are shown as year-over-year percent changes, so that each quarterly point plotted indicates the percent change for the prior 12-month period.

Figure 10.4 *Nonfinancial Output, Hours, and Productivity, IQ 1988–IQ 1998*
(Year-over-Year Percent Change)

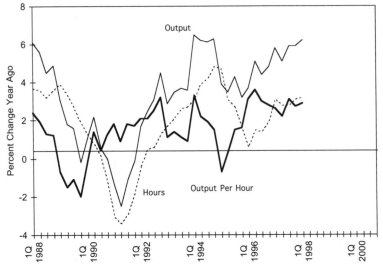

Source: BLS, Major Productivity and Cost Reports

Productivity as used here measures the relationship of output in real terms to the labor involved in its production. It does not measure the specific contributions to output attributable to labor, capital, or any other factors of production. Instead, productivity reflects the joint efforts of many influences: changes in technology; capital investment; the level of output; utilization of capacity, energy, and materials; the organization of production; managerial skills; and the characteristics and efforts of the work force.

Rising productivity indicates less time involved per unit of output, a favorable sign of efficient use of resources in the economy. Gains in productivity reduce costs and can lead to both lower prices as well as higher real wages.

Changes in productivity are also a leading indicator of cyclical changes in the economy. Increases in productivity slow or even turn into declines as the economy approaches a cyclical peak and then moves into recession. Near a cyclical peak, slower productivity increases are due to the use of less efficient labor and equipment. As economic activity peaks and then declines, productivity usually falls as business is slow to cut costs and reduce employment. However, productivity usually resumes an upward path as the economy begins to expand again, because business does not quickly hire more workers and increase overhead.

Examining the figure, productivity changes have been almost always positive since the business downturn in 1990–91. And the performance for 1997 was pronounced. The increase has been accomplished by increased output more than by increasing hours of work.

Figure 10.5 takes the analysis one step further. Changes in *productivity,* or output per hour, in this figure are indicated by the thin solid line. Changes in *compensation per hour* are shown by the dotted line. Compensation includes monetary remuneration plus supplements such as contributions of the employer to social insurance, pensions, health and welfare funds, and compensation for injuries. Combining changes in productivity and compensation equals changes in *unit labor costs,* or the cost to produce one unit of output, represented by the thick solid line.

This figure indicates some sharp contrasts. From early 1988 through the second quarter of 1990, output generally was declining while compensation increased. Consequently, unit labor costs soared. Following that period, the reverse was true; increases in compensa-

Figure 10.5   Nonfinancial Productivity, Compensation, and Unit Labor Costs, IQ 1988–IQ 1998 (Year-over-Year Percent Change)

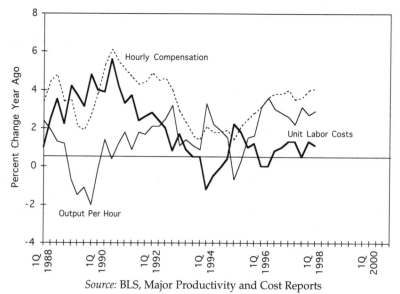

Source: BLS, Major Productivity and Cost Reports

tion slowed and output rose, so that unit labor costs shrank. Since early 1994, compensation has been in an uptrend, but rising gains in productivity have kept unit labor costs under control.

An additional cost factor is show on Figure 10.6. Changes in unit labor costs are indicated by the solid line; changes in unit non-labor costs are indicated by the dotted line. Nonlabor costs are defined as follows:

Capital consumption allowances (depreciation and accidental damage to fixed capital);

Net interest payments (interest paid less interest received);

Indirect business taxes (sales, excise, and property taxes);

Business transfer payments, primarily gifts to nonprofit organizations and consumer bad debts.

The rise in unit nonlabor costs was even more dramatic than for unit labor costs from 1992 to early 1994. One of the reasons for this increase was the dramatic increase in interest costs of nonfinancial corporations, considered in more detail below. In the past year or so, increases have been more moderate. The other interesting development indicated on the chart was the slowing in labor costs when nonlabor costs were rising. Have corporations been able to offset these generally rising costs?

The answer is shown on Figure 10.7, which plots changes in total (labor and nonlabor) costs as well as prices in the nonfinancial sector. As the figure indicates, price increases, although diminishing, have exceeded unit cost increases since 1992. This combination explains the remarkable improvement in profits beginning in 1992.

In addition to the data from the BLS on nonfinancial corporate productivity summarized in the prior figures, the Commerce Department, as a part of the monthly reports on quarterly GDP, provides additional details about costs and profits. The terms used in the analysis are not too familiar and require a bit of explanation, but the rewards are worth the effort to understand the material.

Together with the report for GDP, the Commerce Department reports gross domestic product originating in the nonfinancial corporate sector of the economy (NFGCP). This series represents the contribution of domestic operations of nonfinancial corporations to GDP.

Figure 10.6   Nonfinancial Unit Labor and Nonlabor Costs, IQ 1988–IQ 1998
(Year-over-Year Percent Change)

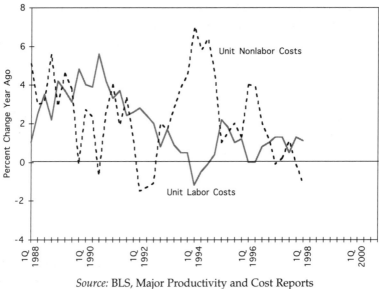

Figure 10.7   Nonfinancial Total Unit Costs and Prices, IQ 1988–IQ 1998
(Year-over-Year Percent Change)

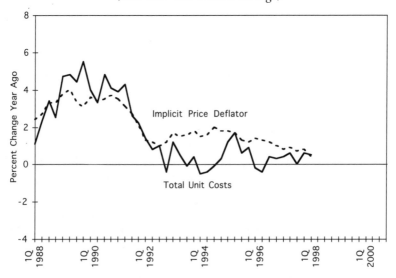

Just as GDP has an income and a product side, so does NFGCP. On the *product* side, NFGCP represents sales of nonfinancial firms to other businesses and consumers, government and foreigners, plus inventory change less purchases from other firms, domestic and foreign. On the *income* side, NFGCP is defined as the sum of:

Capital consumption allowances;

Indirect business taxes less subsidiaries plus business transfer payments;

Compensation of employees;

Net interest;

Corporate profits before taxes and inventory valuation adjustment.

The BLS data described earlier are useful because of the information they provide on the composition of unit labor costs. The Commerce data supplements this information with a more detailed breakdown of unit nonlabor costs.

Commerce provides information on costs and profits in both current and chained 1992 dollars. The price deflator for NFGCP reflects the cost in a particular quarter or year for a unit of chained dollar NFGCP, that is, the costs incurred and the profits earned in producing one chained dollar's worth of output in that period. (This chained dollar equals the current dollar product deflated by the implicit price deflator for goods and services in gross domestic product.)

This cost per unit of NFGCP has been divided into its components of unit costs of capital consumption allowances, indirect business taxes, net interest, and employee compensation; the remaining factor is unit profits. Unit profits are not exactly comparable to the pretax margins (pretax dollars divided by sales) used by financial analysts; unit profits, rather, are current dollar operating profits for a particular period divided by output for that period measured in chained prices. Thus, this measure indicates profits per unit of real output rather than profits per dollar of current sales.

For 1997, the costs and profits per unit of 1997 NFGCP expressed in chained dollars were as shown in Table 10.2.

Table 10.2   Nonfinancial Corporate Unit Costs and Profits—1997

	Unit Cost	Percent
Unit capital consumption allowances	0.101	9.5
Unit indirect business taxes	0.108	10.2
Unit interest costs	0.023	2.2
Total unit nonlabor costs	0.232	21.8
Unit labor costs	0.691	65.0
Unit profits	0.140	13.2
Total unit costs and profits*	1.063	100.0

*This figure equals the price deflator for gross domestic product of nonfinancial corporate business with the decimal point shifted two places to the left.

Source: SCB, June 1998, Table 7.15, p. D-22

One way to utilize this kind of information is to plot the percentage distribution of unit labor and nonlabor costs as well as profits over time. Figure 10.8 plots this information from 1950 through 1997. As the figure indicates, the proportion of unit profits in total unit costs has been volatile. This result might be expected, considering that unit profits are a residual caused by changes in both sales volume and costs. The trend of the share of profits was downward, particularly from 1965 to 1982, as both labor and nonlabor shares went up. The rising share of profits since 1991 was caused first by declining labor costs and then joined by a lower share of nonlabor costs.

One of the causes of the rising share of nonlabor costs from the mid-1960s to 1981 was rising interest costs. Figure 10.9 indicates the percent that interest costs were of combined profits and interest from 1950 through 1997. Part of the cause was rising interest rates; part was the significant increase in corporate borrowing, much of it attributable to the waves of mergers, acquisitions, and corporate restructuring; and part was the tax laws, which encourage corporate borrowing instead of equity financing as a method of raising funds. The decline in the 1990s reflects both lower interest rates and increased internal financing.

Figure 10.10 provides a somewhat different perspective, showing operating profits and operating profits plus interest as a percent of GDP. The widening gap between the two lines indicates

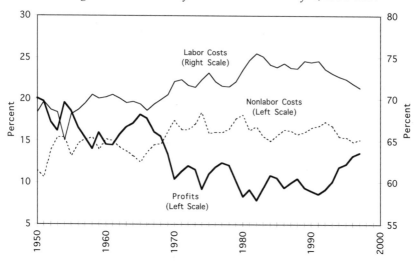

Figure 10.8
Percentage Distribution Nonfinancial Costs and Profits, 1950–1997

Source: Historical NIPA data, Table 7.15

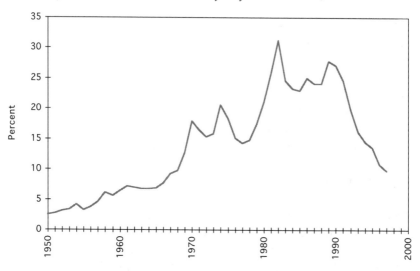

Figure 10.9
Nonfinancial Interest as a Percent of Profits and Interest, 1950–1997

Source: Historical NIPA data, Table 7.15

that, in the period from mid-1960 to 1982, the falling share of output that went to corporate capital (as measured by equity and debt) was not so sharp as the decline in the share to equity only, and the recovery since 1992 has been significant.

Figure 10.10   Profits as a Percent of GDP, 1950–1997

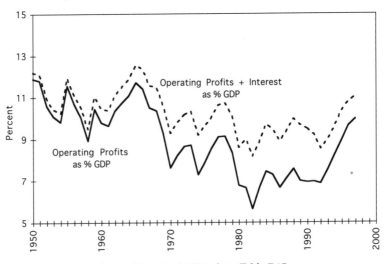

Source: Historical NIPA data, Table 7.15

SUMMARY

Profits are a significant measure of economic well-being and an important determinant of stock prices. Profits are measured in several ways. Perhaps the most familiar are profits reported to corporate shareholders; compilations of these profits are prepared by investment organizations and the financial press. Profits are also reported by corporations to the IRS on their tax returns. Compilations of tax profits are prepared and published by the IRS.

NIPA profits contain reports of several profit aggregates that are based on income-tax profits. These profits are profits from current production adjusted to eliminate inventory profits and to reflect replacement cost depreciation. For nonfinancial corporations, costs and profits can be measured per unit of real output, thus providing a measure of corporate costs and profitability. Following these measures quarterly provides an analysis of factors influencing profits and thus indicates future profit trends.

CHAPTER 11

Tracking the Economy

Business news is reported by the media more often than it used to be; however, that has its disadvantages as well as its advantages. A 30-second slot on TV news does not provide time for interpretation and analysis, just that the numbers be reported in as dramatic a fashion as possible.

At times, the news reporter believes it necessary to have an economist comment on the numbers. Now one thing the economist is *not* likely to say is that this latest piece of economic information isn't terribly significant and that it adds little to what we already know. The economist usually tries to make the data sound important, with far-reaching implications for the future of the economy.

Reporters have their favorite economic interpreters. If the data are up, the reporter finds an optimist who will endorse the new data as supporting a favorable point of view. If the data are down, a pessimistic economist can be relied upon to provide an appropriate negative conclusion.

The end result is confusion to the listener or reader, and disillusionment about the worth of listening to economic commentators at all. The purpose of this book is to provide some perspective against which the daily bits of economic information can be evaluated. The need for looking at the longer term movements of data—for four or five years at least—has been stressed, and for longer periods for some other data. Another aim of this book is to indicate which economic time series are timely and important in following any particular sector. These tools enable one to evaluate the economic news and have less need for economic commentators and their interpretations.

The purpose of this chapter on tracking the economy is to review once again the important statistics to follow, the sources of data, and some pitfalls to watch in their evaluation.

In previous chapters we have described a number of time series that reflect what is going on in the economy. This chapter summarizes the most useful information, so that it can be found all in one place. Professional economists have commercial services that provide economic data, but the cost is well beyond the means of the average individual. Instead, we will list a few relatively inexpensive sources that the individual can use to develop a personal do-it-yourself economic tool kit. In addition, Chapter 12 describes the wealth of economic data available on the Internet, which can be accessed at little or no cost. Finally, although warnings about interpreting economic data were scattered throughout the book, the most important ones will be repeated again, all in one place.

STATISTICS TO FOLLOW

Some economic information is more significant than others. Selection is influenced by the purposes for following the economy: business decision, investment decision, personal finances, and so on.

The total economy should be followed for business decisions, as well as changes in the particular segments such as personal consumption expenditures and their components; residential construction expenditures; business spending for plant, equipment and inventories; government spending; and imports and exports.

In addition, interest rates are important, as well as information on particular sectors or industries. For investment decisions, the economy, interest rates, and stock prices need to be followed. Interest rates, especially mortgage rates and short-term interest rates, are the most useful to monitor for personal finances.

Many figures and tables in this book are examples of the kinds of information that is useful and also indicate ways that the information can be prepared for review and analysis.

Tracking the Total Economy

The broadest measure used to follow changes in the economy is GDP. The most recent quarterly data are provided each month toward the end of the month. The focus is on the output side, that is, how is GDP removed from the market. Each component should be examined to determine the source of changes. Most of the data in the report have been anticipated by statistical releases covering parts of GDP, but this report puts it all together.

The data are revised each month, with annual revisions covering the previous three years. Major revisions are made less frequently. It is useful to analyze the quarterly and annual revisions, especially if the GDP is used as a framework within which to follow the economy. If economic information is followed, regularly, an overall view of the economy and how it is progressing will be set; at times the revisions will significantly change the concept of what was going on.

Another comprehensive statistic available monthly is the industrial production index, which reports on the physical volume of output in manufacturing, mining, and utility industries. While these industries are not the whole economy, they are vital and cyclically sensitive areas. The index is available at midmonth covering the prior month, and thus is a timely indicator of activity. At the same time, the factory operating rate for the past month also is released.

The leading, coincident, and lagging indexes of activity are combinations of data already released and therefore are not "new" information. They are published about one month after the end of the month they cover. However, like GDP, they put together important historical information with appropriate weightings, and thus provide useful clues to interpreting the cyclical position of the economy.

The major limitation of these indexes is that no two business cycles are alike. The analytical value of comparing current data with averages of past performance is not especially worthwhile. Moreover, some important areas of the economy are not covered by the indicators. Consequently, they are useful but not vital tools of economic analysis.

Tracking Prices

The best measures of current prices movements are the CPI and the producer price index (PPI) for finished goods, which generally anticipates changes in the goods components of the CPI by a few months. Examine price movements with and without food and energy components; the latter gives some idea of the underlying or "core" inflation rate. Producer prices of intermediate products and crude materials often foreshadow later movements in finished goods prices. The GDP price index for gross domestic purchases is the broadest measure of prices in the economy. However, it is available only quarterly and is often revised, while the CPI and PPI indexes are changed much less frequently.

Tracking the Consumer

One of the most closely followed economic series is the monthly employment report, which comes out early in the month for the previous month. While most attention is paid to the unemployment rate, the most significant part of the employment report is the information about the changes in jobs on nonagricultural payrolls. Because the data for the two previous months are revised each month, revisions should be examined in interpreting the current report. For example, if prior reports are consistently revised downward, this information is as important as a current decline.

Another early indicator of consumer activity is the report each month of domestic automobile sales, which are provided on a seasonally adjusted annual rate basis by the Commerce Department. These reports are both early and not revised, so that they provide a good clue to consumer spending, especially for durable goods. Another series that should be watched carefully is the monthly series on housing starts and building permits, important indicators of consumer commitments for large expenditures.

The Conference Board index of consumer confidence is also a useful indicator of consumer attitudes. It is of considerable value in anticipating future spending patterns.

Other reports cover the consumer area but are of less value than those cited. Retail sales are very volatile and often revised significantly. Personal income and consumption reports come out at the end of the month and contain few surprises, given other data reported earlier in the month. The consumer credit report is also released late and is more confirmatory than informative.

Tracking the Business Sector

An early and very helpful clue when following the manufacturing sector is the monthly purchasing agents' survey. The strength or weakness of production, new orders, deliveries, inventories, employment, and prices is indicated. The index of these components also has a good relationship to anticipating cyclical changes in business generally. A new survey of purchasing agents of nonmanufacturing companies also may be useful.

Changes in manufacturing activity can be followed by the monthly reports of manufacturers' new orders, sales, inventories, and backlogs. Durable goods new orders are good cyclical indicators; new orders indicate future sales. Backlog changes reflect demand pressures. Inventories and inventory-to-sales ratios indicate possible cyclical pressures in the economy. Business sales and inventories are reported about six weeks late and are subject to revisions, so that the earlier data on the manufacturing sector are more useful.

Business fixed investment can be anticipated by following monthly nondefense capital goods new orders, shipments, inventories, and backlogs as well as monthly capacity utilization reports.

Tracking the International Sector

The monthly trade report, looking at export and import trends separately, is the most current information on this sector. More complete information on the balance of payments is available only quarterly with a three-month lag. Following the dollar can be done on a daily basis; quotations against most major currencies are found in the financial section of most newspapers.

Tracking the Financial Markets

When tracking the financial markets, the problem is not absence of data but rather selecting from the abundance available. The best way to follow monetary policy is to obtain some report that will summarize both key interest rates, as well as indications of monetary policy such as the money supply and the federal funds rate. Reading the statements and testimony of members of the Federal Reserve Board is also helpful. The financial press usually carries a weekly statement of data provided by the Federal Reserve, including the money supply measures, member bank reserve changes, and reserve aggregates. For the stock market, movements of stock prices measured by various market indexes are published in the financial press as well as in many brokerage reports. Again the problem is one of selection. The various stock market indexes will be discussed in Chapter 13.

Table 11.1 summarizes the approximate availability of the various economic releases.

SOURCES OF INFORMATION

One of the problems facing anyone interested in following the economy and the markets is where to obtain the necessary information. As a partial answer, Chapter 12 of this volume lists some primary sources and where information is readily accessible in order to prepare each of the figures and tables in the chapters of this book. For the do-it-yourselfer, suggested basic sources of information are as follows:

The Wall Street Journal or the financial section of major city newspapers. The *Journal* is probably the most complete reference source for daily economic and financial information. However, the *Journal* only occasionally publishes historical charts, so that other sources must be used to get back data for historical statistical series.

The Survey of Current Business (SCB) is a monthly publication of the Bureau of Economic Analysis of the U.S. Department of Commerce. Annual subscriptions are available for $35 from the Superintendent of Documents, U.S. Government Printing Office, Washington, DC 20402.

Table 11.1. Monthly Release Times of Economic Statistics

Early in the Month

Employment report for prior month

Purchasing Managers Survey for prior month

Consumer confidence index for prior month

Automobile sales for prior month

Construction expenditures for two months earlier

Factory orders and shipments for two months prior

Middle of Month

Industrial production and factory operating rate for prior month

Producer price indexes for prior month

Retail sales for prior month

Manufacturing and trade inventories and sales for two months prior

Housing starts and building permits for the prior month

Trade balance for two months prior

Late in the Month

Consumer price index for prior month

GNP and components for prior quarter; profits are released with the
    second and third monthly releases of quarterly GNP data

Durable goods new orders

Personal income and personal consumption expenditures for the prior
    month

Leading, coincident, and lagging economic indicators for the prior month

---

The Survey has several parts:

The first few pages contain a review of the current business situation, with charts and commentary;

A monthly feature is a set of 54 selected tables from the NIPA. Each July the full set of 132 tables is presented, with revisions for the prior three years;

Special articles about economic statistics are featured, as well as special sets of tabular information on subjects such as the balance of payments, regional statistics, and historical data revisions;

The Survey used to be a valuable source of statistical information. However, for budgetary and other reasons, data
availability is primarily through Internet sources, which are
described in Chapter 12. However, the July–August issues of
1997 are valuable because they gather in one place data on the
significant revisions in the NIPA and the international transactions accounts completed in that year. The Surveys are
available at most large public and university libraries, and the
data are also available on the Internet.

Another useful source of information is *Business Cycle
Indicators*, a monthly report of The Conference Board. It is available
by subscription at $120 a year from the Board at 845 Third Avenue,
New York, NY 10022-6679. The Board has assumed from the
Department of Commerce the responsibility for keeping and revising as necessary the leading, coincident, and lagging economic
indicators, and this report provides in tabular and chart form a
wealth of economic information previously contained in the yel-
low insert of the *Survey of Current Business.*

The Economic Report of the President (ERP) is published in
February of each year and is available from the Superintendent of
Documents. Although the economic commentary in the report is
interesting, the extraordinary value of this report is the statistical
appendix. Almost every major economic series is covered, with
most annual data going back to the end of World War II and some
data back to 1929. Monthly or quarterly data are provided for the
most recent two or three years. This book is an invaluable reference for historical economic data that would require hours of
searching to get from other sources.

For current financial data, the weekly report called *U.S.
Financial Data,* available from the Federal Reserve Bank of St.
Louis, P.O. Box 66953, St. Louis, MO 63166-6953. This pamphlet for
$21 a year provides 14 months of weekly reports on interest rates,
money supply components, and other banking data.

Economic Indicators is a monthly publication of selected economic
data available from the Superintendent of Documents for $33 a year.
It provides data and charts on output, income spending, employment
data, production and business activity, money, credit and security
markets, federal finance, and international statistics. Data for many of
the figures described in this book will be found here.

The *Federal Reserve Bulletin* is a monthly report available at $25 a year from Publications Services, Mail Stop 138, Board of Governors of the Federal Reserve System, Washington, DC 20551. The statistical appendix has a wide array of financial and business statistics, although the time periods covered are not very long; other sources must be consulted if data are needed for several years.

Additional References

Two additional books provide more extended descriptions of some of the economic material covered in this book:

The U. S. Economy Demystified, Third Edition, Albert T. Sommers, (Lexington, MA: Lexington Books, D.C. Heath and Company, 1993). This book, by the former Chief Economist of the Conference Board in New York, is an excellent exposition of the U.S. economic system and the significance of economic statistics.

Guide to Economic Indicators, Norman Frumkin (Armonk, NY: M.E. Sharpe, Inc., 1990) provides more detailed descriptions of many of the economic time series described in this book as well as other statistical series that may be of interest.

WATCH FOR PITFALLS

Several problems in interpreting particular economic reports have been mentioned throughout this book, but it is well to summarize them again.

Time Span Covered

Unfortunately, reports in the media stress the month-to-month or quarter-to-quarter percentage changes. Such information can be very misleading, especially for very volatile series. At least several months of data should be reviewed; the best procedure for monthly data is to review it over several years.

For more volatile series, interpretation can be helped by using moving averages of the data; an average of the past three or six months of data can reveal an underlying pattern that volatile monthly changes may conceal.

Revisions

One of the most exasperating jobs in following economic data is to keep up with the revisions. When month-to-month changes are reported, it is not often mentioned that the past two or three months' data were revised. Other times, the prior year's or several years' data are revised. Some reports, like those in the *Wall Street Journal,* usually indicate that the data have been revised, but many other reports do not.

Historical comparisons have to be made carefully when a series is revised for recent months as well as for several years. The revisions should be reviewed to see how significant they are. At times, changes can materially alter the pattern of activity of a particular series. Usually the revised data or at least where earlier data can be obtained are available shortly in the sources mentioned above.

When revisions are made in monthly reports, it is a good idea to keep track of whether the revisions have had a consistent pattern. For example, if for several months data are consistently revised downward or upward, it indicates that later information was weaker or stronger than earlier and less-complete information. Thus the nature of the revisions can provide clues to the strength or weakness of the economy that one month's data alone do not provide.

Keep in mind that almost all series will be revised, often more than once. The few that are not revised include automobile sales, interest rates, and stock prices.

Seasonal Adjustments

Almost all economic data are reported on a seasonally adjusted basis. However, at times the seasonal adjustment may not be adequate. A winter milder than average will cause data influenced by the weather, such as housing starts, to appear stronger than they otherwise would.

At times, data are reported on a year-over-year basis, in order to avoid the seasonal problem. However, this introduces a risk of obscuring recent performance. It is possible for a statistic to be well above year-earlier levels but still plunging for several months! The warning is obvious: Watch for the types of seasonal adjustment and see whether they might have been influenced by unusual circumstances.

Temporary Factors

At times, information can be distorted by unusual factors. For example, the monthly employment report for most of 1990 was influenced by the hiring and later release of temporary government workers for the decennial census. The government did provide information on the number of census workers on the payroll each month, so that an adjustment could be made in interpreting the changes in employees on payrolls. However, this adjustment was not ordinarily reported in the media, and the unadjusted report was unreliable for a good part of the year.

Other unusual factors can affect data, such as strikes, storms and other weather phenomena, earthquakes, and similar events. Contemporaneously, data interpretation can allow for such developments. However, in reviewing data for a number of past years, it is difficult, if not impossible, to know whether a particular month's data were influenced by such a development. The best advice is to be aware of such a possibility and interpret unusual developments with caution.

Don't Count the Same Thing Twice

When interpreting economic data, it is important not to read each piece of information as "new" information. We have mentioned that changes in the components of GNP have been foreshadowed by reports on many of the GNP component areas. Automobile sales heavily influence durable goods retail sales. Building permits reflect future housing starts. Employment changes and average hours worked in manufacturing provide indications of later movements in the industrial production index. Knowledge of these relationships can provide better insights into the economy and prevent unnecessary enthusiasm over something that already has been reported.

Actual vs. Expectations

One of the most confusing developments in recent years is the media practice of comparing the expectations of some group of economists for a particular economic statistic with what the report actually turned out to be. Significant differences between what was expected and what was reported can at times have an unsettling effect on the financial markets, completely losing sight of any interpretation of the data in an historical context. Keep several points in mind:

1. Some data are foreshadowed by other data. Therefore, when you already have a hint of what a number is going to be, someone else's guess doesn't add much to your information about what is going on in the economy.

2. Other data are very difficult to guess beforehand, and expectations are as likely to be disappointed as not. A good example is the data on nonfarm payrolls, which frequently confound the experts.

3. The appropriate emphasis should be on the actual data in an historical context and on the revisions in past data, not on how the number differs from consensus. Remember, they made their guesses on information available *before* they knew what the revisions were and might well have guessed differently if they had had that useful input.

4. Do your own analysis rather than rely on the experts, especially when they are guessing about an area where they have no foreshadowing information to help them.

SUMMARY

This chapter has reviewed the statistics described in earlier chapters, indicating which ones are the most useful in following the total economy and which ones the best in following particular segments. Sources of information were discussed, recommending a few that provide historical economic data that can be used to interpret current economic reports in the financial press. Some cautions in interpreting economic data were also offered, so that these pitfalls would be avoided in determining the meaning of the latest reports.

CHAPTER 12

Tracking the Economy with the Internet*

Creation of the supporting tables and charts for *How the Economy Works'* original publication in 1991 required an extensive manual effort to type data from books and other printed documents into spreadsheets. Since 1991, the tremendous growth of the Internet and the subsequent capability for downloading electronically based data, both historic and current, have greatly simplified the process of locating, gathering, and processing these data. Additionally, the Internet makes new information releases, such as those listed in Table 11.1, immediately available to the individual investor.

For this new edition of *How the Economy Works*, tables and charts were primarily updated with information taken from web

---

* This chapter was contributed by Liam Mennis.

sites on the Internet. For investors or readers who wish to track any of these data going forward, use of a personal computer (PC) and the Internet is strongly recommended. Describing how to do this is at best difficult due to the Internet's fast-paced and constantly changing nature. However, this chapter will provide a brief discussion on the basic tools needed to access data electronically and identify and discuss some of the more pertinent web sites providing data on the economy.

GETTING STARTED

Similar to an individual's selection of the "right" or "best" investments, the choice of a PC is very personal in nature. Just as there are a multitude of investment options, either established or newly introduced to meet an individual's personal investment objectives, risk tolerance, and available capital, PC systems are available to meet an individual's personal and business information-processing needs, technical support requirements, and budget. This selection process is further complicated because the technology of both computer hardware and software changes rapidly. The result is the introduction of newer systems that have greater capabilities and that can cost significantly less than older systems with less capability. Users are faced with the dilemma of deciding if it is better to buy now or to wait for the next "latest and greatest and cheaper" system.

There is no right or best answer to this dilemma, other than the obvious fact that the individual has to "take the plunge" at some point. The longer one waits, the more opportunity is lost by not utilizing the Internet as a potentially more efficient and effective method of obtaining timely information. However, to help approach this dilemma primarily from the objective of using the Internet to locate and process data on the economy, the following suggestions are offered.

CPU, Memory, and Storage

Memory (as measured in thousands of bytes of random access memory, or "K of RAM") and disk storage (measured in millions of bytes or "gigabytes") impact the speed of downloading and space available for storing data. Unless the individual strongly prefers working on multiple tasks at the same time (such as downloading a file, printing a document, and revising a spreadsheet), the speed of the CPU (Central Processing Unit) or chip speed (measured in Megahertz or MHz) is usually less critical than having sufficient memory or disk storage. It should be remembered that economic data are usually presented in text format rather than graphic or multimedia (e.g., sound, movies) format, and therefore less processing power is needed to access and manipulate the data.

Printer

Considerations of color versus black-and-white, speed (in pages per minute), technology (e.g., inkjet versus laser) are personal preferences. Having a printer, however, is recommended unless the individual is accustomed to reading all reports and analyzing data solely on a video terminal.

Modem and Telecommunications Connections

These are perhaps the most critical considerations. As the technology is constantly and rapidly changing, the choice of telephone versus cable or analog (voice grade) lines versus digital data connections is primarily a trade-off of speed versus cost. If affordable, digital connections with higher-speed equipment (e.g., faster modems, cable or ISDN [Integrated Services Digital Network] telecommunication connections) are worth the investment in time saved and lowered levels of frustration. The return is the ability to do more in the amount of time available for connection to the Internet. This may become more of a factor as the Internet becomes more popular, and users vie for limited connections to the same web sites.

It may also become a cost consideration for Internet users if the telephone companies get regulatory approval to begin charging for longer (in time) local calls. One of the initial attractions of the Internet was access to any web site worldwide for the price of a local phone call or connection. As technology advances in terms of the availability and quality of live voice and picture connections between parties on the Internet, the Internet becomes a potentially cheaper alternative to long-distance phone calls and video conferencing. The profits of the long-distance telecommunication providers (primarily the telephone companies) may then be significantly reduced. Also, local telephone service can be negatively impacted as more and more local users remain connected to the Internet for longer periods of time, potentially overloading the local circuits. The cost of upgrading equipment to handle this increasing load, as well as price increases driven by the profit demands of the long-distance carriers (even in fiercely competitive markets) eventually will be passed on to the users.

Software

Along with a word processor and spreadsheet/graphing tools, the most important item is a software application known as a "browser." This software connects the user to the Internet and web sites and provides the Graphical User Interface (GUI) that enables the user to view and interact with the different "pages" of information. Although there are choices in software, the following considerations in selecting software may be useful.

1. Many web sites are designed for ease of use with specific browser software, usually the most widely used. Many sites will list their preference in browser(s), often at the beginning or end of the introductory web page. Users who are unsure of which browser to select should access (on someone else's PC) several sites they may frequent regularly to check for potential preferences.

2. While some of the data may already be available in a file for downloading, often the data are simply listed in a table as part of a document. Although browsers often allow a user to "copy and paste" these data from a web document to either a word processing document or spreadsheet, the results may be unusable. This is due to loss of unseen or unprintable markers that control the spacing of characters or digits on the page. These markers are part of the language used to create the document, such as HTML (Hyper Text Markup Language), which is commonly used to create Internet documents but which is often not readable by standard word-processing software.

   However, software updates from word-processing vendors may be available from the vendor's web site to add the capability of reading (and creating) HTML or similar type documents. These updates may be free, are easily downloaded, and come with fully automated installation procedures.

3. Often the process of copying and pasting data from a web page to a spreadsheet to create tables and graphs requires a great deal of trial and error. Doing this while connected on-line to the Internet can be costly (if telephone toll charges are being incurred) and frustrating if the connection is lost during the process.

A valuable time-saving software tool is a program that supports storing of the actual web pages off-line onto disk. It works with the user's browser and makes the process of copying a web page to disk as easy as printing the web page on a printer. This capability also supports off-line reading and studying of web information without the need for printing paper-based copies. This is especially useful when web pages are wider than the screen (and subsequently wider than an 8½" x 11" page printed in Portrait mode). Printing these pages can require trial-and-error changes of the page setup command in the browser (and sometimes can result in printing numerous sheets of paper in Landscape mode on 11" x 14" paper).

Internet Providers

As its name implies, the Internet is a global network of computers connected by high-speed communication lines. Other than the actual web sites themselves, this network is accessed typically in two ways. One is through Full Service Providers, such as AOL (America Online), CompuServe, and Prodigy. The other way is through Internet Service Providers (ISPs). The main difference is that Full Service Providers offer information services from their own computer systems as well as acting as a gateway to the Internet. ISPs typically act only as a gateway to the Internet and can range from small local companies to national and international corporations, such as the telephone companies. Both usually offer e-mail capability, and some offer the capability to support an individual subscriber's own web site as well as extra disc storage for a subscriber's data on the ISP's systems. Some of the key points to consider when choosing a provider include the following:

1. *Local phone numbers if connecting via a modem.* Beware that phone numbers within the same area code do not guarantee that the call is a local one with no additional or toll charges.

2. *Sufficient capacity to enable connection at any time without hitting busy signals.* This is sometimes difficult to gauge, as service providers with a large national customer base can sometimes be overloaded as easily as a small local provider.

3. *Good technical support.* In addition to providing instructions and help with setting all the proper telecommunication parameters on the PC, there will often be a need to talk with a technical person when a user encounters difficulty getting a good connection or accessing a particular web site. Check with other users for comments on the quality of the technical support as well as the uptime availability of particular dial-up connections to be used for any service provider.

4. *Browsers supported.* This may be especially true with Full Service Providers. Often these providers offer free-trial access and software, and it is worth the time to test access to web sites to be used frequently before signing up for the service.

Other Considerations

Once a user has gained access to the Internet, the most valuable tool in finding any information, from the latest securities (e.g., stocks and bonds) pricing to specific data on the economy, are *Search Engines*, such as Yahoo, Infoseek, Excite, and others. These are actually web sites themselves, accessible via the browser, that provide lists of web sites and direct connections to these sites that may contain the desired information. In using a search engine, users enter a word or phrase that describes what they are looking for. The search engines then locate and list potential sources of information by matching the word or phrase with the contents of the web sites to which it is connected. It is often beneficial to try the same search with different engines, as no one engine has exclusive access or connection to all web sites. Once found, the Internet "address" (the series of characters usually beginning with *http://www.*) of the desired web site can be "book-marked" with a browser command to facilitate immediate access to the site (via the browser) without requiring a repeat of the search with the search engine.

The web sites described in the following section were located utilizing a number of these search engines.

INTERNET SOURCES OF INFORMATION ON THE ECONOMY

It should hopefully be clear at this point that any information provided on specific services and web sites on the Internet carries the caveat of change—what is available today at whatever cost (including free) may either not exist tomorrow or be available (in a different format) at a different location, or carry a different price tag.

Daily News and Securities Pricing

Until the arrival of the Internet, access to timely information, such as government and company daily news releases, daytime stock price changes, world news, and information on global securities markets, required multiple sources such as newspapers, stock tickers, radio, and television. With the Internet, this information is now available almost as soon as it is released.

Search engine web sites (e.g., *http://my.yahoo.com*), newspapers (e.g., *http://www.usatoday.com*), and other sites enable users to set up their own individually styled web page with access to the securities markets (for securities pricing [delayed by 15 minutes]), news releases from the Associated Press and Reuters, and links to sites provided by radio and television and other news sources. Many of these sites are free, although some (e.g., *The Wall Street Journal, http://www.wsj.com*) carry a monthly or annual fee.

Government Sites

Bureau of Economic Analysis (BEA)—*http://www.bea.doc.gov*

This site contains NIPA, industry (e.g., monthly auto sales), and wealth distribution in Regional, National, and International groupings. The data are provided in articles, HTML table format, or spreadsheets available for downloading. Some files are in Acrobat (a document software vendor) format known as PDF, but the site offers the software needed to read these documents free of charge and available for downloading. The BEA site also offers current and historical time series estimates, as well as articles of interest, from the *Survey of Current Business.*

Bureau of Labor Statistics (BLS)—*http://stats.bls.gov*

As an agency within the U.S. Department of Labor, this site provides data on employment, the Consumer Price Index (CPI), and Producers Price Index (PPI).

U.S. Census Bureau—http://www.census.gov

In addition to being the most comprehensive source of data on people (e.g., income, household demographics), this agency also provides data on manufacturing sales, new orders, and inventories by industry and the economy as a whole. In addition to data tables, the site has an "Economic Briefing Room" that provides recently released statistics in summary, full report, and graphical formats.

Federal Reserve Board (FRB)—*http://www.bog.frb.fed.us*

This site contains a wealth of historic data files on U.S. monetary assets (e.g., interest rates; exchange rates; reserves, assets, and liabilities of depository institutions; money stock, liquid assets, and debt measures) in addition to industrial production and capacity utilization, as well as reports to Congress and reports of the Federal Open Market Committee (FOMC). Data are available for downloading or can be purchased on diskettes. Be sure to read the documentation files that describe the file formats and layouts to simplify working with the data. Many of the historic files are in "zipped" or compressed format due to their size. The site provides a link to another web site that contains software to "unzip" the files after they are downloaded.

Additionally, the contents of the Beige Book, published by the Federal Open Market Committee (FOMC), and the text of speeches and testimony given before Congress are available at this site.

STAT-USA—http://www.stat-usa.gov

STAT-USA is a fee-based service run by the U.S. Department of Commerce's Economic and Statistics Administration, and provides probably the best single source of current and historical economic and financial information on the U.S. economy and global trade. Though a government agency, it is run like a business and is not supported by tax dollars, which is why it charges for its services. It is considered the authoritative source for data from other agencies, such as the BEA, BLS, Census, and FRB, *and most government press releases from these organizations are available first at this site.*

Although the web site may be accessed for viewing for free by any user, access to data files is by subscription only. The subscription fee is either $50 per quarter or $150 per year, and is well worth the investment for anyone who needs the most timely access to this information on a regular basis. The site contains information for subscribing and accessing the data files.

White House Briefing Room—
http://www.whitehouse.gov/WH/html/briefroom.html#fsbr

This site provides daily press briefings of the White House Press Corps by the Press Secretary, summaries of press releases from the White House Press Office, and a link to the Economics Statistics Briefing Room (ESBR). This briefing room offers free access to current federal economic indicators from a number of federal agencies on areas such as:

- Production, sales, orders, and inventories
- Output
- Income, expenditures, and wealth
- Employment, unemployment, and earnings
- Prices
- Money, credit, and interest rates
- Transportation
- International statistics

The Economic Report of the President—Council of Economic Advisors

This report is published annually, usually toward the end of February. The appendix of the report contains tables of historical economic data. Although several sites (including one supported by the U.S. Government Printing Office) offer the full text, one site at the University of California at San Diego (*http:www.gpo.ucop.edu/catalog/erp97.html*) includes all the statistical tables from the appendixes in text format. Depending on the user's available spreadsheet tools, it is possible to save this information as a text-type file and import it in columnar format for analysis and graphing.

FEDSTATS—http://www.fedstats.gov

This site offers links to more than 70 agencies in the U.S. federal government that produce statistics, including information on the economy.

Non-Government Sites

The Conference Board—http://www.conference-board.org

This not-for-profit, non-advocacy organization of business and research members produces the Consumer Confidence Index (CCI) and Measure of Business Confidence (MBC), as well as composite, leading, coincident, and lagging economic indicators. Their Consumer Research Center monitors information on major demographics trends and changes in the consumer marketplace. Their information library (available to member organizations) utilizes one of the most extensive collections of business and government data sources. Access to this information is by annual subscription and costs $1,950 for members and $2,500 for non-members. However, the site does provide free access to The Conference Board's latest press releases. Data on economic indicators are also available through STAT-USA.

University of Michigan Documents Center—
http://www.lib.umich.edu/libhome/Documents.center

University of Southern Mississippi—
Resources for Economists on the Internet (Bill Goffe)—
http://coba.shsu.edu/econfaq/EconFAQ.html

There are numerous university web sites on the Internet that offer a wide variety of statistical data, including information on the economy. For example, the above sites offer very comprehensive and well-organized collections of links to government, business, university, and private web sites that provide statistical resources and data. It is well worth viewing and exploring the various links provided by these sites.

SUMMARY

From investors interested in the latest press releases on economic indicators affecting the stock market along with the latest stock prices, to business professionals needing to review the current state of the economy in a historical perspective, the Internet is a most useful and time-saving tool. If technological advances continue to follow historical trends, users should enjoy greater returns for their investment of time and more capability for less capital investment in tools. Given its nature as an evolutionary information network, users should set aside time on a regular basis to seek out and explore new sources of information that may provide more effective methods for tracking the economy.

CHAPTER 13

Suggestions for the Individual Investor

The earlier chapters in this book were designed to help in understanding how the various sectors of the economy relate to each other and how to view changes in the economy with a long-term perspective. The main requirements needed to track the economy is this sense of perspective, access to the financial press, a few government data sources, and some spare time.

Chapter 1 outlined the relationships between the economy, inflation, interest rates, profits, and stock prices. The present chapter will offer further background information for the individual investor to assist in making better-informed investment decisions. No great exposition of financial analysis or portfolio management is intended—nor can tips be provided on how to pick hot stocks or time the market. We offer just a few ideas to give broader perspective for investing, just as earlier chapters were designed to provide broader perspective on the economy.

Four major topics are covered in this chapter:

Understanding *investment objectives,* a process many investors overlook or believe that they are incompetent to do. However, only investors themselves are best qualified to determine their objectives;

Understanding *risk,* a topic often forgotten when establishing and managing a portfolio;

Understanding the advantages of *portfolio diversification;*

Following the *stock market,* a description of the various stock market averages and their advantages and disadvantages.

UNDERSTANDING INVESTMENT OBJECTIVES

What are *investment objectives?* Investment objectives are a description of the purposes of an investment portfolio and the risks an investor is willing to assume to achieve them. In setting objectives, the investor should do the following:

List specific rather than general objectives;

Determine whether these objectives are to be met now or at some future time;

Set an absolute rate of return for your portfolio that you need in order to meet your objectives, and examine that return to see if it is realistic;

Fix a time horizon over which results are to be measured;

Determine your risk tolerance for the portfolio.

Portfolio Purposes

A portfolio may have one or several objectives. The portfolio may be designed to provide current income for someone, or to build a retirement fund. The purpose may be to build an estate that ultimately will be left to someone or to charity. It may be destined to provide a college education for children, or build a fund to buy a house. A corporate retirement fund is designed to provide present and future retirement benefits for employees.

The purpose should be as specific as possible. Objectives such as making as much money as possible or not losing money are too vague and do not consider risk. It is a good idea to commit these objectives to writing, so that they can be reviewed from time to time to see whether they need changing or whether they are being achieved.

Can the Investor Get There?

Once the purpose or purposes of the portfolio are established, the next step is determining when these objectives are to be reached—now, or at some future time. Then it must be determined, using realistic assumptions about future investment returns, whether the funds available are sufficient to reach the objectives set; if not, the objectives may have to be scaled back.

In matching funds versus objectives, the effects of inflation should be kept in mind. For example, when thinking of a fund to be available in the future or one that provides an income stream over a long period of time, be sure to factor in an estimate of future inflation rates. The principal sum or the income needed in dollars of future purchasing power is then determined.

The statement of investment objectives requires determining an *absolute rate of return* that will be needed on the funds available to reach the desired goal. *Relative rates of return,* such as beating the stock market or getting a better rate of return than that available from some other investment, are useful objectives in a subsidiary sense, but an absolute rate of return is essential. Selecting expected rates of return can be materially helped by reviewing historical rates of return, covered in the next section of this chapter.

LONG-TERM INVESTMENT RETURNS

Investors often find it difficult to establish realistic rate-of-return objectives, because they have limited information about what rates of return have been achieved on various types of investments in the past. This section provides, in tabular and chart form, rates of return on several financial instruments for most of the years since World War II and for important subperiods during that time. These rates of return have varied; some explanations for the variations are offered to enable you to estimate expected returns more easily.

The following information covers financial instruments only, that is, stock and bonds. They were selected because these securities are marketable and the records of their prices, as well as interest and dividend payments, are available for long periods of time. Returns for other types of investments are not so readily available.[1]

Long-Term Average Returns

Table 13.1 indicates the average return on various types of financial instruments for the years 1950 to 1997, which covers practically the entire postwar period. The return was computed by taking the total return (income plus appreciation or less depreciation) for each year and computing a simple arithmetic average of the total of the individual year's returns.

Of course, averages can be misleading; the story of someone drowning in a lake with an average water depth of three feet is well-known. Thus, further information as well as an average is needed.

In addition, the results shown in Table 13.1 may seem a bit odd because the returns on long-term government bonds averaged less than the returns on intermediate issues. Ordinarily an investor would expect to receive a higher return to compensate for the longer wait before the principal of the investment is returned at maturity. In actual practice the opposite has been true. How can this anomaly be explained?

---

[1] Returns on real estate equity investment, for example, are available only for shorter periods and cover only limited samples of real estate. Real estate is a unique product that does not have a ready market with frequent transactions; this lack of liquidity results in a return that should be somewhat higher than the return on common stocks. As a rough rule of thumb, real estate equity returns over time have been between 2 and 3 percentage points higher than the return on common stocks. The returns on other types of investments can be estimated in much the same way—returns in excess of the historic returns on stocks or bonds reflect the greater risk taken in these other types of investment.

Table 13.1   *Average Annual Return, 1950 to 1997*

30-Day U.S. Treasury Bills	5.20%
Intermediate (5-year) U.S. Government Bonds	6.40%
Long-Term (20-year) U.S. Government Bonds	6.23%
Long-Term (20-year) Corporate Bonds	6.62%
Common Stocks (S&P 500 Stock Index)	14.42%

Source: Same as Figure 13.1. Used with permission. ©1998 Ibbotson Associates, Inc. All rights reserved. Computation by author.

Annual and Average Returns

Figures 13.1 through 13.5 present the annual returns for each of the financial instruments for the 1950 to 1997 period, with the average return indicated by the dashed line, as a first step toward answering this puzzle. These figures also provide some perspective on returns over time. The vertical scales for the figures are approximately the same, so that the volatility or fluctuations around the average of the annual returns of the various financial instruments can be compared. (Volatility risk is discussed at greater length later in this chapter.)

Figure 13.1 presents the investment returns for U.S. Treasury bills. Year-to-year fluctuations in returns are not very great. Returns trended gradually upward until 1981 and trended downward thereafter; recent returns have been about average.

Figure 13.2 indicates the annual returns and the average return for intermediate government bonds. The year-to-year fluctuations in this series are greater than those for Treasury bills. However, a similar pattern is evident: returns prior to 1970 were generally below average and returns after 1970 were higher than average, although more volatile.

When attention is shifted to the returns of long-term government bonds in Figure 13.3, the most striking characteristic is the greater volatility, particularly in the period after 1969. The very high returns after 1982 pulled the average return up considerably. Presumably something happened in this later period to cause average returns to be much higher.

A similar observation can be made about long-term corporate bonds as seen in Figure 13.4. Returns were quite volatile, but after 1982, returns averaged considerably higher than in prior periods.

Figure 13.1   Investment Returns—U.S. Treasury Bills, 1950–1997

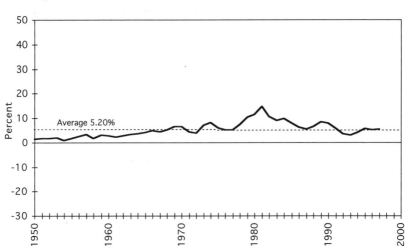

Source: Stocks, Bonds, Bills, and Inflation 1998 Yearbook, Ibbotson Associates, Chicago, IL, Table 2-5, pp. 38–9; computations by author. Used with permission. ©1998 Ibbotson Associates, Inc. All rights reserved. [Certain portions of this work were derived from copyrighted works of Roger C. Ibbotson and Rex Sinquefield.]

Figure 13.2
Investment Returns—U.S. Treasury Intermediate Bonds, 1950–1997

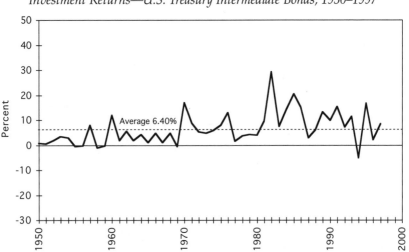

Source: Same as Figure 13.1. Used with permission.
©1998 Ibbotson Associates, Inc. All rights reserved.

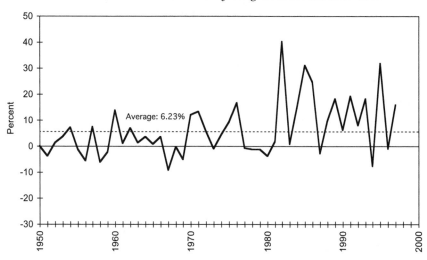

Figure 13.3
Investment Returns—U.S. Treasury Long-Term Bonds, 1950–1997

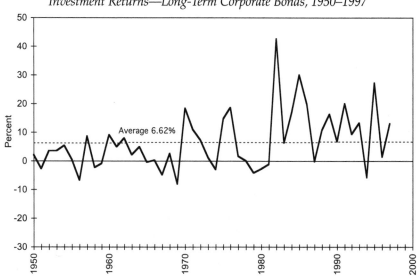

Figure 13.4
Investment Returns—Long-Term Corporate Bonds, 1950–1997

Figure 13.5 indicates the returns for common stocks. Here the volatility is greater than that of any other series, although common stock volatility diminished somewhat after 1980 while the volatility of long-term bonds increased. The average return of common stocks was more than double the return of any of the other investments considered. Returns followed a saucer-shaped pattern—trending downward to 1974 and rising thereafter. Common stocks had fewer years of negative returns than either of the long-term bonds series— 10 negative years out of 48 for stocks and 16 and 14 negative years, respectively, for government and corporate long-term bonds.

Figure 13.5
Investment Returns—Common Stocks, 1950–1997

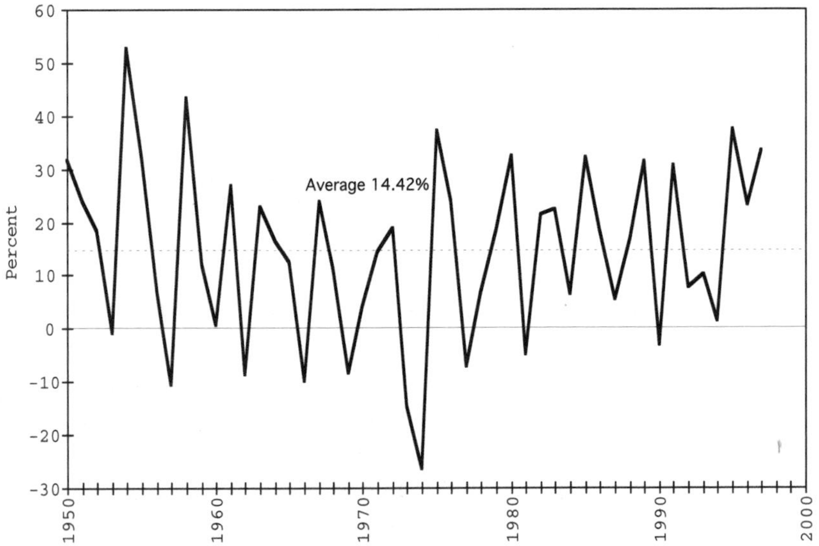

Volatility and Return

Investments with greater volatility have provided higher returns. Is there some way by which these two factors can be measured and then compared among various investments?

A statistical measure called the *standard deviation* measures the dispersion of individual points (in this case, yearly returns) around the average; the method gives greater weight to wider differences than narrow differences. In order to obtain a measure that compares the dispersion and risk of several series, this dispersion or standard deviation is divided by the average return. The result provides a measure of *volatility per unit of return*. This measure for the financial instruments we have surveyed is shown in Table 13.2.

Stocks, which are more volatile than bonds, had a sufficiently larger return so that the risk per unit of return, although greater than Treasury bills and intermediate government bonds, was less than for long-term government and corporate bonds.

Table 13.2   *Volatility Per Unit of Return*
Selected Financial Instruments, 1950 to 1997

U.S. Treasury Bills	0.57
Intermediate U.S. Government Bonds	1.01
Long-Term U.S. Government Bonds	1.71
Long-Term Corporate Bonds	1.53
Common Stocks	1.15

Source: Same as Figure 13.1. Used with permission. ©1998 Ibbotson Associates, Inc. All rights reserved. Computations by author.

The Inflation Rate

The returns discussed previously are called "nominal" returns, that is, they are not adjusted to show the real purchasing power of the dollars of return received. A simple way to illustrate the purchasing power of these returns is to adjust them for inflation by subtracting the annual inflation rate (as measured by the familiar CPI) from the annual returns.

Figure 3.3 in Chapter 3 shows the annual change in the consumer price index from 1950 to 1997. What did these differing inflation rates mean for investment returns? The next few charts show the so-called real returns, or returns less the annual inflation rates.

Figure 13.6 indicates the real return on U.S. Treasury bills for the 1950 to 1997 time period. During the years 1952 to 1972, the bill rate closely followed the inflation rate, running about 1 percentage point above it for most years. From 1973 to 1980, bill returns did not keep up with inflation. In the period 1980 to 1986, returns on bills have averaged more than 4 percentage points above the inflation rate; investors required higher real returns on even the safest securities, probably because their expectations were for higher inflation rates in the future. From 1987 through 1997, the real return averaged 1.95 percentage points above the 1950–97 average of about 1.08 percentage points.

Figure 13.7 shows the returns for intermediate U.S. government bonds. The pattern is much the same as that of bills, with the fluctuations in returns somewhat greater because of the longer maturity of intermediate bonds. Real returns on average were positive from 1950 through 1972 at a level somewhat higher than bill rates. Real returns fell more than 3 percentage points below the inflation rate for the 1973 to 1981 period. Returns from 1982 to 1991 were well-above the inflation rate, averaging 9.43 percentage points. In 1992–1997, returns were 4.1 percentage points higher.

Figure 13.8 shows the same information for long-term government bonds. Here the pattern is both surprising and disappointing; returns averaged below inflation for the entire period up to 1981. A similar pattern is shown for long-term corporate bonds in Figure 13.9, although they did have a return slightly in excess of the inflation rate in 1950 to 1965. Real returns have significantly exceeded those of bills and intermediate bonds only in the period since 1982.

Figure 13.6
Inflation-Adjusted Investment Returns—U.S. Treasury Bills, 1950–1997

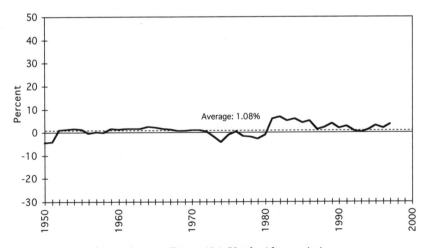

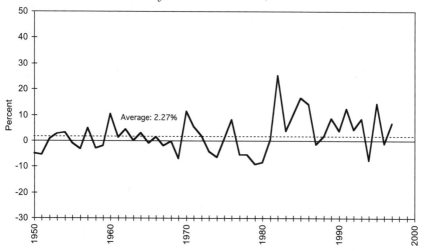

Figure 13.7   Inflation-Adjusted Investment Returns—
U.S. Treasury Intermediate Bonds, 1950–1997

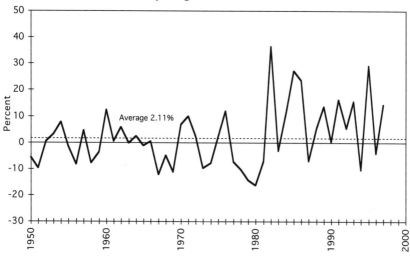

Figure 13.8   Inflation-Adjusted Investment Returns—
U.S. Treasury Long-Term Bonds, 1950–1997

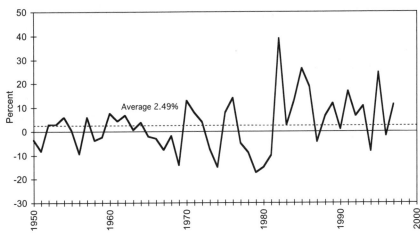

Figure 13.9
Inflation-Adjusted Returns—Long-Term Corporate Bonds, 1950–1997

Why has this pattern for long-term securities occurred? In addition to the long-term debilitating effects of inflation, another reason for this pattern was that in the earlier years of this period, long-term investors such as insurance companies and pension funds bought these bonds for their higher yield and planned to keep them to maturity. Therefore, they carried these bonds on their books at cost and paid little attention to fluctuations in market prices.

However, U.S. insurance companies are no longer major purchasers of long-term bonds. Their product mix has shifted from mostly ordinary life policies to other types where the policyholder shares in the investment return that is linked to the current investment return on the company's portfolio. More recent purchasers of long-term bonds trade them rather than hold them to maturity, attempting to make capital gains on the trades. Therefore, they carry the securities at market, and price fluctuations over time are important. In addition, investors have become aware of the need to receive a real return that compensates for the possibility of higher inflation rates in the future. Capital markets also have become international, and U.S. securities must compete for capital with demands worldwide. Consequently higher real returns are necessary to induce investors to purchase longer maturity bonds.

Figure 13.10 indicates the real returns for common stocks. Although very volatile, common stock real returns were negative on average only during 1973 to 1981, and the average negative return in that period was less than those of all but Treasury bills. Thus, for those investors who can stand the volatility of stock returns, they do appear to provide a good hedge against inflation in all but periods of very high inflation rates.

Figure 13.10
Inflation-Adjusted Returns—Common Stocks, 1950–1997

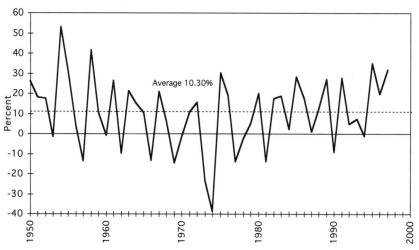

Source: Same as Figure 13.1. Used with permission.
©1998 Ibbotson Associates, Inc. All rights reserved.

Selecting a Rate of Return

When selecting a rate of return for a portfolio, the following ideas may be useful:

In setting return expectations, using absolute numbers based on long-term averages may not be the best guide. Returns in the most recent decade may be more meaningful;

The higher the expected return, the greater the volatility of returns;

Investment returns for financial instruments have varied considerably during the past 48 years, and these variations have been related, in part at least, to the inflation rate;

More recently (1982 to 1990), all types of investments have had returns that were greater than the inflation rate by an amount more than in prior years.

To establish an expected absolute rate of return, the following procedure is suggested:

- Check any nominal rate selected against the past record of returns for various financial instruments to determine how realistic the selected rate is;

- Select an expected inflation rate;

- Estimate the real rate of return, that is, the return above the inflation rate, implicit in the nominal rate selected;

- Review the figures on inflation-adjusted rates of return to see whether the expectations are reasonable relative to past inflation and returns, especially in recent years.

TIME HORIZON

Part of setting investment objectives is selecting an investment time horizon, that is, the period over which investment results will be measured. Most investors are understandably impatient, which puts them at the mercy of the short-term vagaries of the markets, forgetting that short-term results could be due to chance and could cause a switch in investments just at the wrong time.

A realistic alternative is to select a longer time period to measure results, for example, five years or a complete market cycle. Of course, an investor shouldn't wait for five years before determining whether the investment program is on track; investments must be reviewed regularly to see if results are on the path that will achieve the set objectives.

Figure 13.11 may provide some perspective on investment time horizons. The annual nominal investment returns (income plus price gains or losses) for the stock market for each of the years 1926 through 1997 were reviewed along with the average annual results for successive overlapping five-year periods (i.e., 1926 to 1930, 1927 to 1931, etc.) for the same time period. We divided the annual returns into four categories:

1. Negative returns;

2. 0 to 10 percent returns;

3. 10 to 20 percent returns; and

4. Returns of more than 20 percent.

For the entire period, the annual return on stocks averaged 11.7 percent. Focusing on a one-year time horizon (as shown by the four bars at the left side of the figure): approximately 30 percent of the time results would have been negative; about 33 percent between 0 and 20 percent; and about 37 percent of the time more

Figure 13.11
Investment Returns for One- and Five-Year Time Horizons, 1926–1997

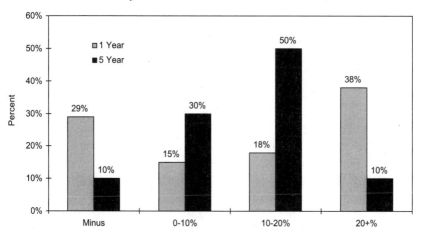

than 20 percent. In short, about two-thirds of the time an investor would have been either very happy with the results, or very miserable and perhaps impelled to make some changes!

However, if a longer term perspective is taken, as shown by the bars on the right side of the figure, almost 90 percent of the time you would have received positive returns between 0 and 20 percent, and negative periods would have been reduced to about 10 percent of the total. A longer viewpoint is a lot easier for peace of mind.

RISK

Risk is an important concept in portfolio management, but it often is overlooked or only partly considered. For example, investors often say they don't want any "risky" investments. However, although "riskless" investments may avoid the loss of dollars, they also may not compensate for the loss of the purchasing power of those dollars because of the effects of inflation. Risk is often defined in terms of portfolio volatility, but in order to avoid volatility you may be assuming a bigger risk—the risk of not achieving the returns needed to reach your investment objectives.

One characteristic of risk, and one that often is the only kind of risk considered, is *volatility*. Volatility is defined as fluctuations in market price or in total investment return (income plus or minus market appreciation or depreciation of the investment). Volatility may be measured in absolute terms or relative to some market average. The investor should separate volatility into principal and income volatility and make a realistic appraisal of how much volatility can be tolerated in each. For example, if income is of primary importance, a fixed-income investment can be purchased and fluctuations in the value of the principal due to changes in the level of interest rates can be ignored. If volatility of principal cannot be tolerated, a short-term investment of the highest quality, such as a U.S. Treasury bill or a high-quality money-market fund is a preferable investment.

Volatility tolerance has two parts:

1. The practical effects that volatility will have on the ability to reach the investment objectives; and

2. The psychological effects of having a smaller investment fund than at some time in the past.

The first part is significant because a financial cost is involved: the funds needed are not available. The second part may not be that critical. For example, if the primary need is income, some volatility in market principal may be tolerable so long as income is assured.

However, other kinds of risks should be considered:

Financial risk is the risk associated with a company itself, that is, a company cuts its dividend or files for bankruptcy, or a real estate venture goes sour.

Interest rate risk is associated with investments whose income is fixed by the terms of the security. When the coupon rate or the designated interest rate of an investment is fixed, changes in the general level of interest rates will cause the market value of the investment to rise or fall to adjust the actual yield on this investment to prevailing interest rates. Although the dollar income remains the same, the value of the principal of fixed-income investments will go up and down as interest rates rise and fall. An additional problem may occur when the security matures, because market yields at which reinvestment is made may be lower than they were when the investment was originally made. Many investors discovered this risk to their sorrow in the 1980s when high-yielding bank certificates of deposit had to be rolled over into lower yielding securities.

Purchasing power risk is the risk caused by the erosion in purchasing power due to the effects of inflation. Figure 3.4 shows the erosion in the purchasing power of $1 in 1950. By the end of 1997, it was worth only fifteen cents in 1950 purchasing power. This risk certainly is one that should be considered in establishing investment objectives.

Meeting Risk

In meeting risk, one fundamental factor should be kept in mind—the higher the expected return, the higher the risk. There is no free lunch. A high return is a good reflection of the risk

assumed. A diversified portfolio reduces the risk of any one investment not living up to expectations.

Volatility risk is the most misunderstood, probably because
investors get upset when the market value of their investments at
some point in time is worth less than it was at an earlier date. In
some portfolios, of course, volatility is undesirable. For example, a
drop in the value of a participant's account in a profit-sharing plan
a year or so before retirement can be a real problem. This risk could
have been offset by gradually shifting more and more of the assets
into cash equivalents as retirement approached.

Alternatively, consider a portion of a portfolio invested in
diversified, well-selected common stocks with a history of and
prospects for increasing earnings and dividends. This portfolio
segment was designed to provide protection against inflation.
Price volatility in the principal of this portfolio should cause little
concern unless the principal will be needed to supplement income.

For *interest-rate risk,* the higher the quality of the security, the
more likely it is to be affected by interest-rate risk rather than
financial risk. Also the longer the maturity of the instrument, the
greater the market volatility. An investor can seek protection
against interest-rate risk by portfolio diversification and staggered
fixed-income maturities.

Offsetting *purchasing power risk* depends on the type of inflation expected. A moderate inflation rate (say 4 percent or less a
year) may be met with a diversified investment portfolio, including well-selected common stocks that have prospects for increasing earnings and dividends. In a higher and accelerating inflation,
financial assets do poorly, as occurred during the 1970s. In that
environment, the assets that did best were real estate and Treasury
bills or other short-term money-market instruments that adjust to
inflation fairly quick.

THE ADVANTAGES OF PORTFOLIO DIVERSIFICATION

One of the important concepts of investment is the advantage
of holding a portfolio of diversified securities. The concept of diversification is simple, summarized by the old adage, "Don't put all
your eggs in one basket." Even safe investments such as Treasury
bills provide a varying income stream over time as interest rates

fluctuate, although the principal is always backed by the full taxing powers of the federal government. In addition, it is well-recognized that not all investments do equally well each year.

Table 13.3 illustrates the concept of diversification. The first column lists various types of fixed-income and equity investments. Treasury bills are used to represent conservative, short-term money-market investments such as certificates of deposit, savings accounts, or money-market funds, which do not fluctuate in value and have a somewhat higher yield than Treasury bills. On a sum invested in guaranteed income contracts, insurance companies guarantee repayment of principal plus interest over a limited number of years, usually three or five.

The remainder of the table gives each type of investment a subjective grade, from A to D, based on how these investments have done in the past in terms of long-term investment returns, price volatility, inflation protection, and marketability. The grading is admittedly subjective and can be modified if wished. However, the main point derived from the table is that no investment

Table 13.3   Types of Investments

Investment	Long-Term Total Investment Return	Price Volatility	Inflation Protection	Liquidity and Marketability
Fixed Income				
Treasury Bills	C	A	A	A
Intermediate Bonds	C	C	C	A
Long-Term Bonds	D	D	D	A
Mortgages	D	D	D	B
Guaranteed Income Contracts	C	A	D	D
Equity				
Stocks	B	C	C	A
Small Capitalization Stocks	A	D	B	B
Foreign Stocks	B	C	C	B
Real Estate	A	B	A	C
Oil and Gas	B	C	B	C

Grading Scale: A (most favorable) to D (least favorable).

receives a perfect score; one type of investment alone does not meet all investment requirements. Each type of investment has its advantages and disadvantages. Consequently, depending on the investor's objectives and circumstances, a blend of several investments is generally the best way to construct a portfolio.

Another way to look at diversification is illustrated in Table 13.4.

Some explanation of Table 13.4 is necessary. The returns are total returns (income plus appreciation), averaged for the 25-year period. The money-market fund was assumed to return about 0.5 percent per year above the Treasury bill rate. The high-grade bonds were represented by an index prepared by Salomon Brothers. Common stocks were represented by the Standard & Poor's 500 Stock Index.

For the diversified portfolio an initial diversification of 10 percent in a money-market fund is assumed, with 30 percent in high-grade bonds and 60 percent in stocks. Whatever the results in any year, the portfolio was rebalanced to the original diversification at the beginning of the next year. Essentially, this process reduced the more successful investments in any particular year and redistributed the proceeds among the less successful investments.

For each type of investment, the average yearly return is shown, as well as the fluctuations around that return (the standard deviation). The last column shows the standard deviation divided by the average, giving a measure of volatility risk per unit of return.

Table 13.4   Total Investment Return, 1971–1997

Investment	Average Annual Return	Standard Deviation	Standard Deviation Divided by Average
Money-Market Fund	7.4%	2.7%	0.37
High-Grade Corporate Bonds	10.0	11.8	1.18
S&P 500 Stock Index	14.6	16.0	1.10
Diversified Portfolio	12.5	11.9	0.95

As one might expect, when moving from safe to riskier investments, the average return increases. However, so does the variations in the return around the average. What happens to a portfolio diversified among the three types of investments? Over time, the results of this portfolio fall between bonds and stocks, but the fluctuations per percentage point of return were reduced considerably and were less than for either stocks or bonds.

A balanced portfolio may not be for everyone. Some investors can't stand losses, even though they may be just on paper and not realized. These investors are willing to sacrifice the higher return from alternative investments for the assurance that the principal of their investments will always be safe. Other investors are risk-takers willing to assume the exposure to greater fluctuations in order to get the highest possible returns. Many others would prefer a higher return than that of money-market investment but also would like to control portfolio volatility. For that investor, a balanced portfolio, historically at least, has given a higher return than either Treasury bills or bonds and has had lower fluctuations than either an all-bond or an all-stock portfolio.

Types of Investments

Finally, in establishing investment objectives, consideration should be given to the types of investments preferred as well as to investments *not* liked and normally excluded from an investor's portfolio. Generally, an investor should understand and be comfortable with the investments chosen. At times, however, it may be worthwhile to be familiar with the characteristics of new investment vehicles that may enable the investor to reach the objectives more successfully. Referring again to Table 13.3, the listed characteristics may be useful in considering the investments to include in a balanced portfolio.

FOLLOWING THE STOCK MARKET

Tracking interest rates is a relatively simple procedure, because both long and short rates are published daily in the financial press. Also, Chapter 11 referred to a St. Louis Federal Reserve Bank publication that provides such information on a weekly basis. Following stock prices, however, is a bit more difficult, because it involves selecting from among a number of indexes with varying characteristics. Which stock market average is best? A review of various stock price indexes and their construction may help answer these questions.

The Dow-Jones Average

Probably the best known average is the Dow-Jones Industrial Average. Although this average is probably the least useful, it is still the most popular because it goes back more than 100 years and is widely quoted in the financial press and the media.

The Dow-Jones Industrial Average represents only a small segment of the market. It is computed based on the daily prices of 30 stocks that account for about 20 percent of the market value of all of the stocks listed on the New York Stock Exchange. The Dow used to be composed mostly of heavy industry stocks, but the average has become more diversified in recent years—although stocks like Disney, JP Morgan, Travelers, McDonalds, and Wal-Mart hardly spring to mind when the term "industrials" is used. But the average does represent large, solid, successful companies. Consequently, movement of the prices of the Dow Industrials may often be different from the movement of the prices of a broad spectrum of NYSE stocks.

Another problem with the Dow arises from its method of construction. When the average first started, it was computed like any other average, that is, add up the prices of the 30 stocks and divide by 30. However, over time stocks were split, stock dividends were declared, and some stocks were substituted for others. Each time that occurred, the *divisor*, which started out as 30, was changed so that, after adding up the prices of the 30 stocks and dividing by the divisor, the value of the average or index would be unchanged.

As a result of using this process over many years, the market value of the 30 stocks now is not divided by 30, but 0.25089. Consequently, a one-point move in one of the 30 stocks can cause almost a four-point move in the Dow! This computation method explains why the Dow index is so much larger than the price of any of the individual stocks in the average. It also explains the seemingly big daily movements of the average—far more than the changes in any component stock.

The Dow's method of computation gives heavier weight to stocks with larger dollar prices, and over the years the lowering of the divisor has distorted daily changes to make them almost meaningless. Moreover, if a stock were split, for example, 2 for 1, the stock suddenly has only half the importance it formerly had.

To get a better feel of the daily movements of individual stocks in the Dow, each day on the NYSE market price page, The *Wall Street Journal* prints a chart showing the daily high-low-close of the Dow averages for the past six months; on that same page yesterday's price change for each stock in the average is also reported.

Dow-Jones averages are also computed in the same manner for 20 transportation stocks, 25 utility stocks, and then a composite for all 65 stocks. The divisors for all indexes are printed regularly in *The Wall Street Journal* or can be obtained on the Dow-Jones web site *http://averages.dowjones.com*

Standard & Poor's Indexes

Among the more widely used price indexes are those prepared by Standard & Poor's Corporation. These indexes are probably the ones most widely used by professional investors because of their long history and also the breadth and depth of their coverage.

Standard & Poor's prepares a composite of the prices of 500 stocks, including 400 industrial, 20 transport, 40 utility, and 40 financial stocks, which is reported daily in the financial section of most newspapers. Most of the stocks in the indexes are listed on the various stock exchanges, although some stocks traded over-the-counter are included.

The composite price index goes back to 1918, although it included only 90 stocks until 1957. It has also been linked to an older index prepared by the Cowles Commission, so that a continuous record of stock prices is available going back to 1871. Information on the industry indexes are reported from 1918.

The Standard & Poor's weekly publication, *The Outlook* (available in many public libraries), reports the values of more than 100 industry components in addition to the weekly values of the broad indexes. Consequently, these indexes are used more than any others to follow the movement of industry groups. However,

Dow-Jones has recently introduced industry indexes of its own, which are published daily in *The Wall Street Journal*.

The computation of the Standard & Poor's data is by market weight, that is, the market price of each stock is multiplied by the number of shares outstanding. The totals for all stocks are then added and reported relative to the value in a base period (1941 to 1943), with the base period set equal to 10. The recent value of the composite index of about 1100 means that the value of the stocks in the index is about 110 times the average value in 1941 to 1943. No adjustment is needed for stock splits, because a split does not affect the market value of all of the shares of the company. Changes resulting from mergers, delistings, substitutions, or rights offerings are adjusted for by a proportionate change in the base value.

The average now accounts for about 80 percent of the value of the stocks listed on the NYSE, including all of the stocks in the Dow. Companies that have a large number of shares, that is, large capitalization stocks, or industries with large capitalization stocks (e.g., office equipment, oils, drugs, and telecommunications), dominate the movements of the index.

The New York Stock Exchange Index

The New York Stock Exchange publishes a daily index that reflects the prices of all of the roughly 1,500 stocks listed on the Exchange, as well as indexes of divisions of these stocks into industrial, transportation, utility, and financial stocks. The index goes back to 1964, and it can be extended back further to 1939 by linking it to a now-discontinued index once prepared by the Securities and Exchange Commission (SEC).

The NYSE indexes are constructed in the same manner as the Standard & Poor's indexes. However, the base period is market value on December 31, 1965, and the base is set at 50, which was reasonably close to the average value of all NYSE stocks on the base date. Because all NYSE-listed stocks are included, changes occur more frequently than for the Standard & Poor's composite index.

The NYSE index is more comprehensive than the Standard & Poor's index in one way because it covers all of the stocks listed on the NYSE. However, it does not cover stocks listed on other exchanges or stocks that are not listed. Because it is constructed in the same way as the Standard & Poor's, it is also dominated by the movement of large capitalization stocks.

Other Indexes

The *American Stock Exchange (AMEX) index* reflects the price movements of all stocks traded on the AMEX as well as American depository receipts of foreign companies traded on the AMEX. These companies are smaller than the companies listed on the NYSE. The index is constructed in the same way as the Standard & Poor's indexes. The index goes back to the beginning of 1969 but has a base level set at 100 on August 31, 1973.

The price movements of *over-the-counter stocks* traded through the *National Association of Securities Dealers Automated Quotation System* (NASDAQ) are reflected in an index that covers more than 5,000 stocks. The index and twelve subindexes are computed like the Standard & Poor's indexes, that is, total market-value weighted, with the base period of February 5, 1971, set at 100. A small number of large capitalization stocks have a significant influence on movements of this index.

The *Value Line Composite Index* is comprised of prices of about 1,700 NYSE and non-NYSE stocks covered in the Value Line Investment Service. The calculations are based on daily percentage changes, so that each stock receives the same weight in the calculation of the index, regardless of the company size or market capitalization. Consequently, its movements can be compared with the market-value weighted indexes to compare the movements of large versus smaller capitalization stocks. The base period and starting point for the index is June 1961. Daily price changes are reported in *The Wall Street Journal* and other financial papers, but historical data must be obtained from Value Line.

The *Wilshire 5,000 Equity Index* is the most comprehensive index available. It now covers about 5,700 common stocks and includes all stocks traded on the NYSE, AMEX, and those included in the NASDAQ index. The construction is the same as the construction of the S&P indexes. Month-end prices are available for this index since 1971, and the index is based on the December 31, 1980 capitalization of the market, which was $1,404 billion.

Figure 13.12 shows the performance of the three indexes that are followed most intensely. The base is the low in stock prices at the bottom of the market decline that ended in October 1987. Since then, stock prices have increased significantly, with the best performance by the NASD market, which also has been the most volatile. All of the indexes made all-time record highs in 1998.

Figure 13.12
Major Stock Market Averages, October 1987 Low June 1998

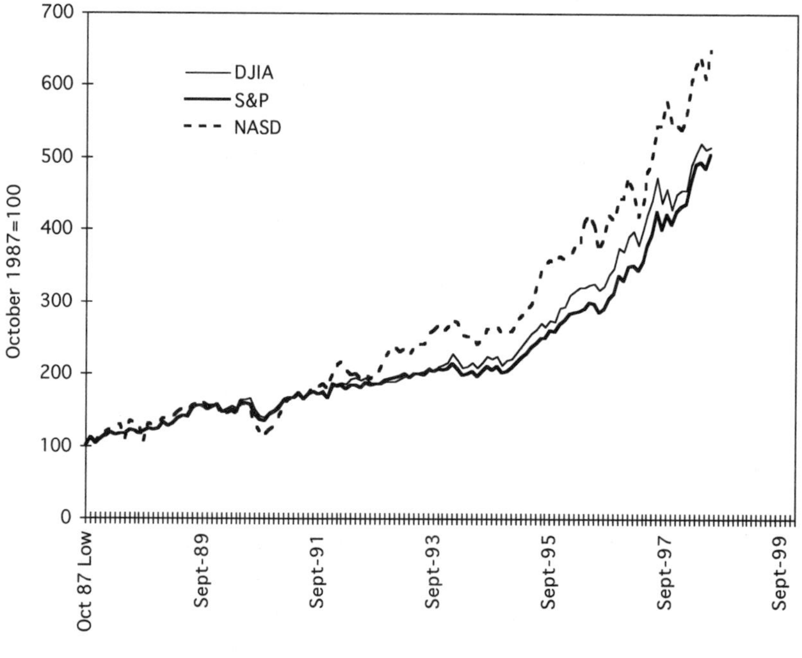

Source: Based on price data from *The Wall Street Journal*.

Which Index to Use?

With so many indexes to choose from, which one should be used? Some guidelines to follow:

Although the Dow often is used to reflect day-to-day stock price changes, it is not representative of the broad market. Its method of construction is unusual, so that changes in the Dow's raw numbers give an exaggerated and at times an inaccurate idea of the general movement of stock prices.

The Standard & Poor's indexes are widely used because of their broader coverage, long history, and many subindexes. The NYSE index is an even broader measure of NYSE-listed stocks than is the Standard & Poor's. The AMEX and the NASDAQ reflect movements of their respective markets and the different types of stocks traded on them. The Wilshire 5,000 is the most comprehensive index available but does not yet have industry components, nor is it as well-known as the others.

The Standard & Poor's, NYSE, AMEX, NASDAQ, and Wilshire indexes are all weighted by the price of individual stocks times the number of shares, and therefore larger capitalization stocks have a greater impact on price changes. An unweighed index, such as the Value Line Index, can provide another view and permit comparison of movements of smaller versus larger capitalized stocks.

Daily percentage changes in the various indexes provide a better way to compare the movements of the indexes and the different views they present of the market. Such percentage changes can be found every day on the market price page of *The Wall Street Journal.*

No one average is good for all purposes. Select an average that will answer particular questions about the movement of broad stock aggregates. It is strongly recommended that price movements be viewed over periods of months and years, rather than too intense a focus on day-to-day price fluctuations.

SUMMARY

The most important step in managing an investment portfolio is to establish a clearly defined set of investment objectives. These objectives include describing the purpose for which the portfolio was established, determining an absolute rate of return needed to meet these objectives, deciding whether this return is realistic by comparing it with historical rates of return for similar investments, and establishing the risk tolerance for the portfolio. Portfolio risk includes more than just price volatility of the portfolio; financial risk, interest rate risk, and purchasing power risk should also be considered. One way of partially offsetting these various types of risk is through a diversified portfolio of securities. Various price indexes are used to follow security price movements. The appropriate index depends on the purpose for which measurement is made.

Index